MALE MATTERS

MALE MATTERS

Masculinity,

Anxiety, and

the Male Body

on the Line

Calvin Thomas

University of Illinois Press

Urbana and Chicago

© 1996 by the Board of Trustees of the University of Illinois
Manufactured in the United States of America
C 5 4 3 2 1

This book is printed on acid-free paper.

Library of Congress Cataloging-in-Publication Data

Thomas, Calvin, 1956–
Male matters : masculinity, anxiety, and the male body on the line
/ Calvin Thomas.
p.   cm.
Includes bibliographical references and index.
ISBN 0-252-02202-5 (alk. paper)
1. Masculinity (Psychology). 2. Anxiety. 3. Psychoanalysis.
I. Title.
BF175.5.M37T46   1996
155.3'32—dc20   95-17447
                                                              CIP

For Liz, with love

Contents

Acknowledgments ix

Abbreviations xi

Introduction: Uneasy Negotiations 1

1. Openings: The Anxiety of Production 11
 Significant Discharge and the Production of Death • The
 (S)tain of the Mirror: Writing the Modernist Male Body

2. Piss Hegel, or Why Sperm Is Never Treated as an *Objet A* 47
 "The Gentleman Seems to Know What He Wants" •
 The Bodily in Hegel Is What Dialectics Never Touched •
 Bataille's Postmodern Prodding

3. Dysgraphia 1: Freud's Anxiety 74
 Masculinity between Cloaca and Castration • An
 Impressive Caesura • Utter(ed) Dismemberment

4. Dysgraphia 2: Deconstruction and the Fear of Mere
Writing 116
 Heidegger's *Durchfall* • Derrida's Hold on Heidegger

5. Not a Nice Production: Anal Joyce 152
 A Phallus Playing Dead • The Only Foolscap Available:
 Shem's Inkenstink • Re: Openings—or Hegel Will Come,
 and Pull out His Eyes • Dispossession: The Initials of the
 Father • Excrementitious Intelligence: Stephen's Lousy
 Aesthetics

6. Closings: Desire and Interpretation in the Porno-House of
Language, or "You Certainly *Do* Know What You Want, Sir" 190

Notes 195

Works Cited 227

Index 243

Acknowledgments

Although it was suggested to me at one point in the writing of this book that "no human reader" would ever get very far with it, a number of very human beings have assisted me with *Male Matters*. I would like to thank Ihab Hassan, Gregory S. Jay, Jane Gallop, Patrice Petro, Bernard Gendron, Jamie Owen Daniel, Kathleen Kirby, Kathleen Woodward, Herbert Blau, Elizabeth Grosz, Michael Warner, Carl Freedman, Daniel Mark Fogel, Dympna Callaghan, Rosaria Champagne, Susan Edmonds, and Gayle Fornataro for their help and advice. A special note of gratitude goes to my two anonymous readers, as well as to Bruce Bethell, my copy editor at the University of Illinois Press, for their editorial and organizational suggestions and, in one case, for the last phrase of the book's final subtitle. My thanks also go to the Center for Twentieth Century Studies at the University of Wisconsin–Milwaukee for an Uihlein Fellowship, and to the Fred L. Emerson Foundation of Rochester, New York, for a Distinguished Faculty Fellowship in Modern Letters at Syracuse University. Portions of chapter 1 and chapter 5 were originally published in *NOVEL: A Forum on Fiction* 23, no. 3 (Spring 1990). Copyright NOVEL Corp. © Reprinted with permission.

Abbreviations

The following abbreviations are used to refer to the most frequently cited texts of the major authors examined in this book. Full bibilographical data on these and on less frequently cited texts by the same authors and others are given in the list of works cited.

Georges Bataille

AS I	*The Accursed Share, Vol I: Consumption*
AS II, III	*The Accursed Share, Vols. II & III: The History of Eroticism & Sovereignty*
E	*Erotism: Death and Sensuality*
G	*Guilty*
IE	*Inner Experience*
OC	*Oeuvres complètes*
VE	*Visions of Excess*

Jacques Derrida

D	*Dissemination*
EO	*The Ear of the Other*
MP	*Margins of Philosophy*
OG	*Of Grammatology*
OS	*Of Spirit: Heidegger and the Question*
P	*Positions*
PC	*The Post Card*
SP	*Speech and Phenomena*
WD	*Writing and Difference*

Sigmund Freud

CL	*The Complete Letters of Sigmund Freud to Wilhelm Fliess*
SE	*The Standard Edition of the Complete Psychological Works* (references give volume and page number)

G. W. F. Hegel

ETW	*Early Theological Writings*

| PS | *The Phenomenology of Spirit* |
| PM | *Philosophy of Mind* |

Martin Heidegger

BW	*Basic Writings*
BT	*Being and Time*
DT	*Discourse on Thinking*
ID	*Identity and Difference*
IM	*An Introduction to Metaphysics*
PLT	*Poetry, Language, Thought*
QCT	*The Question concerning Technology*
OTB	*On Time and Being*

Luce Irigaray

| SW | *Speculum of the Other Woman* |
| TS | *This Sex Which Is Not One* |

James Joyce

CW	*Critical Writings*
DB	*Dubliners*
FW	*Finnegans Wake* (references give page and line numbers)
PA	*A Portrait of the Artist as a Young Man*
SL	*Selected Letters*
SH	*Stephen Hero*
U	*Ulysses* (references give chapter and line numbers)

Julia Kristeva

| PH | *Powers of Horror: An Essay on Abjection* |
| RPL | *Revolution in Poetic Language* |

Jacques Lacan

| É | *Écrits: A Selection* |
| FFC | *The Four Fundamental Concepts of Psychoanalysis* |

MALE MATTERS

Introduction: Uneasy Negotiations

> All that should concern us is the acute and increasing anxiety of the relation itself, as though shadowed more and more darkly by a sense of invalidity, of inadequacy, of existence at the expense of all that it excludes, all that it blinds to.
>
> —Samuel Beckett, *Disjecta*

> What if it were better not to meet any expectation and to offer precisely that which repels, that which people deliberately avoid, for lack of strength: that violent movement, sudden and shocking, which jostles the mind, taking away its tranquility: a kind of bold reversal that substitutes a dynamism . . . for the stagnation of isolated ideas, of stubborn problems born of an anxiety that refused to see.
>
> —Georges Bataille, *The Accursed Share*

> The text is (should be) that uninhibited person who shows his behind to the *Political Father*.
>
> —Roland Barthes, *The Pleasure of the Text*

My family—southern and working-class—lived near a large elementary school. Before I entered the first grade there, I would take advantage of the school's playground, entertaining myself on the sliding board, the monkey bars, and the swings. One day, when I was four or perhaps five, I was down at the playground with a boy about my age, whose name I do not remember. At some point this boy abruptly announced with some urgency that he had to use the bathroom. It was summer, or perhaps a weekend. The school building was closed, and except for us, the playground was deserted. There was no way for the boy to make it home, so we ran over to the big red-brick school building, and the boy hurried down a flight of concrete steps to a landing by a basement door. I remained at the top of the steps, ostensibly to stand guard and call out if I saw any approaching adults, but also to watch. For I have always been intrigued by the body and its functions.

I assumed that he needed only to pee, which I am sure I would have been happy enough to witness. When I looked down the steps, however, I beheld that the boy had lowered his pants and was now squatting down. In broad daylight, at the nether door of the looming school, he began to let fall a dark, coiling figure.

If I say that I remember being thrilled, remember being positively *beside myself* with glee on witnessing this event, it is only to foreground a certain anti-oedipal *jouissance* that was doubtless incommensurable with my own fledgling ego syntony; in other words, whatever the boundaries of my "self" at that moment, the pleasure experienced in watching this boy defecate on school property somehow took me beside or outside them. Furthermore, there must be a sort of *Nachträglich-keit*—deferred action or retrodetermination—at work in my presently endowing this event with a special significance by virtue of its having occurred at the very threshold of the school itself, an institution that I had then yet to enter and, in some form or another, have now yet to leave. What thrilled me as a preschooler, as I remember it, was the thought of adult displeasure and outrage at the sight of this boy's coil of droppings. What thrills me now, as a scholar, is the thought of this event as a metaphor for the way the body can defy and defile certain institutional and disciplinary boundaries, along with the boundaries of ego coherence, even if defiance and defilement must now, at least among adult academicians, take a rather more subdued or sublimated textual form. Granted, it may be stretching the metaphor to say that this nameless boy, in darkening the door of education, was engaged in something like textuality, in some "subversive" sort of writing. After all, he was only doing what he had to. Nevertheless, it may suggest something about *this* text that I remembered the boy and what his body performed—and where—only while I was engaged in producing it.

The subject of this book is not pleasure, however, but male anxiety. I explore here the social construction of masculinity, the repression of the male body that is necessary to that construction, and the way that writing—as a corporeal and material process, a way of putting the body on the line—can disturb or subvert that repression. The book begins with the feminist argument that, in Western culture, the "excessive" question of the body tends to be displaced onto "the feminine": femininity becomes the repository not only for the bodily but for the excessive as such, for everything that masculine subjectivity cannot admit or accept about itself. This displacement of the bodily onto the feminine is particularly pronounced when it comes to the question of representation, of the visibility of the male body. The conditions of possibility for that body's being seen are culturally produced and gendered as well. Those conditions are summed up rather neatly by

John Berger, who in *Ways of Seeing* provides the following paradigm: *"Men act* and *women appear"* (47). The consequences and contradictions of that paradigm will be examined in greater detail in the opening chapter. Here, however, I point out only how the question of writing can become conspicuous in the light of Berger's paradigmatic opposition. Because it is both act and appearance, both process and visible, material result, writing can be thought as a scene of gender ambiguity, and thus a cause of anxiety, for any author invested in preserving the boundaries, institutional or otherwise, of gendered identity and ego coherence.

In this book I examine the ambiguity and anxiety that writing occasions. But the book goes beyond the by now rather time-worn notion that writing for some men is a feminine or feminizing process. Rather, the argument shifts from the question of the body's representation in writing to the role the body plays in the production of representation and writing. The issue, in other words, becomes not writing about the body but *writing itself as a bodily function.* Thus the book concerns an unease about the male body as a material site of linguistic production, a corporeal tension between (gendered) identity and (self-) representation. This tension, particularly as it is exacerbated by the visibility of writing, troubles the construction of normative, hegemonic masculinity; it disturbs what Kaja Silverman calls "the dominant fiction"—the "ideological belief [through which] a society's 'reality' is constituted and sustained, and [through which] a subject lays claim to a normative identity" (*Male Subjectivity* 15).[1] My argument is that males accede to the dominant fiction and identify with normative masculinity and its fictions of dominance by learning how to assuage this anxiety; the mechanisms of assuagement are ideologically embedded in cultural modes of representational containment that govern and restrict the visibility of male bodies and male bodily productions. However, to the extent that the anxiety in question can be left open and unassuaged, a critical intervention can be made into these restrictive mechanisms and new configurations of identity and representation can be performed.

Before I expand on the argument itself, however, some attention to its presentation is warranted. *Male Matters* might be called a performative reading; that is, it not only concerns anxiety but tries discursively to enact it, attempting to do what it would otherwise merely discuss. The book's intent is thus to produce anxiety—particularly in its male readership—rather than to assuage it, for I argue that the foreclosure of anxiety secures male identity within the parameters of masculine domination. It would therefore not be a particularly productive contradiction if the argument itself attempted to transcend the anxiety it describes.

One of my working assumptions in this book is that the most productive way to deal with anxiety is to allow it to remain open, embodied, and discursively excessive. By letting that assumption become a performative principle, this book puts one male body on the line.

Of course, not every reader will be drawn to this examination of or exercise in discursive excess, which may strike some as a sort of linguistic fetishism, overly citational if not compulsive, involuntary, or out of control. But I consider this excess to be, paradoxically, quite indispensable to my argument, which works—to the extent that it does work—less by linear exposition than by gradual accretion, appropriation, juxtaposition, and reinscription, engaging a number of disparate theorists and writers not only on the level of paraphrasable knowledge and argument but also on the level of the "heterological" materiality of the signifier itself.[2]

I stress "to the extent that it does work" because, as a student of Barthes, Bataille, and Beckett, I am attracted to Barthes's shift of value away from the work of textual meaning to the pleasure of the text and "the sumptuous rank of the signifier" (*Pleasure* 65); I am drawn to Bataille's discursive subversion of utility, his disruption of the work of knowledge and argument through "unproductive expenditure"; and I am intrigued by the Beckettian possibility of what Leo Bersani calls a "culturally nonviable" discursive practice, one that never ceases to affirm its own inadequacy and invalidity.[3]

At the same time, however, I am embarrassed by the political liabilities of this seemingly perverse attraction to discursive powerlessness, particularly when faced with Fredric Jameson's sternly utopian admonishments concerning textual pleasures and "the potentialities of the material body." Jameson argues that

> the thematizing of a particular pleasure as a political issue . . . must always involve a dual focus, in which the local issue is meaningful and desirable in itself, but is also *at one and the same time* taken as the *figure* for Utopia in general, and for the systemic revolutionary transformation of society as a whole. . . . So finally the right to a specific pleasure, to a specific enjoyment of the potentialities of the material body—if it is not to remain only that, if it is to become genuinely political . . .—must always in one way or another also be able to stand as a figure for the transformation of social relations as a whole. ("Pleasure" 73–74)

Thus, if I have doubts as to whether my argument about the material body and its potentialities works, I also admit to anxieties about its transformative ability, its capacity, figuratively speaking, "to stand."

Furthermore, however drawn I might be to Beckettian affirmations of inadequacy, I am very much concerned with the utility and viability of my argument, its adequacy and validity if not its utopian urgency, in one particular area of social relations. I would like nothing better than this book's reception as a valuable feminist intervention, a useful contribution to that branch of transformative cultural studies coming to be known, however uneasily, as male feminism: I am anxious for the book to be considered as an example of what Charles Bernheimer calls "a materialist, feminist-informed, straight male reading of male sexuality that works to resist phallocentric cultural symbolizations" ("Penile Reference" 118). And yet, since my argument is that anxiety can and should be left open, and since men (even feminist men) are rarely less anxious than when convinced of their adequacy, perhaps usefulness in this instance might consist less in being theoretically adequate than in challenging the dominant standards of value— of the useful, the viable, the adequate, the valid—by which masculinity ordinarily props itself up, compels itself to stand. This challenge would have to be issued at the performative level as well. As Denis Hollier puts it in *Against Architecture*, "Incompletion and failure from [Bataille's] point of view enter into the tactical arsenal of a writing that tries to escape the rules of mastery: they delineate the critical figures of a rhetoric of non-power" (118).

The irony of arguing for the usefulness of uselessness, of powerlessness, was hardly lost on Bataille, who understood the tension as being between the "sovereignty" of eroticism and "the servility of discourse"(*IE* 113), the utilitarianism of discursive thought itself. In such works as *Inner Experience* and the three volumes of *The Accursed Share*, Bataille links eroticism with "poetry, ecstasy, and laughter," with "the domain of sovereignty," with life "beyond utility," with potlach, the gift, ostentatious and unproductive expenditure, the squandering of resources, waste, "the enjoyment of possibilities that utility doesn't justify" (*AS* III:198). Thought, on the other hand, becomes servile for Bataille, becomes "project" and thus forecloses on erotic sovereignty, when it subordinates itself to *any* consideration of future results, for "it is *servile* to consider duration first, to employ the *present time* for the sake of the *future*, which is what we do when we work" (*AS* III:198). For Bataille, moreover, the subordination of thought to duration is a function not only of work but of politics, since politics—as conscious action or work toward social change, toward "the transformation of social relations as a whole"—is necessarily indentured to some notion of future results. Hence Bataille's opinion that those "committed to political struggle will never be able to yield to the truth of eroticism," a truth that he considers as always "in defiance of politics" (*AS* II:191).

Bataille, then, for this and other reasons, seems an unlikely ally for feminist politics. It appears very much against Bataille's sovereign grain to attempt to enlist him in any political service at all. Nonetheless, Bataille himself did not consider his writing to be apolitical. Moreover, the complexion of politics, the very notion of what political struggle looks like, has changed considerably in the forty-some years since Bataille wrote *The Accursed Share*. This change is partly due to the incursion of poststructuralist discourses (some influenced by Bataille) into more orthodox modes of Marxist analysis, the extent to which questions of the indeterminacies of language and representation, and the possibilities for reinscription those indeterminacies carry, have troubled the more traditional categories of ideology, economics, history, and class (although for some Marxists that extent is rather slight). In addition, the complexion of political struggle has changed because of the way in which feminist, gay, and lesbian theorists have reconfigured poststructuralist, Marxist, and psychoanalytic methodologies to examine the intersections of history, gender, and sexual orientation, opening up a defiant interrogation of the erotics of politics, as well as of the politics of eroticism.

Bataille's share in all these changes may seem accursedly small. Without suggesting that feminist politics should yield to any male-defined erotic truth, however, much less Bataille's, one could submit that the antagonism Bataille perceives *between* sovereign eroticism and servile political thought is comparable to a tension that operates *within* feminist theory itself. In "Upping the Anti (*sic*) in Feminist Theory" Teresa de Lauretis alters the terms but alludes to a similar tension when she suggests that "two concurrent drives, impulses, or mechanisms, are at work in the production of [feminist] self-representation: *an erotic, narcissistic drive* that enhances images of feminism as difference, rebellion, daring, excess, subversion, disloyalty, agency, empowerment, pleasure and danger . . . ; and *an ethical drive* that works toward community, accountability, entrustment, sisterhood, bonding . . ." (266). De Lauretis links the "mutual contradiction" of the erotic and ethical drives with what she elsewhere calls "the tension of a twofold pull in contrary directions—the critical negativity of [feminist] theory, and the affirmative positivity of its politics" (*Technologies* 26). She writes that this tension "is most productive in the kind of critical thinking that refuses to be pulled to either side of an opposition and seeks instead to deconstruct it . . . by analyzing the undecidability, conceptual as well as pragmatic, of the alternative *as given*" ("Upping" 266–67).

One of the things I want to accomplish in this book is to exacerbate the tension of productivity, and the productivity of tension, by foregrounding the undecidability of certain alternatives as given, particularly those given to and constitutive of normative masculinity and its traditionally decisive standards of discursive value. Insofar as this exacerbation in any way disrupts the cultural production of normative masculinity—its political aim—it may be of some use to feminism. Despite what should be this work's clear indebtedness to feminist and queer theory, however, I myself can hardly identify it as feminist, much less queer, without recourse to an identity politics in which I, writing as a heterosexual man, cannot in any obvious way participate. Thus, although I may consider my writing here to be coaxial with feminist and queer theory and hope that women and men working in these fields may find it useful, this coaxial relationship can for me remain only an anxious one—albeit, I hope, a productively anxious one.[4] Once again, the working assumption here is that the anxiety of ego incoherence, if left open, can be mobilized as a disruptive, interventional force, even if (or perhaps precisely because) the disruption necessarily extends to identity politics itself. Here I find Judith Butler's comments pertinent. Butler writes:

> My recommendation is not to solve . . . [the] crisis of identity politics, but to proliferate and intensify this crisis. . . . [The] failure to master the foundational identity categories of feminist or gay politics is a political necessity, a failure to be safeguarded for political reasons. The task is not to resolve or restrain the tension, the crisis, the phantasmatic excess induced by the term, but to affirm identity categories as a site of inevitable rifting. . . . The task . . . is to make that rift, that insistent rifting, into the persistently ungrounded ground from which feminist discourse emerges. ("Force" 124)[5]

Whether or not *Male Matters* can be identified as feminist discourse, then, it is intended to proliferate crisis, to risk ego incoherence, by putting the body on the line, by interrogating and affirming the failure to master certain foundational identity categories, by deconstructing the alternatives as given. I want the book to situate itself not in an identifiable position, or a positionable identity, but rather in a *dispositional* space of rifting between erotics and ethics, between the production of bodies and pleasures and the realm of knowledge and argument—an anxious space perhaps most usefully described as one of radical inadequacy.

In the first chapter, "Openings," I introduce a theory of productive anxiety and situate the argument in relation to current debates about male feminism. I also attempt to historicize male anxiety, speculating on how changes in the technology of representation (such as the invention of photography) may have helped to make this masculine unease a specifically "modern" one. Chapter 2, "Piss Hegel," starts with a discussion of Hitchcock's *Vertigo* and then uses Luce Irigaray's "Mechanics of Fluids" essay to investigate a curious moment in Hegel's *Phenomenology of Spirit* where the philosopher compares *Vorstellung*, or representational thinking, to urination. This chapter also takes up in greater detail the matter of Georges Bataille. In chapter 3, "Freud's Anxiety," I explore the way in which Freud ignores the implications of his own notion of a cloacal theory of birth, as well as how he represses considerations of pre-oedipal anxieties about the maternal body as a site of production in order to posit a castration anxiety that organizes desire along narrowly oedipal, narrative lines. In chapter 4 I begin by positing a masculinist anxiety about the body in Heidegger's "withdrawal" from representation, in his insistence on the ontic/ontological distinction, and in his currently much-discussed political affiliation with National Socialism. In the second part of the chapter I explore the consequences of Derrida's hold on Heidegger for the gender politics of deconstruction; I also offer a reading of Derrida's theory of a "repression of writing," arguing that Derrida himself represses the more bodily and material aspects of *écriture*. Finally, in chapter 5 I examine what might be called the fully abject Joyce, taking up the matter of Joyce's "cloacal obsession" and showing how that obsession might facilitate a productive, feminist reading of Joyce's work. Chapter 6 is offered by way of conclusion.

Although there is a logic, if not a sort of chronology, that brings these chapters and their subjects together, I have provided very little in the way of rhetorical or argumentative connection between them; rather, I have let a profusion of epigraphs serve as markers for the "writerly" reader who is willing to join me in the performance of this text. I should say that I do not pretend to make significant contributions to the scholarship on any of the thinkers under consideration. Rather, I want to trace a particular symptom of masculine identity formation, which I call the anxiety of production, across a variety of discursive fields in order to intervene into that formation. Scholars of Hegel, Bataille, Lacan, or Irigaray may (or may not) appreciate the use I make of those thinkers here, but they are unlikely to learn anything new about them outside of their participation in or challenge to the production of normative masculinity as I examine it. I hope, however, that readers will learn something new about the production of normative masculinity.

The chapters themselves tend to mix rather indiscriminately theory, literature, film, philosophy, versions of psychoanalysis, and references to mass culture. There has, of course, been a great deal of critical agitation over the past twenty years, particularly among practitioners of cultural studies, for just such a loosening of disciplinary boundaries (albeit with a great deal of disagreement about what such loosening means and how and why it should be effected). The assumption behind my own loosening is that if the symptom of masculinity under examination here is as pervasive as I believe it to be, that symptom is not likely to respect disciplinary boundaries any more than my examination of it should.

Theoretical justifications and defenses aside, however, I should say that if *Male Matters* in any way transgresses disciplinary or identificatory boundaries, it does so mainly because I find such transgression thrilling, whatever the anxiety it may produce. And thinking back to that boy in the schoolyard—whose name I cannot remember, but whose bodily act and appearance I suppose I do, after all, take as a productive sort of model for writing itself—I come to see that I always have.

I

Openings: The Anxiety of Production

Significant Discharge and the Production
of Death

The signifying function of the *I* does not depend on the life of the speaking subject. Whether or not perception accompanies the statement about perception, whether or not life as self-presence accompanies the uttering of the *I*, is quite indifferent with regard to the functioning of meaning. My death is structurally necessary to the pronouncing of the *I*.

—Jacques Derrida, *Speech and Phenomena*

Therefore it is accurate to say that when I speak: death speaks in me. . . . I say my name, and it is though I were chanting my own dirge: I separate myself from myself, I am no longer either my presence or my reality, but an objective, impersonal presence, the presence of my name, which goes beyond me and whose stone-like immobility performs exactly the same function for me as a tombstone weighing in the void.

—Maurice Blanchot, *The Gaze of Orpheus*

Speech is a substitute for life: to speak is to lose life, and all effusive behavior is experienced initially as a gesture of dilapidation: by the avowal, the flood of words released, it is the very principle of life that seems to be leaving the body; to speak is to spill oneself, that is, to castrate oneself.

—Roland Barthes, *On Racine*

In one of her contributions to *Men in Feminism* Alice Jardine suggests that, after feminism, men need to learn not only to "speak their bodies" but also to retheorize their own relationship to death ("Men" 61). The epigraphs above, although they indicate no explicit exchange with feminism, also seem to suggest that this retheorization of death needs to confront the problematic relationship, for men, between speaking and the body. For the traditional relationship between men and their bodies has never been a spoken one; rather, it has been marked by a profound if not pronounced anxiety, one that refuses to speak, refuses to see. In the construction of normative masculinity, the question of the body—of its speakability, its visibility, its representability—historically has been displaced onto the other, onto the feminine. Feminization as gendering, as the social and cultural attribution of a certain set of traits (e.g., passivity, vulnerability, dominability) to a biologically "sexed" body, can be read at least partially as an effect of this displacement. Masculinization, the attribution of another set of traits (activity, invulnerability, mastery) to a differently sexed body, is also an effect, although until quite recently one that has not been subjected to critical, oppositional reading.

In *Thinking through the Body* Jane Gallop writes that "men have their masculine identity to gain by being estranged from their bodies and dominating the bodies of others" (7). If this is the case, and I believe it is, then the entire process of this constitutive estrangement needs to be read and relentlessly rewritten. As Gallop makes clear, this estrangement is the price of accession to masculine identity; within the confines and imperatives of that normative or dominative identity, the specific question of the *male* body, the speakability or representability of what Gallop calls "bodily masculinity," cannot arise or can do so only under the auspices of rigorously codified symbolic structures, such as sports and warfare, that guarantee competitive violence. After all, we are allowed to see Arnold Schwarzenegger's naked body in the beginnings of both *Terminator* films only on the condition that he is just about to beat up some other bodies; we are permitted to gaze at Mel Gibson's bare butt in *Lethal Weapon* only on the condition that he will soon be kicking around other butts. These examples of male bodily visibility terminating in lethality are only the most painfully obvious. But from high culture to low, from lyric poetry to hard-core porn, any discursive or representational practice that pays inordinate or "inappropriate" attention to the male body risks falling outside masculine confines and imperatives. Straight male discourse must therefore negotiate itself in relation to that risk, which the producers of this discourse are encouraged to perceive as that of feminization: weakness, vulnerability, powerlessness—a risk ultimately perceived as related to death itself. As Gallop puts it, "Death is a key part of the bodily enigma, perhaps the most violent sign that we live in a nonsensical body which limits the powers of our will and consciousness" (*Thinking* 19).

Nonetheless, if the perceived and perpetuated relationship between men and their bodies has never been a happy one, it could be argued that women's experiences of this tradition of masculine corporeal self-misrelation have been even less happy, if not more deadly. If death speaks in me, as Blanchot puts it, death can also speak *through* me *to* others, particularly to the extent that my identificatory "I" attempts to inscribe the binary opposition of life and death that inheres within my body as a difference between myself and others. Although I am not the one to make the argument, and do not presume to speak for women's experiences, I maintain that historically it is largely (but not only) women who have borne the brunt of the anxieties that underlie and help to overdetermine the construction of normative masculine identity. An interventional rereading of that construction is politically necessary because, as Kaja Silverman puts it, "masculinity impinges with such force upon femininity [that] to effect a large-scale reconfiguration of male identification and desire would, at the very least, permit female subjectivity to be lived differently than it is at present" (*Male Subjectivity* 2–3). This reconfiguration would need to take into account as fully as possible male anxiety about the body because, as Tania Modleski writes, "Women . . . are made to bear . . . the burdens of masculine ambivalence about the body" (*Feminism without Women* 109). Or, to quote Modleski again, "Men's fears become women's fate" (*The Women* 107).

This book deals with a specific instance of men's fears. It concerns what I consider a constitutively masculine anxiety about the male body as a site for the production of language and representation, the role this anxiety plays in constructions of straight male sexuality, and the various ways in which this anxiety can reinforce—or, potentially, disrupt—the representation of masculine identity *in* writing. My emphasis will be on representation and writing, on writing as representation, because the practice of any representational discourse is necessarily "embodied": one thinks, speaks, and writes "through the body," whether the role of the body in the production of thought, speech, and writing is acknowledged or not. Masculinity attempts to construct itself by repressing the acknowledgment of that role (along with other significant debts, most conspicuously that owed to the maternal body). But masculinity cannot represent its supposedly immaculate self-construction without giving itself over to discursive productions in which the always potentially messy question of the body cannot fail to emerge. Thus production—in Jean Baudrillard's sense of "to render visible, to cause to appear and be made to appear: *pro-ducere*" (*Forget Foucault* 21)—becomes a matter of anxiety for masculinity: it becomes the scene of writing in which masculinity faces and, with varying degrees of success, attempts to master its own anxiety. The variation in degrees of success and the stakes of what such success means to the others onto whom masculinity unloads itself are what I attempt to read here.

The anxiety in question, however, is not so much one of *influence*,

as in Harold Bloom's oedipal agons, as one of *exfluence*, of excorporation, a general anxiety about flux and fluidity, an unease not only about
what comes out of the body but also about the way bodies themselves
originally come out. Thus the origins of what I am here calling the
anxiety of production may be located in that pre-oedipal realm of the
abject in which, as Julia Kristeva argues, the masculine subject confronts his fear of an archaic maternal authority. In *Powers of Horror*
Kristeva links abjection with "what disturbs identity, system, order.
What does not respect border, positions, rules" (4). She associates the
abject with "what is jettisoned from the *'symbolic system'* . . . what escapes that social rationality, that logical order on which a social aggre-
gate is based" (65). To the extent that what is jettisoned from any symbolic system relates to what is expelled from the individual body and
its orifices, the abject is for Kristeva always related to fluids and products that traverse the body's boundaries, "polluting objects" that "always relate to corporeal orifices as to so many landmarks parceling-
constituting the body's territory" (71): blood, saliva, milk, urine, semen,
feces, tears. Abjection is thus the general realm of defilement. For
Kristeva, the subject's feeling of abjection in response to these polluting or defiling substances, the anxious ambivalence about their traverse
of the body's boundaries as those boundaries are constituted by the
symbolic, relates to a fear concerning the maternal body and its boundaries. "Defilement is the translinguistic spoor of the most archaic
boundaries of the self's clean and proper body [*corps propre*]. In that
sense, if it is a jettisoned object, it is so from the mother" (73). Abjection as a disruption of these archaic boundaries thus poses a threat of
"engulfment" to the subject, the threat "of being swamped by the dual
relationship, thereby risking the loss not of a part (castration) but of
the totality of his living being," the phantasmatic danger of "his very
own identity sinking irretrievably into the mother" (64).

Kristeva writes that it is the "logic of prohibition," "the simple logic
of *excluding filth*," that founds the abject and that founds "the 'self and
clean' [*corps propre*] of each social group if not of each subject" (*PH* 64,
65). She cites Georges Bataille—who writes that abjection "is merely
the inability to assume with sufficient strength the imperative act of
excluding abject things" (*OC* 2:217)—as having "linked the production
of the abject to *the weakness of that prohibition*, which, in other respects,
necessarily constitutes each social order." Bataille, says Kristeva, is "the
first to have specified that the plane of abjection is that of the *subject/
object relationship* (and not subject/other subject) and that this archa-
ism is rooted in anal eroticism" (*PH* 64). Again, Bataille is hardly a
feminist hero, and many American feminists (not to mention Marx-

ists) have grave problems with Kristeva.[1] Nonetheless, in a move that suggests the urgency for feminism of examining the social, political, and psychosymbolic implications of the way in which this archaic anal eroticism is caught up in the gendering of subject/object relationships, and the still-pervasive cultural denial of subject status to mothers and to women, Kristeva goes on to suggest that

> such an archaic relationship to the *object* interprets, as it were, the relationship to the *mother*. Her being coded as "abject" points to the considerable importance some societies attribute to women. . . . The symbolic "exclusionary prohibition" that . . . constitutes collective existence does not seem to have, in such cases, sufficient strength to dam up the abject or demoniacal potential of the feminine. The latter, precisely on account of its power, does not succeed in differentiating itself as *other* but threatens one's *own and clean self* which is the underpinning of any organization constituted by exclusions and hierarchies. (*PH* 64–65)

What needs to be examined, however, is how the imperative act of excluding abject things functions in the construction of masculinized identity and in the linguistic and representational processes by which the masculinized subject attempts to identify (with) itself.[2] For this exclusion of the abject does more than suppress the threat of the maternal—or the feminine.[3] An abject masculine relationship to the maternal, to the feminine, to the nonidentical, also interprets—and is perhaps overdetermined by—an anxious masculine relationship to the male body, to the visibility of that body, the traverse of its boundaries, the representability of its products, the corporeal conditions of male subjectivity, and the unavoidable materiality of the signifying process itself. This anxiety is an inevitable function of an idealized identificatory formalism, the long-standing patriarchal ideology in which embodiment and femininity are equated, in which male bodies do not matter, in which only women are supposed to have bodies, in which only women's bodies are seen. As Rosalind Coward puts it,

> Our society has been saturated with images of women's bodies and representations of women's sexuality. Under this sheer weight of attention to women's bodies we seem to have become blind to something. Nobody seems to have noticed that men's bodies have quietly absented themselves. Somewhere along the line, men have managed to keep out of the glare, escaping from the relentless activity of sexual definitions. In spite of the ideology which would have us believe that women's sexuality is an enigma, it is in reality men's bodies, men's sexuality which is the true "dark continent" of this society. (*Female Desires* 227)

In *Male Matters* I examine the relationship between the dark continent of male sexuality and masculine anxiety about its own dark incontinence. Exploring the historical invisibility of male bodies and the unrepresentability of male bodily production(s) in dominant signifying practices, I interrogate the way productive anxiety functions in the ideological interpellation of men as subjects supposed to dominate; I examine the deployment of a hegemonic masculinity that can imagine self-preservation only as the mastery of a visible alterity, of the representational Other, the Other as representation itself.

It is this inescapable alterity of the visual—for instance, the materiality of writing as visibilized speech—that makes the project of masculine self-representation an always uneasy process of fluidic self-alteration that calls the solidified boundaries of masculinity itself into question: that is, masculinity does not exist outside representation, yet in the processes of self-representation it risks losing itself, changing itself, seeping out through its own fissures and cracks. Thus, the self-sameness of masculinity depends on the *assuagement* of productive anxiety through a relentless attempt at semiotic self-containment. This assuagement depends on more than a fearful devaluation of the "uncontained," however. It both depends on and helps to overdetermine what Andreas Huyssen calls "the persistent gendering as feminine of that which is devalued" (*After the Great Divide* 53). Consequently, a silence about bodily masculinity must be complicit in the reproduction of that devaluation and hence of oppressive gender relations. Thus I consider the theoretical project of making the production(s) of masculinity and of the male body visible to be an at least potentially transformative political intervention into the social reproduction of gender.

One point, however, needs clearly to be stressed. The constitutively masculine anxieties under examination here originate in, and reproduce themselves as, fears that are often (and often quite ludicrously) phantasmatic. Nonetheless, these socially produced phantasmatic anxieties play a role in reproducing social consequences that are all too hideously real. Masculine anxieties help to produce history itself, which as Fredric Jameson has argued, is not only "the Real" in the Lacanian sense but also, more simply, "what hurts" (*Political Unconscious* 102). The most irreducible real of history may well be the body in pain, and one can intervene into this history only by interrogating the position of power that one occupies and is supposed to occupy within it. Thus insofar as I, writing as a heterosexual white male, have any dispensation to discuss women's anxieties at all (again, I do not presume to speak for women), I submit that whereas masculine anxieties are largely phantasmatic, women's fears of being marginalized and silenced—

indeed, of being raped and murdered—are anything but: men's fears *produce* women's fate. Without replicating the scenario in which women's victimization is unalterably fated, one could say that women's anxieties are real not only in the sense that Modleski suggests but also in the sense described by Freud: "we should call [real anxiety] a reaction to the perception of an external danger, of an injury which is expected and foreseen; it is bound up with the reflex of flight, and may be regarded as an expression of the instinct of self-preservation" (*SE* 16:393–94). Moreover, women's self-preservation might necessarily depend more immediately on anxiety about men and men's actions than on anxiety about the economic, representational, and psychosymbolical structures of power and oppression that must reproduce men as subjects of domination in order to reproduce themselves. No change in the reproduction of masculine subjectivity is possible, however, without close critical attention to these structures and the mechanics of their reproduction. No social change is likely without our transforming the reproduction of a masculinity that continues to imagine its own self-preservation as domination—or, to quote Modleski once again, as long as "man desperately tries to sustain a sense of himself that necessitates the end of woman" (*The Women* 100). As Anthony Easthope puts it, "Social change is necessary and a precondition of such change is an attempt to *understand* masculinity, to make it visible" (*What a Man's Gotta Do* 7).

My critical and political interest, therefore, is in making hegemonic masculinity visible. Although I attempt this visibilization through reading a diverse collection of texts, however, I am concerned not only with masculine anxiety about speaking and writing the body as an exclusively textual phenomenon for which there is no outside. More important, I am concerned with the role this anxiety plays in the patriarchal deployment of men as agents of domination, as those whose main political function becomes quite precisely to silence and to marginalize, if not to rape and to kill. My argument is that male productive anxiety constitutes a psychosymbolic area that can be both used as a site of resistance to patriarchy and exploited for the purposes of furthering male domination. In the former case, which I take to be articulated in work by men (such as Joyce) who wrote under the condition of being "possessed by abjection" (Kristeva, *PH* 208), resistance involves the reactivation of nonsublimated semiotic discursive energies that potentially disrupt the male body's insertion into a fixed masculine/dominative subject position (although it should be stressed that whatever resistance to patriarchy such disruption offers does not by itself constitute a feminist project). In the latter case, perhaps best typified by the "fascist male warrior" mentality examined by Klaus Theweleit in *Male Fantasies* and by Stanley Kubrick in *Full Metal Jacket*, the same energies are channeled so coercively that production itself is tolerated only on the condition that nothing be produced but domination and death.[4] In this most restrictive representational economy, nothing is allowed to come out of the male body except in the name of violence and domination. The male body itself is rigidly overcoded as a lethal weapon. Freedom becomes just "another word for nothing left to kill" (Gitlin 30).[5] The end of all masculine excorporation becomes destruction, not in any supposedly radical Heideggerian sense but in the sense of what Arthur and Marilouise Kroker have called "the search for the killable other."[6] In this worst-case scenario, death becomes not a telos of final rest but rather the ideal of the masculine/dominative mode of subjective agency, an ideal of "being-death," speaking the death that speaks in me to others—an ideal that inhabits and governs the construction of masculine mastery.

Obviously there is nothing phantasmatic or unreal about any man's fear of literal death. Death is rather unavoidably "something to be scared of" (Kristeva, *PH* 32). Nevertheless, there seems to be a powerful and spectral set of psychosymbolic forces at work to generate the thought that pervades the opening epigraphs from Derrida, Blanchot, and Barthes, the idea not only that utterance itself inscribes death but that any act of linguistic self-designation somehow threatens the male body with violence. As John T. Irwin puts it, writing about Faulkner, "A writer's relation to his material and to the work of art is always a loss, a separation, a cutting off, a self-castration that transforms the masculine artist into the feminine-masculine vase of the work" (*Doubling* 171). According to this logic, then, to speak, to identify oneself in language or in art, is to lose oneself, to solidify one's own death, to spill out one's life, to put one's head on the chopping block. But if this logic of linguistic self-mutilation is conflated with the classical psychoanalytic view of women as castrated, as in the passage from Irwin, then to speak or write oneself would also be to feminize oneself, to move from the masculinized activity of producing art to the feminized passivity of being looked at as art, as material, as product. John Berger, in his *Ways of Seeing*, identifies the working paradigm thus: "*Men act* and *women appear*" (47).[7]

What we might also see operating here, particularly in Barthes's conspicuous mixture of phallic dismemberment and seminal spillage, is a strangely abject solidification of seminal loss, a partial solidification that might also be designated as fecal.[8] The excremental becomes a sort of crumbling space of morphic indeterminacy between phallic solidity and seminal fluidity. Situated in the interstices between action and appearance, subverting what Luce Irigaray identifies as the gendered mechanics of fluids and solids,[9] this indeterminacy reveals certain "cloacal" configurations subtending masculine anxiety not only about death and castration (Freud's notion, which I will examine later, of defecation cum part-object loss as a prototype for the fear of losing the penis) but also about ejaculation—and beyond that, about the production of visible language and the representation of masculine identity in that language. This quite material indeterminacy, particularly as it makes evident the threat posed by the visibility of semen to the clean and proper invisibility of the phallus as Lacanian transcendental signifier—"neither a real nor a fantasized organ," writes Gallop, "but an attribute: a power to generate meaning" (*Thinking* 126)—will allow us to see how the paradigm Berger identifies might be disrupted, how the power to generate meaning is potentially undermined, and how "the inability to assume with sufficient strength the imperative act of excluding abject things" (Bataille, *OC* 2:217) is anxiously foregrounded, whenever and however semen appears.

The main if not sole representational arena in which semen regularly makes a literal appearance is the ejaculation scenes, or "money shots," of heterosexually oriented hard-core film pornography. In these scenes, the male sex worker typically withdraws his penis from whichever of the female worker's orifices he has occupied and ejaculates visibly onto some other portion of her body, usually the face, breasts, or buttocks. In her excellent study *Hard Core: Power, Pleasure and the "Frenzy of the Visible,"* Linda Williams provides an extended analysis of the money shot. Following Foucault, Williams designates pornography less as a representation of repressed bodies and pleasures than as a specific deployment of sexuality, a mode of power/knowledge that attempts to capture "the visual evidence of the mechanical 'truth' of bodily pleasure caught in involuntary spasm; the ultimate and uncontrollable—ultimate *because* uncontrollable—confession of sexual pleasure in the climax of orgasm" (101). In the attempt to extract and display this confession, however, porn confronts "the very limit of the visual representation of sexual pleasure" (101), for the truth of bodily pleasure that porn wants to catch is that of women, and although there are exceptions, women's bodies generally do not offer up substantial visual evidence of orgasm.[10]

The irony of the money shot, then, is that what the male sex worker's ejaculation actually represents, or stands in for, is the *woman's* otherwise unrepresentable involuntary spasm. Thus, in this regard, semen is feminized by virtue of being subjected to representation. But unless we as viewers believe that, as Williams puts it, "the sexual performers within the film *want* to shift from a tactile to a visual pleasure at the crucial moment of the male's orgasm," unless we believe the pornographic conceit that "the woman prefers the sight of the ejaculating penis or the external touch of the semen to the thrust of the penis inside her" (101), we can see that not only the woman but in fact *both* participants are excluded from the "uncontrollable" pleasure that the money shot purports to display: his ejaculation becomes the verifiable sign of the orgasm she is not really having (and could not visibly prove even if she were), while her performed convulsions signify the uncontrollable *jouissance* to which he, as a man, has no access (except through watching her). For men, as they are constructed in and out of mainstream (straight) pornography, do not have involuntary, uncontrollable spasms; they do not have, or at least are not represented as having, pleasures that fall outside the margins of control. Arguably, men are not represented as having sex at all; rather, they are represented as having power. As Kathy Acker puts it in *Great Expectations*, "Most men don't like sex. They like being powerful and when you have good sex you lose all power" (111).

I believe, however, that we need to dismantle this gendered opposition between a "bad power" that really has nothing to do with sex and a "good sex" that could be located at some utopian remove from the effects of power. The problem is not simply that men like power more than sex, although that is obviously the form the problem takes and in which it is historically reproduced; rather, the problem is that sexuality inscribes a tense oscillation between power and powerlessness to which all bodies are subjected but that is culturally split into the gendered subject positions by and as which men and women are ideologically interpellated.

In "Is the Rectum a Grave?" Leo Bersani critiques the "redemptive" notion that "the sexual—involving as it does the source and locus of every individual's original experience of power (and of powerlessness) in the world: the human body—could somehow be conceived of apart from all relations of power, [as if it] were, so to speak, belatedly contaminated by power from elsewhere" (221). Bersani begins his brilliant essay with the assertion that "there is a big secret about sex": it is not just men but "most people" who "don't like it" (197). For Bersani, however, the problem lies not with sex but with people, or more closely with "the self," which cannot possibly like a sexuality whose main function is precisely to shatter it. In *The Freudian Body: Psychoanalysis and Art*, Bersani follows Freud in arguing that "the pleasurable unpleasurable tension of sexual excitement occurs when the body's 'normal' range of sensation is exceeded, and when the organization of the self is momentarily disturbed by sensations or affective processes somehow 'beyond' those compatible with psychic organization." Sexuality, then, writes Bersani, "would be that which is intolerable to the structured self. From this perspective, the distinguishing feature of infancy would be its *susceptibility to the sexual*. The polymorphously perverse nature of infantile sexuality would be a function of the child's vulnerability to being shattered into sexuality" (38). In "Is the Rectum a Grave?" Bersani also posits sexuality as self-shattering and the "self-shattering into the sexual as a kind of nonanecodotal self-debasement . . . in which, so to speak, the self is exuberantly discarded" (217–18). Bersani goes on to write that

> the self which the sexual shatters provides the basis on which sexuality is associated with power. It is possible to think of the sexual as, precisely, moving between a hyperbolic sense of self and a loss of all consciousness of self. But sex as self-hyperbole is perhaps a repression of sex as self-abolition. It inaccurately replicates self-shattering as self-swelling, as psychic tumescence. If, as these words suggest, men are especially apt to "choose" this version of sexual pleasure, because their sexual equipment appears to invite by analogy, or at least to facilitate, the phallicizing of the ego, neither sex has exclusive rights to the practice of sex as self-hyperbole. For it is perhaps primarily *the degeneration of the sexual into a relationship that condemns sexuality to becoming a struggle for power*. As soon as persons are posited, the war begins. It is the self that swells with excitement at the idea of being on top, the self that makes of the inevitable play of thrusts and relinquishments in sex an argument for the natural authority of one sex over the other. (218)

Again, then, the problem is not that sexuality is contaminated by power but that the hyperbolic self, the phallicized ego, cannot experience sexuality as anything but power, cannot give itself over to the "strong appeal of powerlessness, of the loss of control" ("Rectum" 217). It cannot exuberantly discard and shatter itself into sexuality and so can have contact with sexuality only as the shattering discard of the other. Phallocentrism, therefore, writes Bersani, is "not primarily the denial of power to women (although it has obviously also led to that, everywhere and at all times), but above all the denial of the *value* of powerlessness in both men and women. I don't mean the value of gentleness, or nonaggressiveness, or even of passivity, but rather of a more radical disintegration and humiliation of the self" (217). Bersani takes this subversion of phallocentrism through radical self-disintegration to be not only sexual but political, for he says it is "the sacrosanct value of selfhood [that] accounts for human beings' extraordinary willingness to kill in order to protect the seriousness of their statements. The self is a practical convenience; promoted to the status of an ethical ideal, it is a sanction for violence" (222).

Bersani's definition of phallocentrism as a denial of the value of powerlessness in both men and women allows us to reread "the persistent gendering as feminine of that which is devalued" (Huyssen, *After the Great Divide* 53) as possibly pertaining to both men and women, however differently—and violently—women have experienced that persistence (and the difference is considerable). It allows us to think of phallocentrism as the opposite of abjection, since phallocentrism does in fact assume with sufficient strength the imperative act of excluding abject, powerless, devalued things.

But this definition also brings us back to the matter of the money shot in porn. If semen, the putative essence of biological maleness, is potentially feminized at the moment when it is given over to representation, feminized and hence devalued by virtue of its visibility—if semen in its very movement from invisibility to visibility undergoes a change in value that corresponds to the movement from the hyperbolic self to the exuberantly discarded self—then the money shot functions to assuage male anxiety about the lack of value, lack of power, and lack of masculinity that accrue to the hyperbolic act of ejaculation at the very moment of the ejaculate's self-shattering appearance. The division between masculine act and feminine appearance, the movement from hype to humiliation, is momentarily revealed as a purely homosocial split between male orgasm and male ejaculation, but only so that the split may be sutured immediately and redistributed along rigidly gendered, reheterosexualized lines. In other words, since the visibility of semen in the money shot moves it outside the frame of normative reproductive heterosexuality (insemination necessarily being invisible), the money shot depends on the cinematic apparatus to reproduce masculine power by other means, ensuring that semen always ends up where it "belongs" (or, to use another language, that "a letter always reaches its destination").[11] The female sex worker's function is not only to guarantee the heterosexuality of the erotic visual exchange between the male sex worker and the male spectator but also to conceal the change in value and to bolster male hyperbole by taking on the role of the discarded, humiliated self, staging what Scott McDonald calls "aggressive acceptance" ("Confessions" 41). In her performance she positions her body as a reassuring surface for the male's ejaculatory inscription—reassuring precisely because powerless, valueless, convulsive, involuntary, out of control—and so reaffirms the male, both worker and spectator, in the position of power and value from which she herself is excluded. As Williams points out, "it is always quite evident that this spectacle is not really for her eyes. She may even close her eyes if the man comes on her face; and, try as she might, she cannot possible see the ejaculate when he comes, as frequently he does, on her buttocks or the small of her back. The man, in contrast, almost always sees himself ejaculate; the act seems much more clearly intended for his eyes and those of the viewer" (101). The camera also functions to conceal the change in value, cutting away before the recuperative illusion that the woman performs becomes untenable—cutting away, that is, before that inevitable moment, which pornography rarely reveals but which the masturbating male spectator perhaps glumly perceives, when the ejaculate must finally be wiped away, when it reveals itself as what Bataille calls an "object of horror" or anguish, a "fetid, sticky object without boundaries, which teems with life and yet is the sign of death" (AS II:95).[12] The camera's cut conceals that moment when the essence of masculinity assumes the status of valueless, powerless, and hence feminized waste.

What the money shot makes explicit, then, is the status of woman in the processes of specularization that allow man not only to see himself ejaculate but to see himself and identify (with) himself in the first place. Given the conflation of femininity with waste on which the money shot clearly depends, however, we might return to the Bataillean/Kristevan contention that an archaic *anal* eroticism subtends any (gendered) subject/object binary opposition and suggest that it is perhaps not only or originally what is feminine but rather, as Freud puts it, "what is 'anal' [that] remains the symbol of everything that is to be repudiated and excluded from life" (SE 7:187).[13] The function of the money shot is ultimately to prevent the change in value, to maintain the distinction between phallocentrism and abjection; more bluntly, it is to help keep the processes of specularization that produce masculinity from turning it into shit. The price of the hyperbolic self's coherence is thus the consistent shattering, disintegration, and humiliation of the other; the terms of accession to the *corps propre* of the phallicized ego are the abjection or fecalization of the other. As Judith Butler puts it in *Gender Trouble*, abjection is "the mode by which Others become shit" (134).[14]

The anxiety that the choreography of the money shot attempts to assuage hinges on an abject identification; it is excremental, scatontological. Exploring that anxiety will allow us to examine the persistent gendering of the devalued as feminine, the denial of the value of powerlessness in both men and women, but particularly *in* men as it is deployed *against* women, not simply in pornography (which will remain only a subtext here), but throughout the entire realm of phallocentric specularization. As feminist critiques of pornography have been insisting for some time now, pornography is only the most explicit form of the phallocentric mechanism that pervades and dominates the present cultural domain.[15] If in porn the money shot functions to assuage male anxiety about the visible production of masculinity by displacing the devaluation of the product onto the body of the other, by displacing the whole question of the body onto the scene/seen of the other, the same function may be at work in less explicit ways in the more mainstream areas of masculinist specularization. The stakes, however, would remain the same: to protect the economy of the same from a change in value, to protect the phallus from the threat of abjection inscribed in representation itself. If, as Bersani puts it, "sex as self-hyperbole is perhaps a repression of sex as self-abolition," as self-disintegration and self-abjection, might not the same repression, the same "redemptive" project, be supported (or challenged) in other productions of masculinist representation as well? If "the pleasurable unpleasurable tension of sexual excitement occurs when the body's 'normal' range of sensation is exceeded, and when the organization of the self is momentarily disturbed by sensations or affective processes somehow 'beyond' those compatible with psychic organization" (*Freudian Body* 38), might this description of sexuality as self-shattering also describe a certain experience of modernity? The specific language of Marshall Bermann's *All That Is Solid Melts into Air: The Experience of Modernity* is interesting here:

> There is a mode of vital experience—experience of space and time, of the self and others, of life's possibilities and perils—that is shared by men and women all over the world today. I will call this body of experience "modernity." To be modern is to find ourselves in an environment that promises us adventure, power, joy, growth, transformation of ourselves and the world—and, at the same time, that threatens to destroy everything we have, everything we know, everything we are. Modern environments and experiences cut across all boundaries of geography and ethnicity, of class and nationality, of religion and ideology: in this sense, modernity can be said to unite all mankind. But it is a paradoxical unity, a unity of disunity: it pours us all into a maelstrom of perpetual disintegration and renewal, of struggle and contradiction, of ambiguity and anguish. (15)

Are the anguished ambiguities, the struggles and contradictions, and the disintegrations and renewals of modernity related to those of sex? Is modernity as self-hyperbole a repression of modernity as self-aboli-

tion? That is, are those philosophical, political, and aesthetic respons-
es to and projects of modernity that gather themselves into self-hyperbole a repression of the experience of modernity as self-shattering? Is
this hyperbolic gathering of modernity into a totalizing project staked
not only on the repression of self-abolition but on the active abolition
of the other? And is the acceptance or even celebration of the self-
shattering experience of modernity the necessarily unorganizing ral-
lying cry for the impossible communities of the postmodern?

I take up these rather large questions throughout this text. Here,
returning to the matter of male porn, and focusing briefly on literary
modernism as a response to modernity, I will pose a more specific but
still quite large question: given the familiar list of male modernist writings prosecuted or vilified as pornography—*Ulysses, Sanctuary, Lady
Chatterly's Lover, Tropic of Cancer*—might such charges indicate not only,
or simply, the priggishly conservative Comstockery of the prosecutors
but also a "pornographic" anxiety at work in those writings, if not in
modernist male writing itself? It is at least worth noting that one such
prosecuted and persecuted male modernist, D. H. Lawrence, relied on
the distinction between phallocentrism and abjection on which porn
is predicated to distinguish his work from pornography. In his essay
"Pornography and Obscenity" Lawrence writes:

> Sex is a creative flow, the excrementory flow is toward dissolution,
> decreation. . . . In the really healthy human being the distinction be-
> tween the two is instant, our profoundest instincts are perhaps our
> instincts of opposition between the two flows. But in the degraded
> human being the deep instincts have gone dead, and then the two
> flows become identical. *This* is the secret of really vulgar and porno-
> graphical people: the sex flow and the excrement flow is the same
> thing to them. It happens when the psyche deteriorates, and the
> profound controlling instincts collapse. Then sex is dirt and dirt is sex,
> and sexual excitement becomes a playing with dirt, and any sign of
> sex in a woman becomes a show of her dirt. . . . And this is the source
> of all pornography. (39)[16]

Here Lawrence assuages his own anxiety by setting up an "us-them"
distinction between creation and dissolution that pits "our" profoundly
healthy and instantaneous instincts against "their" psychic degradation,
deterioration, and collapse.[17] What is most conspicuous in this passage,
however, is Lawrence's assumption that in this decreative collapse any
sign of sex can be a show only of *feminine* dirt, as if there were never
any sign or show of masculinity in pornography, as if men never appear there. Lawrence, that is, takes the word *pornography* at etymolog-
ical face value—*pornē* for "whore" and *graphos* for "writing"—and as-

sumes that only women can be depicted graphically as whores who show their dirt.

The deeper assumption at work here, however, and not only in Lawrence, is that any *graphos* turns its subject to *pornē*, and this anxious assumption is indentured to the repressed perception not only that any sign of sex is potentially a show of dirt but that *any sign is a sign of sex*, teeming with life and yet signifying death. There is always something sexual at stake in signification, for the signifying process itself, like sexuality, inextricably involves "the source and locus of every individual's original experience of power (and of powerlessness) in the world: the human body" (Bersani, "Rectum" 221). The signifying process locates every body on the side of the accursed share: it always already corporealizes, sexualizes, thanatosizes, or otherwise stains any subjectivity that proudly imagines itself as the immaculate or immortal origin of that process, locating the subject in a perpetual movement, an oscillating tension, between power and powerlessness, control and collapse, coherence and shattering, hyperbole and humiliation, activity and appearance, identity and difference, renewal and disintegration, phallocentric value and abject waste.

A reconfiguration of the gendering of these oppositions into masculinity and femininity would require a disruption of the standard of value that supports and maintains that gendering. It would require an interrogation of what abjection, waste, anality, death mean to normative masculine subjectivity. Bersani writes that "if the rectum is the grave in which the masculine ideal (an ideal shared—differently—by men *and* women) of proud subjectivity is buried, then it should be celebrated for its very potential for death" ("Rectum" 222). He also suggests, in what I consider the most valuable statement ever produced on the subject, that "the value of sexuality itself is to demean the seriousness of efforts to redeem it" ("Rectum" 222). I submit that if the masculine ideal is to be de-meaned, if not buried in the end, the radically irredemptive revaluation and celebration of which Bersani speaks needs to be extended to the level of signification itself, to the entire domain of cultural semiotics in which and by which the masculine (as) ideal is produced. The anxiety of production, as an anxiety about signification, is an effect of the irrepressible perception that the signifier, like the sexual, is always potentially de-meaning, unredeemable, always subject to a certain rectal gravity. The assuagement of that anxiety is the attempt to foreclose it, to enforce the meaningful boundary between phallocentrism and abjection, while the refusal to foreclose on anxiety may open up a potentially subversive space in which certain standards of value and redemption—of "life" itself—are discursively undermined. The tension between anxiety and its assuagement, foreclosure and its refusal, is what I attempt to read here.

As the opening epigraphs suggest, this anxiety about the potential for abjection embedded in the signifying process seems to involve masculine anxieties about castration and death. As I argue throughout this work, however, abjection is a greater, more uncontainable threat to the phallic, hyperbolic self—the self that would kill to protect the seriousness of its statements—than either castration or death, both of which are finally rather phallus-friendly. After all, it is by virtue of the figure and fear of castration that the phallicized ego is allowed to see the other not even as shattered but as castrated, its own symmetrical other; castration anxiety thus becomes a roundabout ticket to a final phallic coherence, an alibi for its own overcoming and the possession of that symmetrical other in what Bersani refers to as the "teleologically narrativized" sexuality subtended by the oedipus complex (*Freudian Body* 64). As Charles Bernheimer puts it, "The function of the castration fantasy is not to discredit the childhood story of universal maleness but to support it ("Penile Reference" 123). Death, on the other hand, is not something that happens to the phallicized ego at the very end of that teleological narrative. It is not even, or exactly, that Freudian state of quiescence and absolutely reduced tension, far beyond the pleasure principle, to which the phallus longs to come in its own sweet time. Rather, as I will show, death is the subject position of "absolute master" that the phallus occupies and from which it produces the deaths of others.[18] Anxieties (Freudian or Heideggerian) about castration and death are privileged precisely because they function to install individuals in phallic subject (or metasubject) positions by virtue of the promise of their resolution. The phallicized ego thus knows how to handle itself, has always handled itself, in the face of death and castration; death and castration are the figures by which the phallicized ego is produced. Abjection, however, is another matter, and so is the anxiety that surrounds it.

But again, what needs to be stressed constantly is the status of women and other others in this uneasily phallic self-relation that is always threatened by the abject. By virtue of Berger's paradigm, the appearance of femininity and the femininity of appearance are inextricably mingled in the actively anxious masculine imaginary not only with castration and death—which, after all, are both aesthetically redeemable (the female body as devivified aesthetic object, Faulkner's vase, which the masculine would have and the feminine would be, or Poe's beautiful dead woman as "the most poetical topic in the world")—but also with an irrecuperable excrementality, with powerless matter itself (the abject dis-contents of the vase as chamber-pot, which smudge the margin between having and being, the feminization of an ejaculation that wastes itself by simple virtue of its appearance). To install masculinity on the active and proper side of the boundary between phallocentrism and abjection, the association between the feminine and dead matter must always be maintained. The *femme fatale*, the fecal female, the analized mother, the sexualized woman as engulfing swamp, and the porn actress who stages her body as the money shot's surface all become the necessary props of the male *corps propre*, the inextricable nightmare/fantasy figures of masculine paranoia and desire. This paranoid desire—as it obsessively, aggressively, and even globally enacts itself—becomes in turn the nightmare of history for women and for the rest of the world, for all those constituted as other by a heterosexist white male hegemony. Thus, in the closing shot of Kubrick's *Full Metal Jacket*, Joker, whose shooting of a Viet Cong "rifle-woman" has assured his solidarity with the "hard corps" of the fearless Marines, announces his hyperbolic self-affirmation as a full-metal subject: "I'm in a world of shit . . . yes, but I am alive, and I am not afraid."

What are the terms of this "fearlessness"? How do they indicate the sexual, textual, and political stakes of the phallicized self as a sanction for violence, sanctioned to kill to protect not only the seriousness but the propriety of its statements, and to guard its identification with itself in the production of those statements? Again, there is nothing phantasmatic or unreal about men's fears of death: bodies die. The phantasms symptomatically emerge in the question of how various and divergent forms of alterity and heterogeneity come to *figure* death in the masculine imaginary, how sexual, cultural, and material differences inscribe masculinity in a relation to what Derrida calls "visibility, spacing, death" (*OG* 234), and how masculine production handles itself in the mark or shadow of this inscription. The problem of death, castration, and the abjection that lies behind them becomes a problem of writing, a question of the objectification, mutilation, and contamination to which, in the very process of representing identity in language, the anxious male writer imagines that he submits his being. Writing becomes a problem not only because it "causes the subject who ventures in it to confront an archaic [maternal] authority" (Kristeva, *PH* 75) but because it causes the subject who ventures in it to confront the abject production(s) of his own body.

The repression of writing and the foreclosure of productive anxiety collude with the exclusion of all that phantasmatically figures death. This exclusion "aspires" toward an ideal state in which death and being become purely identical. This pure identity is rather ironic, since the ostensible purpose of the original exclusion was to protect being from the threat of death—to protect male essence from the excremental (m)other, to protect the *corps propre* from contaminating abjection. But this irony becomes deadly serious when "being-death" becomes an active subject position, the agency for the death of others, a sort of fortified and spotless bunker from which the masculine subject, like Theweleit's fascist warrior, polices the boundaries and frontiers of his own masculinity and, when these are threatened, narrows his vision, sets his sights, and fires. Tracing the mechanisms by which being-death can become the dominant paradigm for any significantly masculine discharge shows how the rigid foreclosure of productive anxiety can lead to the production of death. It suggests the stakes of the ongoing construction of a masculinity unafraid in a world of shit and the need to examine the repression of the visibility of the male body that continues to subtend that fearlessness.

The (S)tain of the Mirror: Writing the Modernist Male Body

> . . . an anxiety about language—which can only be an anxiety of language, within language itself.
>
> —Jacques Derrida, *Writing and Difference*

> They are, to put it bluntly, enemies of production. Production makes them uncomfortable. You never know where you are with production; production is the unforeseeable. You never know what's going to come out.
>
> —Bertolt Brecht, to Walter Benjamin[19]

> For this subject, who thinks he can accede to himself by designating himself in the statement, is no more than such an object. Ask the writer about the anxiety that he experiences when faced by the blank sheet of paper, and he will tell you who *is* the turd of his phantasy.
>
> —Jacques Lacan, *Écrits*

The relationship between language and the body is a relation of production, of causing to appear and being made to appear: bodies produce language, just as language helps to produce the field of cultural intelligibility in which bodies make their appearance. As the preceding epigraphs suggest, however, this productive relation is not without a certain amount of anxiety for a particular speaking subject. This anxiety can stem from the way in which conceptions and to some extent even experiences of the body are produced by and inscribed within an inherently unstable linguistic system. More important for this discussion, however, is the extent to which language inscribes the body as its own productive site, a corporeal matrix of openings for the reception, reproduction, and re-presentation of words. The subject's struggle for identity in language, the subject's attempt to accede to itself by designating itself in a statement, involves its mediation in a complex dialectic of internalization and externalization for which its body and the bodies of others serve as boundaries.

It is, however, on externalization that the burden of productive anxiety most heavily falls. Some system of "ideal receptacles" that channel or contain whatever the body produces and externalizes from itself—biologically, libidinally, or linguistically—always lies in wait for the speaking subject. For the disposal of urine and feces, for example, there are codes of appropriate social behavior that vary from culture to culture but that in the West have devolved largely on the segregation of public facilities according to gender—and, at some specific historical and regional junctures, according to race.[20] For male ejaculation, there are masturbatory, coital, marital, and other proscriptions that enact a heterosexual imperative by directing the flow of semen toward the interior of a female body (preferably ovulating but definitely not menstruating) or toward the exterior of that body as reassuring surface (the money shot), but in any case *not* toward the interior or exterior of another male. Finally, for signifying practice itself, there lies in wait, anterior to any act of speaking or writing, a conventional system of meaning that at the most basic level ensures simple communication but that, at the level of ideology (literature, art, politics, family, church, state), works to ensure the transmission of culturally dominant values.

On a number of levels, then, civilization works to contain the incontinence of its discontents. To be a subject, whatever else it might mean, always involves being subjected to civilized economies of production. Arguably, the more *developed* the civilization, the greater the collapse of these various and heterogeneous economies into one another. Their insistent organization as a homogeneous, unified front works to narrow the space for social, sexual, and linguistic difference, resulting in what Bataille calls a "restricted economy."[21] Socialization— or as Althusser puts it, the transformation of "the small animal conceived by a man and a woman into a small human child" (*Lenin* 205)— thus involves the subject's ongoing negotiation of this corporeal and "tropaic matrix"[22] of receptacles, of which its own body is always already a function: learning to use language, learning to use the bathroom, learning to occupy a socially constructed and gendered subject position are all intricated functions of this ideological negotiation. It is scarcely an accident that Freud's claims arose from his examinations of the discourses of hysterics, in which deviations in conventional linguistic meaning (parapraxes, etc.) indicated failures to negotiate conventional or normative sexual meanings—in the case of the hysterical woman, often a "failure" not to use but rather to *be* such a receptacle for a male. Psychosis, the most complete refusal of socialization, a thoroughgoing breakdown of all negotiations, often involves a refusal to be subjected to any social economy, to use any of the ideal receptacles: the psychotic soils him- or herself, masturbates in public, talks in babble, stops making sense.

Between two hypothetical poles, then—the one of absolute socialization, which would involve a complete mastery of (and hence complete subjection to) the dominant social codes, and the other of absolute psychotic breakdown—the subject attempts to negotiate an identity in language. Nonetheless, given on the one hand the challenge posed to the stability of this negotiation by the unconscious—to which the subject can only partially relegate what it must forgo to learn its social lessons (the pleasures of anal pulsion, for example, or of a presymbolic babble free from the burden of meaning anything at all)—and on the other the radical heterogeneity of language itself (the now widely acknowledged inability of signification to come to full closure in a transcendental signified), this negotiation can be neither stable nor finished. It can be only a process of constant renegotiation without promise of final settlement, endless rearticulation without hope of what Conrad calls "full utterance."[23] No utterance, that is, can be full because the act of uttering empties out that utterance. Nor does the subject ever fully possess an identity that it then somehow renegotiates through a transparent rational process of meditation and decision. Rather, subjectivity is the effect of this ongoing process of renegotiation, a process that produces subjectivity and that can be discerned only in terms of such effects. Thus, we "read the text" of any subject not as a unified and self-identical whole but as an always breached social contract.

These tropes of legality and rupture—contract, negotiation, settlement, breach—resonate with the works of Lacan and Kristeva. For Lacan, all symbolization (and hence all socialization) orders itself according to the logic of the phallus, the primary signifier of sexual difference that functions as both the Name and the Law of the Father (*nom du père* and *non du père*): to accede to the symbolic order of language, to become a speaking subject, is to assume a subject position predictated by the phallogocentric law. For Kristeva, however, the subject can never completely take this dictation.[24] The radical heterogeneity and play of difference of all signifying practice, as well as the way semiotic or psychosomatic energies disrupt symbolic formations, ensure that no subject position is ever finally fixed; the subject, which can signify or represent itself only within the dialectic of semiotic and symbolic, is never fully present either to itself or to the law, but is rather always put *en procès*—the term Kristeva uses to designate both "in process" and "on trial."[25]

A subject *en procès* can well be imagined as a subject of anxiety, an anxiety in, of, and about language that is also in, of, and about the body: an anxiety of production that collapses all those heterogeneous processes for which bodies are sites—fecal, urinal, seminal, fetal, menstrual, glottal, lingual—into an undifferentiated and abject flux. The anxiety is that this flux will somehow either miss, overrun, or otherwise exceed the prefigured social containers and channels, the restricted economy of the ideal receptacles. The flux might either disseminate, pitching itself into the abyss in a gesture of pure expenditure in which the subject experiences the externalization of its essence as radical loss, or contaminate, lingering or returning as a hostile presence to threaten the prophylactic boundaries of the subject's insular ego, engulfing the subject in its own material corruption. In either case the anxiety of production is clearly indentured to a binary, prophylactic, hierarchal logic of internal and external, subject and object, identity and alterity, propriety and contamination, appropriation and loss. This anxiety is specifically masculine and in ways identifiably modern in the broadest sense. That is, it functions in the ideological interpellation of biological males as masculinized subjects of domination within the historical problematic of modernity. This anxiety not only contributes to that interpellation but reaches a sort of critical mass when the masculinized subject confronts representation itself, the irreducible and unsublatable materiality of signifying practices—when, in the attempt to secure a stable identity by producing a self-representation, to accede to himself by designating himself in a statement, he fa(e)ces himself on the blank white page.

In *Inhibitions, Symptoms and Anxiety* Freud provides a possible sexual etiology for what he elsewhere refers to as "dysgraphia," or "an incomprehensible disinclination to write" (*CL* 48). "As soon as writing, which entails making a liquid flow out of a tube onto a piece of white paper, assumes the significance of copulation . . . writing [is] stopped because [it] represent[s] the performance of a forbidden sexual act" (*SE* 20:90). Leo Bersani has examined how psychoanalysis tends "to domesticate its own discoveries" (*Culture* 44).[26] Here Freud domesticates, oedipalizes, and hence normativizes the dysgraphic anxiety he describes, assuming that writing will naturally take on the significance only of heterosexual copulation and not of other problematic sexual or bodily functions or interactions. Lacan is perhaps closer to the mark: the subject who thinks he can accede to himself by designating himself in the statement in fact turns himself into an object: "Just ask the writer about the anxiety he experiences when he faces the blank sheet of paper, and he will tell you who *is* the turd of his phantasy" (*É* 315). Elsewhere Lacan writes of "that vertigo . . . of the white page, which, for a particular character . . . is like the centre of the symptomatic barrage which blocks off for him every access to the Other. If, quite literally, he cannot touch this white page at which his ineffable intellectual effusions come to a stop, it is because he apprehends it only as a piece of lavatory paper" (*FFC* 268–69).

This anxiety, as it is pronounced in the masculinized writer—that in trying to represent himself by or accede to himself through the written statement, he inadvertently but unavoidably turns himself into shit—is what I am calling the anxiety of production. But this anxiety obtains not only for writing, which only exacerbates it, but for speech itself. As Kristeva puts it, giving matters a more oral spin, "I expel *myself,* I spit *myself* out, I abject *myself* within the same motion through which 'I' claim to establish *myself*" (*PH* 3). One way of understanding this self-establishment as self-expulsion is to relate it to Benveniste's notion of an inevitable linguistic split between the subject of an enunciation and the subject of a statement, between the "I" that speaks and the signifier "I" that the speaker uses, loses, and vainly attempts to regain in the act of self-representation: "I—mark(s) the division," as Derrida writes in *Glas* (165).

The question that arises in trying to consider this split psychoanalytically, however, is to what extent this split or division—which relates to that primordial lack or loss of the real that for Lacan constitutively marks subjectivity itself—can still be thought, as Lacan indeed thinks it, as castration and to what extent castration functions to formalize and reify this notion of a primordially constitutive lack.[27] My interest here will be in the way castration domesticates, oedipalizes, and thus heterosexualizes this linguistic split between enunciation and statement, the way an insistence on castration disavows other more abject forms of separation, excorporation, and loss that may be involved with it. The question that extends throughout this study concerns what the vertiginous anxiety of the blank white page that Lacan describes so well has to do with castration and whether castration is not finally a means of papering over that corporeal and linguistic unease.

To be sure, the anxious male writer who wants to stabilize and fortify the boundaries of his own masculine identity fears that he gives himself over to death and castration in the attempt to re-present himself through writing. But he also fears that he shits himself, confronting himself as the turd of his own anxious fantasy. Unable to bear the scatontological anxiety opened up by the vertigo of writing, the anxious male writer projects his fears about himself onto others as a way of fixing the boundaries of his own *corps propre*. To avoid abjecting himself, to avoid spitting or shitting himself out in the same motion by which he claims to establish himself, the anxious male writer turns on the other. This abjecting puts into writing the mode by which others become shit. Writing masterfully becomes the means of both mastering and assuaging the anxiety of production opened up by the materiality of writing, the abject corporeality of language itself.

I will be examining what I believe to be the cultural consequences of this anxiety as it is variously articulated in different but corresponding areas of male textual production: speculative dialectics (Hegel), psychoanalysis (mostly Freud), deconstruction (Heidegger and Derrida), and literary modernism (Joyce).[28] I use the word *production* not to rehearse the classical Marxist vocabulary based on nineteenth-century industrial manufacture but in the sense that Baudrillard develops in *Forget Foucault:* "to render visible, to cause to appear and be made to appear: *producere*" (21). The term will designate any process of externalization by which something is made or allowed to appear. Production thus discloses not only linguistic and representational processes (speaking, writing, painting, photography, even what Hegel calls "picture-thinking") but also those corporeal processes not generally considered productive—urination, defecation, wayward ejaculation, vomiting, even Stephen Dedalus's depositing of a lonely booger on a rock on Sandymount Strand in *Ulysses*. By collapsing linguistic, representational, and corporeal processes of externalization under this generalized rubric of production, I examine the restricted economy of sexual, textual, and political representation that hails men as masculine subjects in history.

This hailing depends on a certain repression and disciplining of the male body, of the bodily in the male. A major aspect—perhaps *the* major aspect—of this repression is the conversion of an arguably indifferent bodily organ, the penis, into the primary or transcendental signifier, the phallus. Indeed, Kaja Silverman writes that the "collective make-believe in the commensurability of penis and phallus" so overdetermines "our 'dominant fiction'"—the "ideological belief [through which] a society's 'reality' is constituted and sustained, and [through which] a subject lays claim to a normative identity"—that "our society's entire 'reality' depends upon the maintenance of that equation" (*Male*

Subjectivity 15, 8). Silverman's comments suggest that a reconfiguration of the dominant fiction and normative identity might be effected by disrupting the equation or commensurability of penis and phallus. In *Thinking through the Body* Jane Gallop writes that the phallus in the Lacanian sense is "neither a real nor a fantasized organ but an attribute: a power to generate meaning" (126). In *Homosexual Desire* Guy Hocquenghem refers to the phallus as "the dispenser of meaning between the sexes" (65). And Judith Butler, in *Bodies That Matter*, asserts that "insofar as the male genitals become the site of textual vacillation, they enact the impossibility of collapsing the distinction between penis and phallus" (61). If these descriptions hold, then the incommensurability of penis and phallus might be foregrounded to the extent that the penis joins with other bodily openings (most gravely, perhaps, the rectum) in having the (non)power to produce a (non)meaning that substantially de-means phallic reproduction, no longer dispensing meaning but dispensing with it—and along with meaning, normative identity itself, for as Hocquenghem comments, "Only the phallus dispenses identity; any social use of the anus, apart from its sublimated use, creates the risk of a loss of identity" (*Homosexual Desire* 87). Here we might recall and augment Bersani's definition of phallocentrism in a way that reveals why it is always a phal*logo*centrism working hard to maintain meaningful identity: it is not primarily a denial of power to women (though always that) but a denial of the value of powerlessness, and of meaninglessness, of nonidentity or disidentification, in both women and men.

Commenting on "the endless repetition of failed efforts to clearly distinguish phallus and penis" (*Thinking* 127), Gallop writes that "if the phallus is distinct from the penis, then feminism's battle against phallocentrism is not a battle against men. But if it is nearly impossible to keep the distinction phallus/penis clear, that may account for the constant return of the assumption that men are the enemies of feminism" (125). She writes that "to distinguish penis from phallus would be to locate some masculinity that does not necessarily obliterate the feminine. Yet it remains an open question . . . whether there is any masculinity that is beyond the phallic phase" (125). Gallop concludes:

> I cannot disintricate the penis from phallic rule but neither is it totally synonymous with the transcendent phallus. At this point in history I don't think they can be separated, but to insist on bodily masculinity is to work to undo the heterosexist ideology which decrees the body female, to be dominated not by a male body (too disorderly to rule) but by an idealized, transcendent phallus. I want to render that idealization impossible. (*Thinking* 131–32)

I agree with Gallop that at this point the two cannot be distinguished; the production of (non)meaning can take place only within structures still dominated by the phallic generation of meaning, the meaning of a still predominantly phallic generation (men, that is, are for the most part still such a bunch of mean-ies, not to mention outright enemies of feminism, that any male effort to de-mean the phallus, including this one, should remain suspect). At the same time, I also agree that one of the most productive ways of rendering phallic idealization impossible would be to insist on bodily masculinity, to insist on a male body that is too disorderly to rule—that is, both too disorderly to be ruled and, more important, too disorderly to allow the easy assumption of the subject position of the one who is supposed to rule.

Gallop's point seems lost on Stephen Heath, however, at least in his leading essay in *Men in Feminism*. Forestalling the whole question of the male body as utopian, Heath writes that "the truth about men and their bodies *for the moment* is merely repetitive . . . : the regime of the same, the eternal problem of the phallus, etc. . . . Taking men's bodies away from the existing representation and its oppressive effects will have to follow women's writing anew of themselves: for today, telling the truth about the male body as freeing subject is utopia, about the female body *actuality*" (26). Cary Nelson, in his contribution to *Men in Feminism*, joins Heath in dismissing as utopian Alice Jardine's suggestion that men learn to speak and write their bodies. Although he concedes that to enact such a project would be "to overturn our whole notion of academic writing" and admits that if this project could be enacted, "the social construction of gender will itself begin to change," Nelson argues that Jardine's suggestion is "a utopian aim [that] we are unlikely to achieve . . . for some time. It is useful as a provocation and a basis for reflection and self-critique, but it is unrealistic as a condition for feminist writing by men" (158).

I am suspicious of these caveats and wonder whether they are not themselves indentured to a certain inherently phallogocentric maneuver. In the passage from Heath, for example, the truth of the male body is elevated to the realm of an ideal, unseen, unrealistic utopia, whereas the question of actuality (corporeality or materiality) gets displaced onto the feminine. Heath writes that "female sexuality is a bad question from a rotten history," whereas "'male sexuality' [note the scare quotation marks] is a good question from a rotten history that could not pose it" (14). His implication is that history is still too rotten for feminist men to pose the question of male sexualities, male bodies. I suggest that it is not simply that history is still too rotten for men to pose the question but rather that men's refusal to think, speak, and write their bodies helps to make history rotten in the first place. The refusal to tell the truth about the male body is the precondition not only for the effacement of those bodies in the existing representation—that is, in the truth according to the phallus—but also for the continuing displacement of the question of the body onto an actuality coded as feminine. Nothing could be more repetitive. The longer male theorists forestall attempting to tell the truth or say something specific about the male body, the longer we continue to bear witness to the truth of the phallic law and to reproduce ourselves as the agents of patriarchal domination.

Such, I think, is the point of Hélène Cixous's assertion that "men still have everything to say about their sexuality, and everything to write" ("Laugh" 247). Such also is Alice Jardine's point in her essay in *Men in Feminism* when she suggests "a moratorium on male discourse about feminism/women/femininity/female sexuality/feminine identity/ etc." and reiterates Cixous's remark by saying to men who would be feminists, "*You still have everything to say about your sexuality*" ("Men" 61). The fact that what has been said most recently by men about male bodies comes predominantly from gay male theorists indicates not only the increasing vitality of queer theory but also the extent to which the idealizing repression of bodily masculinity in male discourse is a function of what Gallop refers to as a heterosexist ideology. A silence about bodily masculinity is a structural necessity in the interpellation of men as heterosexual if not heterosexist subjects, homophobic as well as misogynistic. In an ideology in which the body is always female, "to have a body" can only mean to be a woman or to possess one. The question of the bodily in the male is thus what must be excluded in a heterosexualized narrative of masculine self-possession. As Elizabeth Grosz has written, "the masculine can speak of and for the feminine largely because it has emptied itself of any relation to the male body, its specificity, and socio-political existence. This process of evacuating the male body from (an oedipalized) masculinity is the precondition for the establishment of the 'disinterested' neutered space of male specul(ariz)ation" (*Jacques Lacan* 173).

In *Gynesis* Jardine writes "it is highly probable that 'we' (?) won't awaken from that nightmare [of history] until male theorists awaken from their illusion that 'masculinity imagines itself poorly or imagines itself, at the most, only by feminizing itself,' until men speak their sexuality instead of speaking about it—or about 'ours'" (144).[29] This constitutive illusion on the part of hegemonic masculinity, that it imagines or images itself only at the peril of feminization, operates within the boundaries of the anxious process of evacuation Grosz describes.

Jardine is quite right to point out that male theorists can hardly awaken from this illusion by continuing to theorize women's sexuality and women's bodies and refusing to speak their own. Learning how and why not to theorize about women is apparently a difficult lesson for male theorists to learn. More difficult still, I think, is learning the difference between speaking one's sexuality and speaking about it. In *Men in Feminism* Jardine provides an example of what she means by this distinction.

> What else [can men theorize]? Well, there's men's relationship *after feminism,* to death, scopophilia, fetishism . . . the penis and balls, erection, ejaculation (not to mention the phallus), madness, paranoia, homosexuality, blood, tactile pleasure, pleasure in general, *desire* (but, please, not with an anonymously universal capital D), voyeurism, etc. Now this *would* be talking your body, not talking *about* it. It is not essentialism; it is not metaphysics, and it is not/would not be representation. As Luce Irigaray put it, "The bodily in man is what metaphysics has never touched." ("Men" 61)

Jardine's list is very useful, not only because it groups in the same sentence both death and ejaculation, but also because it suggests that to mention ejaculation is *not* to mention the phallus (and if the phallus in some sense does not ejaculate, the question may be less "why not?" than "where not?": a question of destination).[30] Conspicuously, however, Jardine does not mention anality—unless, supposing the rectum to be both a grave and an exclusively homosexual province, she intends the tropes of death and homosexuality to include it. Is this omission a function of Jardine's reassuring promise to the male theorist who would speak his body that such talk would not be representation? Whether it is related to the foreclosure of anality or not, this promise of evading representation—not simply Heath's existing representation but representation itself—is dangerous enough, for the repression of the bodily in the male has always been in structural solidarity with the fond hope of either escaping representation or mastering it, making sure that representation, like abjection, befall only others, not oneself. Nothing could be more essential to both the existing representation and the whole history of masculinist metaphysical assurance.

Although I have used the word *history* several times now, it has probably not escaped the reader's attention that very little of what I have said about productive anxiety thus far lends itself in any obvious way to Fredric Jameson's famous dictum "always historicize" (*Political Unconscious* 9). In speaking the body or speaking about it, there seems to be a danger that one might lapse into ahistorical formulations, naïve empiricism, or worst of all, biological determinism. Nevertheless, no discourse about the body, and no bodily experience, ever takes place outside history and historical determination.[31] Locating discourse about the body in the body itself, however, putting the body on the line, is one unorthodox way of historicizing that discourse. To quote Gallop once again: "Locating thinking in a desiring body is also, in another vocabulary, locating thinking in a subject in history. To read for and affirm confusion, contradiction is to insist on thinking in the body in history. Those confusions mark the sites where thinking is literally knotted to the subject's historical and material place" (*Thinking* 132).

There is a very real sense in which our bodies give us history and history gives us our bodies, our sense and understanding of what it means to be in our bodies and of what the productions of our bodies mean. For example, even with such a seemingly ahistorical concept as the split between the subject of the enunciation and the subject of the statement, one can say that the affective meaning of being linguistically split is always a historical, socially mediated construction. If we acknowledge that the notion of a linguistically split subjectivity can be a function only of the concept of identity (i.e., the split can become apparent only in relation to the vision of some unified, self-identical whole), then we can also point out the ways that identity is itself a historical construct. In an essay on Thoreau in *Comparative American Identities*, for example, Michael Warner writes that in the nineteenth century, "integrating the ego had become normative for market culture, and only against the strength of this imperative does erotics come to be understood as self-dissolving. . . . The dissolution and waste of erotics is understood as feminizing for Thoreau because it undoes the ascesis of his self-regard . . ." (171). In *Late Marxism: Adorno, or the Persistence of the Dialectic*, Jameson goes further in locating identity as ego-integration in the imperatives of market culture. Jameson argues that for Adorno, the difference between identity and nonidentity is equivalent to the Marxian distinction between exchange and use values. In *Negative Dialectics*, says Jameson, Adorno

> identifies "what cannot be subsumed under identity"—that is to say, everything that has been evoked . . . variously under the notions of difference and heterogeneity, otherness, the qualitative, the radically new, the corporeal—as "what is called in Marxian terminology *use value.*" . . . This is the decisive clue . . . to the ultimate identity of "identity" itself, which . . . take[s] on the forms of psychic identity and of logic and epistemology before coming to rest (at least provisionally) in the economic realm of exchange and the commodity. (23)

Jameson eventually drops this salutary provisionality, however, and goes on to state conclusively and unequivocally that "exchange value . . . the emergence of some third, abstract term between two incomparable objects . . . constitutes the primordial form by which identity emerges in human history" (23).

Jameson's formulation of Adorno is in its own way quite valuable and will no doubt appeal to those who take their ultimate theoretical satisfaction in last-instance economic primordiality. Ironically, however, this abstract identification of identity and nonidentity with, respectively, exchange and use values itself seems to be a function much more of exchange than of use. Doing little to affirm confusion and contradiction, this identification sets up its own closed circuit of exchange and forecloses on certain questions that perhaps cannot be subsumed under an exclusively Marxian terminology, particularly the question of the gender politics of identity and nonidentity, as well as related corporeal matters that Jameson, in his determination to purify Adorno of any poststructuralist taint, shortchanges when cashing in on Adorno's critique. Jameson, that is, constricts rather than extends Marxian analysis in the same movement by which he attempts to allow it, like identity in Adorno's critique, to subsume everything.

Jean-Joseph Goux, in his *Symbolic Economies: After Marx and Freud*, deals more extensively with the question of identity in relation to economic value. Like Jameson and Adorno, Goux follows Marx in locating both psychic identity and philosophical idealism on the side of exchange value and in the rise of the developed money form as universal abstract equivalent. Goux, however, also links the development of abstraction with Freud's conjecture that conceptuality itself arose primordially from the patriarchal attempt to establish by conjecture the paternal identification of produced male offspring (for the purposes of bequeathing property) over and against the merely visible or empirical proof of maternity provided by the mother's productive body.[32] Goux writes that whereas for Marx,

> use-value is determined solely by the "physical properties of the commodity"—that is, by the empirical object, as a prop, with the diverse and accidental qualities inherent in corporality—exchange-value, on the other hand, expresses the commodity's substantial, permanent base, its essential, universal identity; it rests on the elimination of all empirical determination. What equivalence affirms, Marx shows, is an *identical essence.* . . . This difference between use-value and exchange-value, then, exposes all the oppositions between body and soul. . . . Use-value is the physical, incarnated, perceptible aspect of

the commodity, while exchange-value is a supernatural abstraction, invisible and supersensible. (19)

Jameson stops here, but Goux extends Marx's diagnosis of exchange value not only into what Jameson calls the forms of psychic identity but more explicitly into the forms of sexual identification and libidinal investment as well. Goux writes that Marx "offered an analysis not only of the exchange of commodities but also of the whole theater of evaluations, substitutions, and *social supplementations*. The institution of FATHER, PHALLUS, AND LANGUAGE, of the major 'signs' that regulate the values market, in fact stems from a genesis whose necessity and whose limits are doubtless most pronounced, theoretically, in the origin of MONEY" (13). Goux then examines a structural homology between the four-phased development of value leading to the money form in Marx (elementary, extended, general, and money) and the four stages of libidinal development leading to normative masculine sexuality in Freud (oral, anal, genital, phallic). I will not rehearse Goux's admirable exegesis of that homology in any greater detail here except to note how what he calls "the parallel history of these two accessions" establishes both money and the phallus as the economical/libidinal standard of value, the abstract, invisible, and supersensible universal equivalent of normative male libidinal economy.

Asserting that this parallel "is not the result of some fluke that would resist theoretical investigation" (24), Goux stresses the need to interrogate the historical intrication of economics and sexuality in "the dialectical logic of the symbolization process" (50). He suggests that "only at a certain logical point in the history of symbolization can purely economic exchanges and relations come to pass: precisely when, through the withdrawal of primary investments, a conscious, disaffected, depersonalized symbolism is reached. Only then can 'economic exchange value' be extricated and severed from the investment of significations" (125). Goux goes on to argue, in effect, that the process of oedipalization not only inserts the subject into the symbolic order of language but primes it for capitalist economic relations: "it is only *after* what is termed the oedipal phase that the child acquires the perception, the concept, of this purely abstract exchange value" (126). For Goux these insertions and acquisitions are part of the same process of symbolization.[33] He maintains that this particular slant on *"the logic of the symbolization process* . . . a logic of the successive forms taken by the exchange of vital activities in all spheres of social organization" is what "enables us to conceive *the dialectic of history*" (24). As Goux examines it, however, this logic also enables us to conceive what Jameson, with his well-known reluctance to consider gender and sexual difference as major categories of critical analysis, apparently cannot: namely, that the opposite of materialism is not simply idealism but what Goux calls *"paterialism"* (213), that history as it has been examined by certain male historical materialists remains *"the history of man"* (215). Without this realization, Jameson's dictum "always historicize" will always carry an unspoken masculinist imperative.

Nonetheless, locating identity in history, by whatever primordial form it emerges, helps to historicize and materialize what would otherwise seem to be an ahistorical and uncorporeal linguistic split, as well as that split's concomitant productive anxieties.[34] The anxiety of production can therefore be considered as a symptomatic and constitutively masculine unease about language and the body that is subject to particular historical exacerbations, depending on what specific pressures are brought to bear on socially and economically constructed and gendered formations of identity.[35]

What historical factors, then, might exacerbate the unease of the anxiously masculinized subject? What happens—and the question of exchange value and the commodity form is certainly not evacuated here—when identity becomes a matter of economic, narrative, and representational self-possession? I have suggested that the anxiety of production is not only symptomatically masculine but in ways identifiably modernist. How so? One can, of course, cite various inaugurations of economic modernization, philosophical modernity, and aesthetic modernism. In terms of the aesthetic modernism as a self-conscious practice, a conventional reference is Baudelaire.[36] In terms of modernity as a general problematic, however, one could also cite Sterne's *Tristram Shandy,* in which a comic conflation of textual and anal production registers an early modern anxiety about the subjection of the body's productions to a properly bourgeois discipline of profit maximization and means-ends rationality.[37] One might go further back and examine the adumbration of a modern crisis of legitimation, of a breakdown of the paternal metaphor, in *Hamlet,* in which the prince realizes both that "the king" is an empty signifier that one can manipulate in a murderous will to power (Rosencranz and Guildenstern learn this the hard way) and that "the king" is also a body that can make a progress through the guts of a beggar.

As these examples suggest, questions of the body, its productions, its role in representation and signification, and its potential disruption of identity, authority, and cultural legitimation can loom large in the discourse of modernity. Concerning this modern disruption of culturally legitimating narratives, Jardine writes that "legitimacy is part of that judicial domain which, historically, has determined the right to govern, the succession of kings, the link between father and son, the necessary paternal fiction, the ability to decide who is the father—in patriarchal culture. The crises experienced by the major Western narratives have not, therefore, been gender-neutral. They are crises in the narratives invented by men" (*Gynesis* 24). One might question whether it is simply that the men invented the narratives and not also that the narratives invented the men. Jardine's point, nonetheless, is that the breakdown of the paternal metaphor in Western culture has brought into play that process she calls *gynesis*, a "putting into discourse of 'woman'" that is "never stable and has no identity" and that is "intrinsic to the condition of modernity" (*Gynesis* 25).

For some modern male writers, Jardine suggests, this destabilization of identity opened up new and liberatory discursive possibilities, while others more or less retrenched into their own hysterical paranoia. Masculine paranoia and aggression are prominent features of literary modernism, particularly in that familiar list of male modernists—Eliot, Pound, Yeats, Lawrence, Marinetti, Lewis—who flirted with or embraced authoritarian or fascist ideologies. This prominent paranoia is of the utmost concern to contemporary theorists writing about the gender politics of modernity. In *The War of the Worlds*, for example, the first volume of *No Man's Land*, Sandra M. Gilbert and Susan Gubar argue that the aggression against women that pervades male modernist texts indicates a reaction to both the women's suffrage movement and the success of women writers in the late nineteenth and early twentieth centuries. On the other hand, Andreas Huyssen, in the essay "Mass Culture as Woman: Modernism's Other," explores high modernism's "anxiety of contamination" regarding a mass culture that it genders as feminine, an anxiety that plays into other related fears. For Huyssen, high modernist practice is distinguished as a prophylactic effort to seal itself off from a doubly threatening alterity. He writes that in masculine high modernism "the male fear of woman and the bourgeois fear of the masses become indistinguishable."

> Male fears of an engulfing femininity are . . . projected onto the metropolitan masses, who did indeed represent a threat to the rational bourgeois order. The haunting specter of a loss of power combines with a fear of losing one's fortified and stable ego boundaries, which represent the *sine qua non* of male psychology in that bourgeois order. . . . Thus the nightmare of being devoured by mass culture through co-option, commodification, and the "wrong" kind of success is the constant fear of the modernist artist, who tries to stake

out his territory by fortifying the boundaries between genuine art and inauthentic mass culture. Again, the problem is not the desire to differentiate between forms of high art and depraved forms of mass culture and its co-options. The problem is rather the persistent gendering as feminine of that which is devalued. (*After the Great Divide* 52–53)

Here one might say that while the problem *is* the persistent gendering of the devalued as feminine, that problem is more persistent than, and historically anterior to, both the anxious conflict between high modernism and mass culture and male paranoia about the successes of women's suffrage and women's writing. Gendering the devalued as feminine is the dominative and constitutive maneuver of a patriarchal hegemony that pre-curses those specific developments. The more historical problem, then, may be not simply how the devaluation of the feminine operates in the modernist male reaction against specific forms of representation within modernity (i.e., mass culture and women's writing) but rather how the devaluation of the feminine subtends the devaluation of representation itself. The specific historical developments that Jardine, Gilbert and Gubar, and Huyssen discuss exacerbate an underlying masculine anxiety about the abject relationships among representation, the feminine, and the production(s) of the male body. This anxiety pervades and helps to operate the history of Western patriarchal metaphysics even as that history collides and colludes with the metanarratives of modernity.

Kristeva writes in *Powers of Horror* of abjection as that "which modernity has learned to repress, dodge, or fake" (26). How, though, does abjection figure as "what is jettisoned from the '*symbolic system*'" of specifically modern exclusions and hierarchies, if such jettisoning is endemic to patriarchy as a transhistorical system of symbolization? How does abjection threaten the *corps propre* of the specifically masculine subject of modernity, and how is this threat caught up with historical developments in signifying and representational processes that disrupt the margins of a specifically modern masculinity? According to Jürgen Habermas, philosophical modernity begins when self-reflection becomes the epistemological and ontological foundation of thought (see *Philosophical Discourse*). Martin Heidegger, in "The Age of the World Picture" (*QCT* 115–54), speculates that modernity begins when the world becomes representation and man constitutes himself as a subject for representation. If these two assertions obtain, then the subject of modernity makes its historical appearance in ways remarkably similar to the subject of the Lacanian mirror stage: irreducibly or constitutively alienated in and by representational self-reflection, the modern subject is launched on a teleological fiction leading toward the projectively imagined ideal unity of the *corps propre* and away from the retroactively imagined fragmentation of the *corps morcelé*. And this fiction, to echo Jardine, is male-invented/inventing, a new story or script for the interpellation of a masculinized subject in history.

Jardine also gives us a way of historicizing this new script when she remarks the emphasis that the question of technique comes to bear within the sociocultural disruptions of legitimation in modernity. Jardine writes in *Gynesis* that "at the end of the nineteenth century the possible relationships between technique and its spaces began to change radically . . . at the same time as the radical upheavals in familial, religious, and political structures seemed to accelerate. Suddenly, technique was engulfed by the very spaces that until that time had remained its passive sources, its objects. Technique itself became an object of both fear and wonder; space and matter were beginning to speak a language that Man did not want to hear" (74). Using a formulation indebted to Barthes's *Camera Lucida*, Jardine goes on to identify photography as one of the technical developments by which space and matter began to speak a language "Man" did not want to hear (or see). Photography "actually turned Man into an object. . . . A new space, which was suddenly larger (or smaller) than Man, found a language, began to objectify Man, to turn him into an image" (74).[38]

> The anguish of Man—faced with this particular technique—has not diminished. . . . [Technique] evokes the violent experience of becoming and then being an object . . . of being turned into an Image, nothing but a source for others' use. And beyond a solely existential anguish, the instantaneous slippage between subject and object . . . sounds remarkably similar to how *women* have described the process they undergo in patriarchal systems of representation. It is almost as if technique, as concept and practice, has turned Man into an Object-Woman. (75)

Given Bataille's notion, however, that the subject/object polarity that obviously subtends this anguish is archaically rooted in anal eroticism, could we not pose the questions Jardine raises in a different way? If, as Jacqueline Rose puts it, "The Imaginary itself, through which the subject sets itself up as subject and the other as object, can be seen to contain a potential reversal [in which] the subject is constituted as object by the Other" (*Sexuality* 190), as what sort of object might this subject be phantasmatically constituted in the materiality of this reversal? If man accedes to modern subjectivity by becoming the self-alienated object of his own reflection, just what sort of object has he there-

by become? By what abject gesture of representational self-establishment has he lost or expelled himself, and how can that objectified self
be regained without smudging the margins of a purely masculine identity? Why does man have to resort to the mode by which Others become shit to maintain his masculine purity, and how does this mode
of identity maintenance through constitutive exclusion subtend other
matters of masculinized bodily production—such as, say, the politics
of ejaculation, the trajectories of seminal destination, the grim choreography of the pornographic money shot—and their place within a
heterosexualized representational economy?

As I show in the next chapter, which discusses Hegel's curious critique of a representational "picture-thinking" that he relates to urination, there is a stain on the tain of the mirror stage of modernity, a mark
or trace that hopelessly fouls the modern metanarrative of man's rational and representational self-repossession. For if, as Hegel contends,
Enlightenment modernity inaugurates itself as the vindication of "the
human ownership of the treasures formerly squandered on heaven"
(*ETW* 159),[39] then questions of ownership, (private) property, and the
proper—in all the many senses of that word—become the crucial
matters of modernity (with a Bataillean squander or expenditure as its
repressed). This is particularly the case when the bourgeois philosophical metanarrative of self-repossession (with Hegel as its major repo
man) is aligned with and compounded by a capitalist rationality of
production, acquisition, and profit maximization.[40] What happens,
within the confines of this heavily restricted economy, when the material processes of reflection and representation produce the subject not
as a *corps propre*, a properly pristine identity with stable and fortified
boundaries, but rather as an improper object, an abjection that can be
neither treasured nor squandered, a letter that can be neither kept nor
sent away?

This question disturbs and demeans the masculinist writing of that
historical trauma called modernity, for after the breakdown of the
paternal metaphor, such writing can neither send its full utterance like
a disembodied prayer to the ideal receptacle of a patriarchal heaven
nor fully justify its human ownership. Haunted by the fear that he can
only send, rend, or soil himself as an abject letter, always potentially
dead, partitioned in its very inception—a letter that can always not
arrive at its dest(a)ination and of which he himself is never the punctual origin—the modern male writer is brought into contact with the
production(s) of his own body, with what an anxious metaphysics had
never allowed itself, or him, to touch.

2

Piss Hegel, or Why Sperm Is Never Treated as an *Objet A*

"The Gentleman Seems to Know What He Wants."

> Perhaps the conflict is always between body—as the inadequate name of some uncommanded diversity of drives and contradictions—and Power, between body and Law, between body and Phallus, even between body and Body. The second term in each pair is a finished, fixed representation. The first that which falls short of that representation.
>
> —Jane Gallop, *The Daughter's Seduction*

> In this "phallocratic" power, man loses something too: in particular, the pleasure of his own body.
>
> —Luce Irigaray, *This Sex Which Is Not One*

In *This Sex Which Is Not One* Luce Irigaray identifies phallogocentrism as an "economy of the same" that depends on the "reabsorption of otherness in the discourse of sameness" (130). Following Irigaray, one might describe the paradigmatic mechanism of this reabsorptive economy as the process by which *an* other is converted into *the* Other of a same. This same, however, is only a particular instance of the Same, an instance that can stake itself as same only by virtue of its identity with the One, that is, the phallus as the Name and the Law of the Father, the power to generate meaning. Two reabsorptions thus seem necessarily to be at work in this unary process: the reabsorption of *an* other into *the* Other of the Same and the reabsorption of a same into *the* Same as or identical to the One.

We can see the first aspect of this mechanism laid bare quite clearly in the second half of Alfred Hitchcock's *Vertigo*. In that film a woman named Judy (other with a small *o*) is forced to remasquerade as the phantasmatic Madeline (Other with a capital *O*) to gain the recognition and desire of a man named Scotty. Scotty, however, has to overcome his own vertiginous sexual ambivalence—his own strong attraction to the self-shattering powerlessness of falling—to possess and master Madeline's body and thus finally to identify with the discourse of masculine "power and freedom" represented by the murderous Gavin Elster. Indeed, in his plot to murder his wife, Elster exploits Scotty's "weakness" in order to deploy or interpellate Scotty as the one who will desire Madeline and bear witness in court to Elster's "truth"— that is, his version of the story of Madeline's death.

This brief and obviously inadequate sketch of *Vertigo* allows us to examine the way in which the economy of the same subtends not only what Irigaray calls feminine masquerade—"an alienated or false version of femininity arising from the woman's awareness of the man's desire for her to be his other" (*TS* 220)—but also the ideology of masculine masquerade, or masculine masquerade as ideology and ideological interpellation. To begin with, my emphasis on the indefinite and definite articles in the preceding description of this economy indicates its basic mechanism, which works to convert all that is multiple, heterogeneous, and indefinite into the singular, homogeneous, and definitive. The structure, however, should also indicate the sites for intervention into this economy. On the one hand, subjects who are constituted as others—by gender, race, class, age, ethnicity, or sexual orientation—can resist being scripted as the symmetrical Others of the Same by recognizing and insisting on their difference from that paradigm, by asserting their difference from what Irigaray calls "the old dream of symmetry" (Judy, for example, initially resists her reinscription as Madeline but resigns herself on realizing that it is only as the Other that she can appear to Scotty's desire). On the other hand, however, subjects who are interpellated as and called on to identify themselves with the Same are also called on to uphold the old symmetrical dream. If these subjects can somehow assert their sameness differently, however, then perhaps this sex which is one may not be One either.

The extent to which the Same can be used as a site of resistance— the extent to which there may be something multiple, heterogeneous, and indefinite about the Same, making it only a potential instance of the Same—is much less obvious, much less visible, than in the case of the other. Here it is the question of visibility, of vision, of visual pleasure and unpleasure, that comes to the foreground. What we *see* in *Vertigo*, in painful and painstaking detail, is the conversion of Judy (who just wants to be desired) into Madeline, the coercive transformation of an other into the Other of the Same, and the deadly consequences of this enforced feminine masquerade. What we do not see in *Vertigo*, what we perhaps cannot see because it cannot be made visible as such (without transforming itself), is the conversion of Scotty (who thinks he wants only to desire) into *Scotty*—that is, the conversion of Scotty as an instance of the Same into Scotty as identical (or desiring identity) with the One.[1] What we see in *Vertigo* is the difference between the production of Madeline as what Gallop calls "a fixed, finished representation" and the reality of Judy as a desiring body that "falls short of that representation" (and here, given the ending of the film, the verb *falls* is all too disturbingly appropriate). We see the manufacture of Madeline as a commodified fetish object to be exchanged between two men,[2] but we do not see the production of the men. We do not see the process that Marx describes in the *Grundrisse*, namely, the production of a desiring subject for the produced object, the construction of a consumer for the manufactured representation. "Production," writes Marx, "not only creates an object for the subject, but also a subject for the object" (92).

What we do not see, in short, is the production of the phallus, and its invisibility ensures that the phallus is not a fixed and finished representation but rather the power that attempts to stand behind all representations in order to fix and to finish them (if not to finish them off). To be sure, we do see a stand-in for the production of the phallus in the manufacture and manipulation of Madeline. In "The Signification of the Phallus" Lacan asserts that "one may, simply by reference to the function of the phallus, indicate the structures that will govern the relations between the sexes. Let us say that these relations will turn around a 'to be' and a 'to have'" (*É* 289). Judy's remasquerade as Madeline in the second half of the film clearly marks her alienated desire to be the phallus for Scotty. On the other hand, Scotty's obsession with and possession of Madeline's body as fetish object—indeed, as dead object—stands in for his possession of the phallus and indicates his desire to have what Gavin Elster has had. Scotty's vertigo, however, marks his possession of a contradictory body, an abject, feminized body that can fall. Thus it also marks the way he falls short of the fixed and finished representation of masculinity—or, more closely, the fixing and finishing *non*representation of masculinity, for it is exactly when the phallus allows its "essence" to be represented that it has to fall short. In any case, Scotty's final possession of Madeline's body would have not only signaled the conquest of his own vertiginous abjection but also guaranteed his position of power and freedom and hence his identity with Gavin Elster. This identity indicates that for Hitchcock, there is perhaps something inherently murderous about phallic self-possession and about the patriarchal law of property rights that Elster, in murdering his wife, has not so much broken as asserted.

We do not see the production of the phallus itself, however, because we do not see the production of Scotty's desire to disavow the ambivalent and vertiginous abjection of his own body, his desire to identify with Elster, his desire to possess what Elster possesses in order to feel powerful and free. This desire is simply assumed and thus to a large degree naturalized—a naturalization that tends to get reproduced in some undertheorized feminist criticism as the assumption that men essentially and naturally want to objectify, fetishize, and dominate women because that's just what men want to do, just how they are.

On the contrary, however, one cannot historicize and denaturalize the visibility of feminine masquerade, the proliferation in this culture of images of women's bodies as fetishized and dominated objects, without also attempting to historicize and denaturalize the *invisibility* of masculine masquerade, the disappearance of male bodies in the construction of men as fetishizing and dominating subjects. In fact, the visibility of the former may be a condition of possibility for the invisibility of the latter. The deployment of women as objects of visual pleasure allows the masculine subject to hide himself behind his own gaze. The production of Scotty's desire to be identical with the One is a function of the production of the phallus, and hence we are allowed to see neither. As Lacan puts it, the phallus "can play its role only when veiled, that is to say, as itself a sign of the latency with which any signifiable is struck, when it is raised (*aufgehoben*) to the function of signifier. The phallus is the signifier of this *Aufhebung* itself, which it inaugurates (initiates) by its disappearance. That is why the demon of . . . shame arises at the very moment when, in the ancient mysteries, the phallus is unveiled" (*É* 288).

Lacan's suggestion that visibility shames the phallus is particularly interesting in the light of Sandra Bartky's work investigating the West's cultural feminization of shame, the predominant perception of shame as a woman's emotion.[3] This conflation of femininity with shame is historically and linguistically indicated by the fact that one word for female genitalia, *pudenda*, has for its Latin root the word *pudere*, "to be ashamed." Lacan seems to be aware of this linguistic enforcement of shame, for after noting that the unveiling of the phallus constitutes its shame, he writes, "it is in order to be the phallus . . . that a woman will reject an essential part of femininity, namely, all her attributes in the masquerade" (*É* 290). Lacan then goes on to say that "the fact that femininity finds its refuge in this mask, by virtue of the fact of the *Verdrangung* [repression] inherent in the phallic mark of desire, has the curious consequence of making virile display in the human being itself seem feminine" (*É* 291).

Thus, in the demonology (by) which Lacan exposes (himself),[4] visibility not only shames but feminizes the phallus, transforms it into its opposite, alienates it from itself. Given the importance of alienation in the discourse of modernity—and particularly in that of Hegel, whose terminology Lacan conspicuously employs—we would perhaps do well to explore the relationships among visibility, alienation, and the shameful feminization of a phallus that must remain veiled to play its role. This emphasis on visibility, on appearance, will make clear the anxious relationship, within the phallogocentric economy, between *producere* and *pudere*, to produce and to be ashamed. It will show us why the written trace marks an expense of spirit in a waste of shame. We will see how a relentless emphasis on the visible production(s) of the phallus can align itself with that insistence on bodily masculinity that helps render certain phallic idealizations impossible. The question of visible production is what drives a wedge between the bodily penis and the transcendent phallus, which the penis must "mortgage" a part of itself to become.

What is it exactly that gets mortgaged in this exchange? Again, my possession of a penis marks only the potential for my identification not with my biological father's body but with the power to generate meaning that his name and law supposedly represent within the patriarchal symbolic order. This indicates that the phallus can do what our respective penises by themselves cannot—not, that is, without a patriarchal history of ideological support. It also indicates that any man's penis is generally capable of doing certain things, going certain places, and producing certain substances that the phallus shall not. The complex relationship of this proscription to shamefully visible production, and hence to a vertiginous feminization in which the penis falls short of the phallus, needs to be further explored.

The Bodily in Hegel Is What Dialectics Never Touched

> There looms, within abjection, one of those violent, dark revolts of being, directed against a threat that seems to emanate from an exorbitant outside or inside, ejected beyond the scope of the possible, the tolerable, the thinkable. It lies there, quite close, but it cannot be assimilated. It beseeches, worries, and fascinates desire, which, nevertheless, does not let itself be seduced. Apprehensive, desire turns aside; sickened, it rejects. A certainty protects it from the shameful . . .
>
> —Julia Kristeva, *Powers of Horror*

> This, then, is a symptom: . . . an inert stain resisting communication and interpretation, a stain which cannot be included in the

circuit of discourse, of social bond network, but is at the same
time a positive condition of it.

—Slavoj Žižek, *The Sublime Object of Ideology*

If we were to resituate Hegelian philosophy with respect to history, we would say, in brief, that it belongs to the turning point
where, with the utter dematerialization of general equivalents,
the exchange of productive vital activities themselves behind the
phenomenal representation of the exchange of "products" begins
to be able to be reflected. It is the culmination of the logico-his-
torical trend toward reducing the material, toward "disembodiment" or dematerialization.

—Jean-Joseph Goux, *Symbolic Economies*

In a chapter of *This Sex Which Is Not One* called "The
'Mechanics' of Fluids," Irigaray writes of phallogocentrism not only as
the process of converting an other into the Other of the Same but also
as "a symbolization that grants *precedence to solids*" (110). She writes that
"if every psychic economy is organized around the phallus (or Phallus), we may ask what this primacy owes to a teleology of reabsorption of fluid in a solidified form." She then goes on to suggest that "the
lapses of the penis do not contradict this [reabsorption]: the penis
would only be the empirical representative of a model of ideal functioning; all desire would tend toward being or having this ideal" (110).

Irigaray's description of the difference between fluid and solid mechanics is invaluable for investigating and disrupting the workings of
phallogocentrism, if not for interrogating the permutations of those
workings within the parameters of modernity. What the precedence
given to solids actually solidifies and seals, according to Irigaray, is the
triumph of rationality, a triumph some consider coterminous with
Enlightenment modernity. For Irigaray, the relationship between solid mechanics and Western rationality goes further back; she writes that
the two "have maintained a relationship of very long standing, one
against which fluids have never stopped arguing" (*TS* 113). A fluid
argument, for Irigaray, is one that resists being subjected to the reified
Western *ratio*, resists having its fluid qualities segmented and parceled
out in a quantifiable and rigidified form. The formal rigidity of the
phallic *ratio* dictates that whatever fluids escape this form be considered not only as nonphallic, and therefore feminine, but also as irrational, if not as madness itself.

Here, however, Irigaray may in a sense reinscribe the very teleology of reabsorption that she describes. She asserts that "the lapses of the
penis do not contradict" that teleology, and that the penis is always only

"the empirical representative of a model of ideal functioning." Although elsewhere in her work she seems to allow for the possibility of masculine contradiction (see the epigraph at the beginning of this chapter), here Irigaray suggests that there is no working or workable difference between ideal phallic identity and its bodily representative, between the general rule and the particular application. I suggest that it is exactly the lapses of the penis that generate the contradictions that a reabsorptive and reappropriative teleological economy must overcome. It is when its productions as such are allowed to be made visible that the penis lapses, shames itself, falls short of its ideally phallic function. Visibility aligns the productions of the penis with other excorporated substances that are excluded, devalued, and abjected by the restricted economy of phallogocentrism. This visibility and its concomitant alignment with abjection constantly threaten to rend the veil that allows the phallus to play its role. I will show how the phallus perceives and answers that apparent threat—the threat of appearance, of its own appearance, which it can never properly claim as its own and which always marks its failure to have come into its own.

The question of visibility allows me to address Irigaray's inquiry regarding the problematic status of semen within the mechanics of solids. Irigaray wants to know

> why sperm is never treated as an object *a*. Isn't the subjection of sperm to the imperatives of reproduction alone symptomatic of a preeminence historically allocated to the solid (product)? And if, in the dynamics of desire, the problem of castration intervenes—fantasy/reality of an amputation, of a "crumbling" of the solid that the penis represents—a reckoning with *sperm-fluid* as an obstacle to the generalization of an economy restricted to solids remains in suspension. (*TS* 113)

Recasting the way Irigaray formulates sperm's subjection to reproductive imperatives, one could say that if the phallogocentric economy converts all fluids to solids, then this mechanics, insofar as it is dedicated to a heterosexual genital finality, works primarily to convert the sperm that flows out of the male body into the hard skull of the (preferably male) child that finally emerges from the female's conscripted womb (a skull we might bear in mind when we come to Hegel's assertion that the being of spirit is a bone). But between the fluidity of semen and the hard-headed imperatives of reproduction falls the crumbling impropriety of abjection. Irigaray speaks of "laws that subject sexuality to the absolute power of form" and writes *"what is in excess with respect to form—for example, the feminine sex—is necessarily rejected as beneath or beyond the system currently in force*" (*TS* 110–11). There are other examples of excess, however, and Irigaray's reduction of all excess with respect to form to this one example rehearses as well as identifies the formal process by which the excessive as such is gendered as feminine and thereby devalued, the process by which femininity becomes the repository of masculinity's excess and waste.

The susceptibility of an ideally phallic (and hence invisible) transmission of semen to shameful visibility suggests the excessive ambiguity of sperm-fluid, the "vital flow" itself. This ambiguity lays bare the fluid contradiction that a solid mechanics must constantly strive to reabsorb: within a heterosexual economy of genital finality and imperative reproductivity, the same seminal substance, depending on the invisibility or visibility of its production, means either everything or nothing, either means or does not. Sperm, that is, if it goes where it is "supposed" to go, is never *seen*. Only the effect of seminal production is beheld, and this "little one" is then reappropriated not by the father's body but by the Law of his Name. In regard to always only potentially phallic productions, then, the difference between the invisible and the visible provides a distinction (perhaps even *the* distinction) between meaning and meaninglessness, absorption and expenditure, the essential that is beyond and the excremental that falls beneath. When the penis lapses and allows its productions to become visible, it does not assert but rather collapses the rigid distinction between the essential and the excremental, the beyond and the beneath. This collapse provides the very contradiction that phallogocentrism must efface or displace to go about its powerful business of generating meaning, reproducing not only itself but the conditions of production that prevail and predominate at the historical moment. This is where Irigaray's one example returns as this culture's dominant and dominating example, for it is largely (but not only) onto the feminine that these abject masculine anxieties about visible production are displaced or projected. Examining this displacement gives us one way of reading the (non)-representation of masculinity and of the male body within the history of modernity.

This examination might begin with the matter of Hegel. Very roughly and reductively put, the basic problem of Hegel's *Phenomenology of Spirit* is how rationality, or subject-centered reason, can dialectically identify with itself and recuperate itself in relation to its other, to the negativity, externality, and materiality of its determination, and how this operation takes place in the unfolding of historical time. Derrida asserts that "the position-of-the-other, in Hegelian dialectics, is always, finally, to pose-oneself by oneself as the other of the Idea, as other-

than-oneself in one's finite determination, with the aim of repatriat-
ing and reappropriating oneself, of returning close to oneself in the
infinite richness of one's determination" (*P* 96). Derrida offers the word
hetero-tautology as the "definition of the Hegelian speculative" (*PC* 301).

Of course, it is very difficult to follow Hegel, to read Hegel, and not
become immersed in this hetero-tautology. Jameson, for example,
suggests that "the attempt to do justice to the most random observation of Hegel ends up drawing the whole tangled, dripping mass of the
Hegelian sequence of forms out into the light with it" (*Marxism and
Form* 306). I do not hope to do justice to the entire Hegelian sequence
of forms here. Rather, I am interested in Jameson's choice of adjectives
in describing that dialectical mass. By focusing on one of Hegel's seemingly random observations in the *Phenomenology*, specifically, that moment when he likens "picture-thinking" to urination, I hope to unveil
an anxious relationship, for Hegel and the phallogocentrism in which
he participates, between dripping and observation. I want to explore
the conditions under which phallocentric speculation can observe itself drip. My concern here is with the mechanics that make Hegel's
analogy between picture-thinking and urination possible and with the
displacements and projections that the analogy in turn allows.[5]

By the end of the chapter of the *Phenomenology* called "Observing
Reason," Hegel's dialectic has progressed or negated its way through
the sequential forms, or "vanishing moments," of sense-certainty and
self-certainty. It has sublated Stoicism, scepticism, and the unhappy
consciousness and made short work of physiognomy. Hegel then tar-
ries for a while with phrenology and flirts with the assertion that the
being of Spirit may be a bone—a skull, to be precise: "Of course," Hegel writes, "the intention here is not to state that Spirit, which is represented by a skull, is a Thing; there is not meant to be any materialism . . . in this idea; rather Spirit must be something more and other
than these bones. But to say Spirit *is*, means nothing else than that it
is a Thing" (*PS* 208). Hegel concludes that it is valid to assert that "the
being of Spirit is a bone" provided that the boniness of Spirit is finally
grasped in its concept or notion (*Begriff*). The material boniness of
Spirit's being is thus recognized and sublated.

Then, in a curious example of what Terry Eagleton calls Hegel's "austere Protestant iconoclasm" (*Ideology of the Aesthetic* 142), Hegel ends the
chapter with the following denunciation of representation, or picture-
thinking:

Reason, essentially the Notion, is directly sundered into itself and its
opposite, an antithesis which for that reason is equally immediately

resolved. But when Reason is presented as its own self and its opposite, and is held fast in the entirely separate moment of this asunderness, it is apprehended irrationally; and the purer the moments of this asunderness, the cruder is the appearance of this content. . . . The *depth* which Spirit brings forth from within—but only as far as its picture-thinking consciousness where it lets it remain—and the *ignorance* about what it really is saying, are the same conjunction of the high and the low which, in the living being, Nature naïvely expresses when it combines the organ of its highest fulfillment, the organ of generation, with the organ of urination. The infinite judgement *qua* infinite would be the fulfillment of life that comprehends itself; the consciousness of the infinite judgement that remains on the level of picture-thinking behaves as urination. (*PS* 210)

Again, the basic problem of the Hegelian speculative is how subject-centered reason can identify with itself in relation to its other. As the word *speculative* suggests, this relation concerns visibility; indeed, if the problem of specularity is somehow related to the problem of alterity itself, then the goal of speculative dialectics is to overcome or sublate (*aufheben*) the alterity that the visible as such represents in order to reach the imageless telos of absolute knowing and the hetero-tautology of self-reappropriation, to turn the image into a concept. In the passage just quoted, the difference between reason and its irrational other seems to hinge on the visibility or invisibility of thought, between a thinking that resorts to visual aids and one that goes beyond them. This difference corresponds to that between the imaginary and the symbolic in Lacan, or between the pleasure and reality principles in Freud (particularly since both Lacan and Freud figure this difference in the context of a teleological progression, with Lacan from the spatial lures of the imaginary to the supposed dereifications of the symbolic and with Freud from passive contentment with hallucination to active thought processes). This difference could also be said to inhere in language itself, in the form of the distinction (to which Derrida has drawn our attention) between invisible speech and visible writing. Hegel recognizes that language (as speech) functions as mediation, as the necessary—and to some extent necessarily embodied—medium of reason. Hegel considers language as both the scene of and requirement for reason's self-alienation and for the sublation of that alienation in absolute knowing. As Slavoj Žižek comments, "Language is . . . the very medium of the 'journey of consciousness' in *Phenomenology*, to such a point that it would be possible to define every stage of this journey, every 'figure of consciousness,' by a specific modality of language" (*Sublime Object* 210).[6] Thus in the chapter on "Self-alienated Spirit," Hegel writes:

This alienation takes place solely in language. . . . The power of speech . . . is the *real existence* of the pure self as self; in speech, self-consciousness . . . comes as such into existence, so that it exists *for others*. Otherwise the "I," this *pure* "I," is non-existent, is not *there*; in every other form of expression it is immersed in a reality, and is in a shape from which it can withdraw itself; it is reflected back into itself from its action . . . and dissociates itself from such an imperfect existence . . . letting it remain lifeless behind. Language, however, contains it in its purity, it alone expresses the "I," the "I" itself. (*PS* 308)

Here we might recall Kristeva's formulation from *Powers of Horror:* "I *expel* myself, I *spit* myself out, I abject *myself* within the same motion through which 'I' claim to establish *myself*" (3). This comparison with Kristeva gathers resonance in connection with another Hegelian passage, this one in the *Philosophy of Nature*, where the philosopher notes a specifically corporeal ambiguity: "In many animals the organs of excretion and the genitals, the highest and lowest parts in the animal organization, are intimately connected: just as speech and kissing, on the one hand, and eating, drinking and spitting, on the other, are all done with the mouth."[7]

A certain difference, then, that seems to inhere in language is exemplified for Hegel by the ambiguous conjunction that nature "naïvely" expresses in combining two antithetical functions in the same (re)-productive organ or orifice, in one case the penis and in the other the mouth (the one doing its part in sexual reproduction, the other acting in the reproduction of meaning through speech, but both capable of emitting substances—urine and spittle—of no value to either). In the *Phenomenology* Hegel aligns thinking that remains on the level of pictures with the function of urination. At the same time, he privileges as life's highest fulfillment that thought which goes beyond the merely imaginary. In the *Philosophy of Nature* he moves up to another orifice that also ambiguously combines "high" and "low," reproductivity with excrementality, and kissing and speaking with eating, drinking, and spitting. What allows Hegel to make these alignments? What does picture-thinking have to do with pissing?

Picture-thinking in the *Phenomenology* translates the German *Vorstellung*, often rendered simply as "representation." Mark C. Taylor writes that in *Vorstellung* "the subject 'places' (*stellt*) itself 'before' (*vor*) itself." For Hegel, says Taylor, *Vorstellung* "is the mean that mediates the extremes of sense experience and conceptual thought. This mean is, in effect, the incarnation of the Logos in which reason descends into space and time (i.e., nature and history) and space and time ascend to reason. If the Mediator remains a *Vorstellung* that is not translated into a *Begriff* (concept), opposites coincide but are not truly reconciled. The complete reunification of opposites becomes actual only in the total transparency of the concept" (*Altarity* 12).

For Hegel, then, it is the murky opacity of *Vorstellung* that mars the clarity of absolute speculative reflection; picture-thinking stains the tain of the mirror, occludes the total transparency of the concept—a concept clearly indentured to a heterosexual teleology of fetal conception, for as Taylor contends, "Hegel's systematic philosophy is, among other things, an extended effort to secure the legitimacy of copulation and conception" (*Altarity* 4–5).[8] For this conceptual copulation to occur, for *Vorstellung* to be sublated by the *Begriff*, "it is necessary to transform moribund exteriority into vital inwardness. The proper conception of the Hegelian concept is possible only if the complex interrelation of identity and difference is reconceived" (15). In this proper reconception the vital inwardness of the absolute subject of reason is finally reflected, after the reversion to the imaginary is worked through, by the vital inwardness of the fetus in the womb. All fluid contradiction is reabsorbed in the solidity of conception and in the transparency of the universal concept.[9]

Nevertheless, in the reversion to the merely representational that Hegel posits as a necessary step in the self-alienation leading to absolute knowing, there is a risk that moribund exteriority will threaten life's highest fulfillment with defilement. Having momentarily risked its essence to the self-alienation or self-externalization of *Vorstellung*, subject-centered reason may slip on what it has placed—or spilled—before itself. Such is the slippery threat of abjection that visibilized language poses, for language's corporeality and materiality also encompass the imaginary opacities that threaten to cloud the subject of reason's vision, preventing that subject from seeing itself, and from seeing an "other" as *its* Other, in a totally transparent, hetero-tautological concept.

Picture-thinking, then, threatens pure transparency because it is neither completely inside nor outside, neither subject nor object. Because it relies on images, it is tainted by the outside, but because it remains a form of thinking, it is still on the inside; picture-thinking thus constitutes an abject and ambiguous space in which the boundaries of the body are traversed and the line between vital inwardness and moribund exteriority is blurred. The goal of the Hegelian *Aufhebung* is therefore an imageless truth that has dialectically mucked its way through its own encounter with a devalued picture-thinking, with the merely representational in language, and has emerged high and dry on the other side of that abyss. Interestingly enough, for Hegel the effacement of the imaginary in language is effected by the name. In the *Philosophy of Mind* Hegel writes, "Given the name lion, we need neither the actual vision of the animal, nor even its image: the name alone, if we *understand* it, is the simple imageless representation" (220). One would be hard-pressed to think of a better lionization of the phallus as *nom du père* and *non du père* than this: given the Name of the Father, we need neither the actual vision of the animal (the real father, the father's body) nor even his image; the name alone, if we understand it—if we have successfully internalized it—is the simple imageless representation, the transcendental signifier.

This phallic differentiation between name and image, between the symbolic and the imaginary, between meaning and sense, leads us back to Hegel's differentiation between generation and urination in his critique of picture-thinking. I submit that the difference Hegel is alluding to is one he could neither speak nor name: not that between semen and urine but that between *invisible and visible semen*. It is a sort of purely speculative money shot, unspeakable as such, that Hegel negotiates here, for in evoking the ambiguity of the male organ, Hegel clearly alludes to the two different substances that pass through the same urethral defile. Quite significantly, however, he *names* only the one that he has already aligned with visibility and hence degraded. He never names that substance whose emission leads (or can lead) to life's "highest fulfillment." In Hegel's passage, the word *semen* never appears, as if even to commit the thought to writing would call forth an image and thus align that precious substance with the very picture-thinking that Hegel relegates to the *pissoir*. This omission suggests Hegel's anxiety that, contrary to what he asserts in the case of the lion, we may never reach that simple imageless representation, that the appearance of the name, even to the understanding, always threatens to carry with it the image of the referent. Language is never purely symbolic but always mired in the imaginary; thinking can always fall back into picture-thinking, and vital inwardness can always be stained, is always already stained by moribund exteriority as its constitutive other. Thus the proscription against allowing sperm to become visible—a proscription that seeks to ensure insemination and to discourage disseminative or nonprocreative sexual expression—prevails even to the point of proscribing the visibility of semen's name. Semen must remain invisible both sexually and discursively, both to perception and to apperception, to the eye and to the mind's eye. That this proscription works on the discursive level as well as the sexual reveals the involvement of the latter with the former in the production, reproduction, and valuation of meaning itself.

Given the clear relationship for Hegel between the fetal solidification of conception and the vital transparency of the concept, the sexual and discursive invisibility of semen is "of the essence" in Hegel's system. The essence of Hegelian dialectics is none other than reason— "Reason is Spirit when its certainty of being all reality has been raised to truth, and it is conscious of itself as its own world, and of the world as itself" (PS 263)—and reason, which with the Enlightenment ostensibly replaces a patriarchal God, thus validating what Hegel calls "the human possession of the treasures formerly squandered on heaven" (ETW 159), is nonetheless still traditionally identified with masculine thinking. On the other hand, by virtue of its visibility alone, visible semen is aligned not only with urination but with the irrational, and the irrational, as Irigaray and others have shown, traditionally has been identified with the feminine.

Thus we see a philosophical variation on the pornographic economy of the money shot: the same substance, depending on its invisibility or visibility, is coded as either essential, rational, and masculine or excremental, irrational, and feminine. This economy regulates what comes out of male bodies both sexually and discursively. The crazy and scandalously abject notion of feminine semen, of semen that can fall, that can appear only in drag, provides the vertiginous contradiction that a phallogocentric economy must masterfully sublate whenever it is called on to externalize its essence. It is this femininity and excrementality of unsublatable semen that indicates why what Irigaray calls a reckoning with sperm tends to remain in suspension.

Hegel's critique of picture-thinking as urination suggests that, for Hegel as for Lacan, the phallus can play its role only while veiled.[10] For Hegel, the phallus that allows its productions to become visible can no longer be considered a phallus worthy of the name. The phallus must veil and reveil itself to relève itself, but it can never reveal itself (much less relieve itself) without at the same time shaming and reviling itself. The being of Spirit thus is not a bone; it is the imageless Begriff of a boner. In Hegel's conceptual/copulative scenario, this "boner" brings its vital inward essence up from the depths and allows it to spill out into the material world. Without the safety net of a proper and properly feminine "receptacle" that would reveil that spillage, however, and thus ensure a hetero-tautological reabsorption, that essence becomes simply moribund exteriority. In fact, it turns to crust. This abject solidification could signal the phantasmatic alignment of visible semen not only with urine but also with feces, for between the vital and the fetal falls the shadow of the fecal, which, contra Irigaray, is no particularly close friend of the phallus.[11]

In Joyce's *Ulysses* Leopold Bloom learns from a Mrs. Breen that her husband has received an anonymous postcard on which someone has written "U.P.: up" (*U* 8:258). Richard Ellmann suggests that this enigmatic message "implies that in erection [Breen] emits urine rather than sperm," that he pees up. Ellmann writes that this message "brings the processes of generation and corruption as close as [can be] imagined" (*Ulysses on the Liffey* 75–76). Thus, in D. H. Lawrence's terms, the postcard accuses Breen of being a "really vulgar and pornographical" person for whom the creative flow and the excrementory flow have literally become identical. The accusation, of course, makes Breen quite angry. This message, however, is not only an insult to Mr. Breen's procreative powers; it also seems to be the abject worry of Hegel's dialectics, which locates itself, in this instance, in the mainstream of phallic masculinity.

Bataille's Postmodern Prodding

> Above all, heterology is opposed to any homogeneous representation of the world, in other words, to any philosophical system. The goal of such representations is always the deprivation of our universe's sources of excitation and the development of a servile human species, fit only for the fabrication, rational consumption, and conservation of products. But the intellectual process automatically limits itself by producing of its own accord its own waste products, thus liberating in a disordered way the heterogeneous excremental element. Heterology is restricted to taking up again, consciously and resolutely, this terminal process which up until now has been seen as the abortion and shame of human thought. In this way it leads to the complete reversal of the philosophical process, which ceases to be the instrument of appropriation, and now serves excretion; it introduces the demand for the violent gratifications implied by social life.
>
> —Georges Bataille, *Visions of Excess*

> Renegotiating our relation to the Law of Language would . . . hinge first and foremost upon the confrontation of the male subject with the defining conditions of all subjectivity, conditions which the female subject is obliged compulsively to reenact, but upon the denial of which traditional masculinity is predicated: lack, specularity, alterity. It would seem to necessitate, in other words, dismantling the images and undoing the projections and disavowals through which phallic identification is enabled.
>
> —Kaja Silverman, *Male Subjectivity at the Margins*

In *Inner Experience* Georges Bataille comments on Hegel's "horror of the blind spot" (*IE* 111). In *Minima Moralia: Reflections from Damaged Life,* Theodor Adorno also comments on "what might be called the waste products and blind spots that have escaped the dialectic" (151).[12] The various wasteful spots to which dialectics seemingly turns a blind eye—the come stain, the pee spot, the skid mark—are all produced through the openings of the body, marks or traces that a body might leave lifelessly behind. Nonetheless, given the difficulty of making any neat and tidy distinction between these traces of moribund exteriority and the substances and processes they signify, it would be a mistake to suppose that for Hegel, or for phallogocentrism itself, the dialectical sublation of external determination involves a reabsorption of fluid into solid form that would in any simple way privilege feces, as Irigaray argues. Despite the rationality of Hegel's system, and despite the amenability of fecal matter to phallomorphism and a quantifying *ratio*—the turd, writes Jane Gallop, is as "solid and countable as money" (*Daughter's Seduction* 84)—there is still small welcome for the asshole and its products within the closed system of a phallocentric speculative dialectics that remains conceptually invested in life's "highest fulfillment." As Bersani puts it, anality "is the mode of sexuality that most closely literalizes the affinities of the sexual with death" (*Culture* 45), and as Gallop puts it, "the turd will not be *aufgehoben*" (*Intersections* 47). In fact, the turd and the site of its origin may prove to be bigger scares for dialectics than urine, despite the latter's feminine and irrational fluidity, its threatening urethral proximity to an essentially masculine vital flow.

The political ramifications of this deadly fear of rectal gravity can be seen in Hegel's fierce abjection of the Jews in the *Early Theological Writings.* Taylor points out that one of the ways in which Hegel represents the three moments of the dialectic—identity, difference, and absolute identity, or possession, loss, and repossession—is as Greek, Jew, and Christian: "In Hegel's speculative dialectic, we are first . . . Greek, then Jew, and finally Christian. As the mean that reconciles extremes, Christianity takes up into itself both Hellenic unity and Hebraic separation. What the Greek enjoyed and the Jew lost, the Christian regains" (*Altarity* 5). The identification of the Jew with the second step of the dialectic, with separation and loss, links the Jew not only with the visible but with the divisible, rather than the in(di)visible—that is, with what visibly divides or separates itself from the body, or what is jettisoned from the "symbolic system," but cannot be regained through dialectical reappropriation or repatriation. For Hegel, Taylor writes,

> the wandering Jew is the most extreme example of a form of experience he later describes as "unhappy consciousness." . . . Never at-

taining the lofty status of the eagle, the Jew is not simply immature but is actually abject. . . . Unhappy consciousness's realization of its infinite *difference* from everything other than itself exposes outer and inner wounds that never heal. Plagued by division within and without, the Jew is impotent to recognize salvation when it truly arrives. (*Altarity* 8–9)

Figuring the Jew as the embodiment of unhappy consciousness allows Hegel to read the Jewish refusal of Christ as Messiah as a sign of abjection, to read Jewishness as abjection, to abject the Jews. Furthermore, the site of Semiticized abjection is not, for Hegel, simply that of a metaphysical gulf between the Jews and God but rather the homeless home of fecality itself. Hegel puts this quite bluntly:

How were *they* to recognize divinity in a man, poor things that they were, possessing only a consciousness of their misery, of the depth of their servitude, of their opposition to the divine, of an impassable gulf between the being of God and the being of men? Spirit alone recognizes spirit. They saw in Jesus only the man. . . . More he could not be, for he was only one like themselves, and they felt themselves to be nothing. The Jewish multitude was bound to wreck his attempt to give the consciousness of something divine, for faith in something divine, something great, cannot make its home in a dunghill. (*ETW* 265)

For Hegel, the Jews cannot recognize the truly messianic because of what he considers their abject association with the messy anus.

I cite this stunningly anti-Semitic formulation not simply to vilify Hegel, make an atrocious pun, and claim the moral high ground but rather to stress what can be at stake in the political deployment of the male anxieties I am attempting to describe. The cultural logic of abjection, of the anxiety of production, demands that the male subject's anxieties about what comes out of his body be phantasmatically projected onto others who are already socially, culturally, and economically marginalized, jettisoned from the symbolic system—in my reading usually onto the woman and in Judith Butler's reading onto the queer, but with Hegel, also onto the Jew. Whenever the assuagement of productive anxiety depends on such projection, this anxiety constitutes a psychosymbolic area that can be exploited by a status quo that also depends on such marginalization to reproduce its own conditions of production, its own misogyny, homophobia, and racism. The relationship between Hegel's anti-Semitic passage and his critique of *Vorstellung* as urination suggests the solidarity between the denigration of the culturally marginalized other and the effacement of the abject trace, of figuration or representation itself. Hegel's figuring of the Jew as abject suggests that figuration and abjection—the mode by which others become shit—can be gravely intricated processes and hence why the project of *self*-representation is for masculinity always potentially "something to be scared of" (Kristeva, *PH* 32).

In the *Phenomenology* the explicit identification of the Jew with unhappy consciousness occurs not in the chapter called "Stoicism, Scepticism, and the Unhappy Consciousness" but rather in the chapter entitled "Physiognomy and Phrenology," in quite close proximity to Hegel's urinization of picture-thinking. At work in that passage is a covert proscription against the visibility of the production—both physical and mental—of seminal fluid. But this proscription against visible seminal production could be related not only to austere Protestant iconoclasm but also, ironically, to the ancient Judaic injunction against uttering the name of God. Indeed, the injunction against uttering the name of God, if not the whole conception of an "invisible, unseizable, unnameable"[13] deity, may be read as an effect of the prohibition against the visibility of phallic production, a visibility that threatens to align both God and phallus with less than divine substances, marking the potential slide from deification to defecation, from the unary to the urinary. Both prohibitions seem invested in securing sacred identity from defilement, protecting the in(di)visibility of something divine, something great, life's highest fulfillment, and so on. Both prohibitions involve "a withdrawal of primary investments" (Goux, *Symbolic Economies* 125) away from heterogeneous difference and a corresponding reinvestment in the economy of the same. For the proscription against uttering the name of the one God obtains exclusively for monotheism; polytheistic forms depend on a taxonomy and an iconography to establish the differences—hierarchical but also terrifically conflictual—among the various deities. Goux writes that

> in the history of religions, the logic of symbolization allows us to grasp the dialectic of the passage first from animism to polytheism, then to increasingly abstract monotheism. That Marx must have conceived money and Freud the phallus in accordance with the logic of the "one God," subordinating and excluding "part objects" and "relative forms" [of value] just as the multiple gods of polytheism are subordinated and banished by the rule of the One, is not a matter of indifference. (*Symbolic Economies* 43)[14]

In *Dialectic of Enlightenment* Adorno and Horkheimer also argue that the historical movement from polytheism to monotheism is one of the initial steps in the demythologization that can lead to enlightenment as instrumental reason, that is, to a rationalized form of thinking that can imagine self-preservation only as the domination of nature. In enlightened thinking, Adorno and Horkheimer write, "men distance themselves from nature in order thus imaginatively to present it to themselves—but only in order to determine how it is to be dominated" (39). In a dialectical thinking that remains indentured to enlightenment as instrumental reason, they assert, "man imagines himself free from fear when there is no longer anything unknown. That determines the course of demythologization, of enlightenment. . . . Enlightenment is mythic fear turned radical. . . . Nothing at all may remain outside, because the mere idea of outsideness is the very source of fear" (15–16).

To the extent that he urinizes the (di)visibility of representation and fecalizes the Jew who wanders interminably on the outside of an impassable gulf, Hegel might be said to retain this mythic fear of the mere idea of outsideness. How, though, might the excrementalization of alterity as the site/sight of homelessness, of utter outsideness and unsublatable dispossession, figure in what Jean-François Lyotard would call Hegel's metanarrational conception of Enlightenment modernity as the teleological process of totalization leading to absolute knowing? As was already shown, Hegel maintains that Enlightenment modernity attempts to legitimate "the human ownership of the treasures formerly squandered on heaven" (*ETW* 159). Following that formulation, one could describe modernity as the failed or abandoned metanarrative of "Man's" total, rational self-repossession. This description opens the question of postmodernity and allows us to begin to consider in more specific detail the matter of Bataille.

Taking postmodernity first, I will elaborate on a suggestion made earlier—namely, that Bersani's description of sexuality as self-shattering, as a pleasurable unpleasurable tension exceeding and disturbing those processes that are compatible with the psychic organization of the structured self, also fits a certain experience of modernity, an experience that, as Marshall Bermann puts it, "pours us all into a maelstrom of perpetual disintegration and renewal, of struggle and contradiction, of ambiguity and anguish" (*All That Is Solid* 15). Here we might distinguish between modernity as anguished experience and modernity as a certain narrative conceptualization or organization of that experience, between experiential modernity as maelstrom and philosophical modernity as a project that aims "to make men and women the subjects as well as the objects of modernization, to give them the power to change the world that is changing them, to make their way through the maelstrom and make it their own" (*All That Is Solid* 16).

But how might this distinction relate to the one Bersani makes when he asks whether sexuality as self-hyperbole is a repression of sexuality as self-abolition, as what he elsewhere calls "the desire to be shattered out of coherence," or "the excited dismantling of identity" (*Culture* 45)? The relation becomes more plausible when we consider Bersani's argument throughout *The Freudian Body* that this repressive self-hyperbole primarily takes the form of teleological narrativization—in Freud, the oedipal story of normative genital finality forecloses on the destabilizing excess of pre- or non-oedipal corporeal sensation—whereas the "antinarrative eroticizing of conciousness" (*Freudian Body* 43) takes place not only in sexuality but also in aesthetic experience (hence Bersani's argument *for* an aesthetics of masochism, with masochism serving as a tautology for sexuality, and *against* a "culture of redemption" that attempts to use art to redeem our damaged lives, damage being more or less the point). To retrope Bersani, then, we might ask whether modernity as self-hyperbolic, coherent, teleological project— the project of making this maelstrom into which we are poured our own—is the repression of (post)modernity as self-shattering antinarrative experience. Is this so even if the self that is being teleologically hyped is not the individual subject but the collective subject-object of history, and even if the narrative organization is not of the individual psyche but of the life-world itself through the rationality of intersubjective communicative action? My reference here is to Jürgen Habermas, who argues that the metanarrative of modernity has been prematurely abandoned, who, perhaps not coincidentally, has little to say about sexuality or aesthetic experience, and who specifically locates Bataille at the "French turn" from modernity as an incompleted project to postmodernism as a project of incompletion.[15]

Why blame Bataille for postmodernism? To begin with, the description of modernity as the failed or abandoned metanarrative of "Man's" total repossession of treasures formerly squandered on heaven can be made only from a postmodern perspective.[16] Such a description allows us to designate three possible elements of modernity and its discontents: (1) a progressive element that projects and attempts to enact globally an egalitarian and revolutionary narrative of human self-repossession and classless unalienation (orthodox Marxism); (2) a reactionary/nostalgic element that tries to recuperate heaven, or at least the hierarchical social order that the idea of heaven had previously legitimated (the fascists and the fascist-friendly high modernists); and (3) a third element that mobilizes its energies toward neither heaven nor rational self-repossession but rather toward absolute squander.

Bataille is close to both of the first two elements. He affiliated him-

self, albeit somewhat marginally, with communism, and like his sur-
realist adversary André Breton, wanted, as Walter Benjamin puts it,
"to win the energies of intoxication for the revolution" (*Reflections* 189).
His opposition to fascism, on the other hand, was troubled by his fascination with the heterogeneous element that the fascist leadership
seemed to him to embody.[17] It is the element of squander or expenditure, however, that Bataille most wants to express. Bataille writes that
"humanity recognizes the right to acquire, to conserve, and to consume
rationally, but it excludes in principle *nonproductive expenditure*" (*VE*
117). He links such expenditure with modes of eroticism or sovereignty
that remain insubordinate to servile thoughts of duration and future
results, with "luxury, mourning, war, cults, the construction of sump-
tuary monuments, games, spectacles, arts, perverse sexual activity (i.e.,
deflected from genital finality) . . . activities which, at least in primitive circumstances, have no end beyond themselves" (*VE* 118). Claiming, then, that "energy cannot in the end but be squandered" (*OC* 7:20–
21),[18] Bataille insists that something crucial to human experience is
excluded or repressed when the rational becomes the actual and the
actual the rational, when a relentlessly reappropriating reason takes
over the space once occupied by a sense—for Bataille, rigorously athe-
istic—of the sacred. Thus, against a Hegelian speculative dialectic in
which all positivities are negated only to be sublated, Bataille champi-
ons a recalcitrant, Nietzschean negativity that eludes dialectical reappropriation. Against Hegel's movement toward absolute knowing and
the totality of meaning in the transparency of the concept, Bataille
asserts that "the fundamental right of man is to signify *nothing*" (*OC*
6:429).[19]

Although Bataille stresses that "the realm of sacred things is composed of the pure and the impure" (*E* 121), he gives his heaviest heterological emphasis to the soiled impurity of the sacred—"the identical attitude toward shit [and] gods," "the elementary *subjective* identity
between types of excrement (sperm, menstrual blood, urine, fecal
matter) and everything that can be seen as sacred, divine, or marvel-
ous" (*VE* 94). Indeed, after defining *heterology* as "the science of what
is completely other," Bataille goes on to say, "The term *agiology* would
perhaps be more precise, but one would have to catch the double
meaning of *agio* (analogous to the double meaning of *sacer*), *soiled* as
well as *holy*. But it is above all the term *scatology* (the science of excrement) that retains in the present circumstances (the specialization of
the sacred) an incontestable expressive value as the doublet of an abstract term such as *heterology*" (*VE* 102). If for Bataille it is man's fundamental right to signify nothing, that right, at least for the early Ba-

taille, is generally asserted through the fundament. If energy cannot in the end but be squandered, such energy is for Bataille squandered not only *in* the end but *out* the butt. Indeed, anyone possessing a passing familiarity with Bataille's notion of expenditure will have noted his relentless emphasis on the anality of *dépense*. Some of Bataille's commentators recognize and appreciate Bataille's anal troping, whereas others do not seem to see any particular point in dwelling on the matter. But what if, against all better judgment, we not only limited our strategic interest to Bataille's anal emphasis but declared it to be the most important, most valuable aspect of his work, the only thing worth discussing? What if we reversed the normative process by which the anal "remains the symbol of everything that is to be repudiated and excluded from life" (Freud, *SE* 7:187) and focused on Bataille's "solar anus" to the exclusion of everything else? The results would doubtless be mixed. In fact, one would probably have to be oblivious to future results altogether to make such a useless rhetorical move.

Indeed, Bataille suggests that one would have to risk being considered "less than human." In both *Erotism* and the second volume of *The Accursed Share*, Bataille writes, "one doesn't even speak of the horror of *excreta*, which is a uniquely human trait. The prescriptions that generally concern our foul aspects are not the object of any focused attention and are not even classed among the taboos. So there exists a mode of the transition from animal to man so radically negative that it is not even spoken of. . . . The negation is so completely successful on this point that merely to note and affirm that something is there is deemed less than human." Bataille posits the transition from animal to man as involving three related prescriptions—concerning sexuality, waste products, and death—and says that Hegel "stresses the first and the third aspects [but] shuns the second, thus submitting (by silence) to the universal prohibitions that we are examining" (*E* 215; *AS* 53). Hegel is hardly alone in this silence, however. Not surprisingly, Habermas barely gives the matter a passing murmur in his critique of Bataille in *The Philosophical Discourse of Modernity* (although Habermas's analysis does have the benefit of distinguishing Bataille's project from that of Heidegger).

What is surprising, however, is to find one of Habermas's main philosophical adversaries, Jacques Derrida, in strange complicity with this silence. In fact, although scant, there is more reference to the excremental in Habermas's treatment of Bataille than in Derrida's well-known essay in *Writing and Difference* entitled "From Restricted to General Economy: A Hegelianism without Reserve," wherein Bataille's solar anus is almost totally occluded. Commenting on Derrida's essay,

Allan Stoekl writes that "we must attempt to understand not only what Derrida affirms in Bataille, but also what he strips from him," and points out that for Derrida, "the really determining, overarching (non)concept of [Bataille's] general economy is in fact *writing*" (*Politics* 112). What Derrida's overarching determination primarily strips from Bataille is his potentially subversive emphasis on anality (I argue later that this stripping, this disembodiment, is symptomatic of Derrida's entire approach to the repression of writing). In *Writing and Difference* Derrida distinguishes Hegelian lordship from Bataillean sovereignty. Whereas the former subordinates itself to its own self-reproduction through meaning, through meaning *as* self-reproduction, the other gives itself over "to the absolute loss of . . . meaning, to expenditure without reserve" (*WD* 268). Unlike the project of Hegelian lordship, Bataillean sovereignty "has no identity, is not *self, for itself, toward itself, near itself . . . must* subordinate nothing . . . be subordinated to *nothing or no one* . . . must expend itself without reserve, lose itself, lose consciousness, lose all memory of itself and all the interiority of itself" (*WD* 265). Derrida goes on to translate the difference between Hegelian lordship and Bataillean sovereignty into a difference between two forms of writing: a "minor" writing that "projects the trace," that "seeks to maintain itself within the trace, seeks to be recognized within it and to reconstitute the presence of itself," and a "major" writing that "produces the trace as trace," that "constitutes itself as the possibility of absolute erasure" (*WD* 265).

What strikes me, however, is how disembodied all this loss and expenditure becomes in Derrida's treatment of Bataille, how the Bataillean corpus itself—not as referent, not as empirical guarantor of presence, but as the site or sight of *dépense*—is erased. This erasure is particularly evident in the early part of the essay, where Derrida is much occupied with the figure of Bataillean laughter. Here Derrida is at pains to show that Bataille, despite his propensity "to laugh at philosophy (at Hegelianism)" (*WD* 252), nonetheless "'takes it seriously'" (253). If "a certain burst of laughter exceeds it and destroys its sense, or signals . . . the extreme point of 'experience' which makes Hegelian discourse dislocate *itself*," "this can be done only through close scrutiny and full knowledge of what one is laughing at" (253). After scrutinizing several Hegelian formulations that elicit a "burst of laughter from Bataille" (255), Derrida writes, "Laughter alone exceeds dialectics and the dialectician: it bursts out only on the basis of an absolute renunciation of meaning, an absolute risking of death, what Hegel calls abstract negativity. A negativity that never takes place, that never *presents* itself, because in doing so it would start to work again. A laughter that literally never *appears,* because it exceeds phenomenality in general, the absolute possibility of meaning" (256). Furthermore, "This burst of laughter makes the difference between lordship and sovereignty shine, without *showing it*" (256).

Derrida's effacement of the visibility of Bataillean laughter seems to follow from statements from Bataille himself, such as his assertion in *Inner Experience* that "what is hidden in laughter must remain so" (155). What neither shines nor shows in Derrida's treatment of Bataille's laughter, however, is the scandalous fact that, at least for the early Bataille, the evolutionary prototype of all human facial expressiveness, including the convulsive effusions of laughter, is nothing other than "the shit-smeared and obscene anuses of certain apes" (*VE* 75). If what is hidden in human laughter must remain so, Bataille's writings from the late twenties tell us why. Let us look, then, at an earlier appearance of Bataillean laughter:

> Anal obscenity, pushed to such a point that the most representative apes even got rid of their tails (which hide the anuses of other mammals), completely disappeared from the fact of human evolution. The human anus secluded itself deep within flesh, in the crack of the buttocks, and it now forms a projection only in squatting and excretion. All the potential for blossoming, all the possibilities for the liberation of energy, now under normal conditions found the way open only toward the superior regions of the buccal orifices, toward the throat, the brain, and the eyes. The blossoming of the human face, gifted with . . . diverse modes of expression . . . is like a conflagration, having the possibility of unleashing immense quantities of energy in the form of bursts of laughter, tears, or sobs; it succeeded the explosiveness that up to that point had made the anal orifice bud and flame. (*VE* 77)

To be fair to Derrida, there is next to nothing in the main texts by Bataille under his consideraton—*Inner Experience* and the essay "Hegel, Death, and Sacrifice"—to link laughter with anality. *Inner Experience,* characteristically and by comparison somewhat blandly, associates laughter with "poetry" and "ecstasy," whereas the Hegel essay makes only a passing reference to "defilement" ("Hegel, Death, and Sacrifice" 23)."[20] As Michèle Richman points out, there is in the Bataille of the 1940s and 1950s a "shift of interest away from the sexual extravagances of the early writings" (*Reading Georges Bataille* 127). Nonetheless, if Bataillean laughter can be aligned with "major" writing, with *écriture* in Derrida's sense (which, to an extent, I do believe it can), the early Bataille's obscene emphasis on the protoanality of laughter lets a light shine on the repression of writing different from that which Derrida's own probings let show. At one point, for example, Derrida writes that when Bataille laughs at Hegel, his laughter bursts out "dryly" (*WD* 252). Perhaps sometimes it does, but what makes the "magnificent but stinking ejaculation" (*VE* 77) of Bataillean laughter most subversive for the *corps propre* of Hegelian dialectics—and what finally makes it different from Derridean *différance* and dissemination, more heterologically material—is that such explosiveness can also be moist, runny, and *spluttering* (to use one of Joyce's favorite words). Perhaps one could remind Derrida—while at the same time insisting that the reminder serves no purpose, will not have been a critique, will have meant absolutely nothing—that Bataille does not want simply to laugh at Hegel, or to make Hegel laugh and play, or even to make Hegel *write;* he also wants to give dialectics a prod, in order, as Denis Hollier succinctly puts it, "to make reason shit."[21]

We have seen that Hegelian reason has not only an aversion to observing itself drip but also, by extension, a hard time bringing itself to shit. We have also seen that for Hegel the phallus cannot allow its productions to become visible and still remain the phallus. If reason is inherently phallocratic, then these aversions and proscriptions may all be related. Taylor writes that "Bataille is convinced that when reason is pushed to its limit, it inevitably slips and falls" (*Altarity* 131). The limits of reason, however, the limits of a philosophical modernity founded on reason, seem to be also the limits of the masculinist *corps propre*, of the phallic, hyperbolic self. The slip and fall of reason is a vertiginous *Durchfall*, a German word that means both "failure" and "falling through," as well as uncontrollable diarrhea. In the *Durchfall* of dialectics that Bataille's laughter enacts, reason craps out: the hyperbolic self not only shatters but splatters. If the penis lapses by allowing its productions to become divisible, then it not only fails to uphold the phallus but falls through the gaps in the trampoline of reason. The collapse of the penis is the *Durchfall* of the phallus: if one comes a cropper, the other becomes a crapper, muddling abstract equivalence with material ambivalence.

It is the representational trace of this abject and ambivalent relation between visible semen and divisible feces that the reversion to an ideally "essential" in(di)visibility strives constantly and relentlessly to repress. This repression plays its part in overdetermining the anxious disappearance of productive male bodies from mainstream cultural and representational scenes. As Elizabeth Grosz puts it:

> The masculine . . . has emptied itself of any relation to the male body, its specificity, and socio-political existence. This process of evacuat-

ing the male body from (an oedipalized) masculinity is the precondition for the establishment of the "disinterested" neutered space of
male specul(ariz)ation. Within this (virtual or imaginary) space . . .
the male can look at itself from outside, take itself as an object while
retaining its position as a subject. It gains the illusion of self-distance,
the illusion of a space of pure reflection, through the creation of a
mirroring surface that duplicates, represents, everything *except* itself.
(*Jacques Lacan* 173)

I can think of no better description of the Hegelian speculative, outside of Derrida's "hetero-tautology," than as the attempt of a disembodied masculinity to take itself as an object while retaining its position as subject. As I have shown, however, it is precisely the question
of male bodily production, of the bodily in Hegel that dialectics never
touched, that reveals the (s)tain or crack of this mirroring surface. An
insistence on bodily masculinity is therefore not simply an infantile
celebration of the excremental but rather an attempt at disrupting
abstract phallic idealization. Such an insistence exposes the speculative mechanisms by which hegemonic masculinity reproduces itself,
and only itself, in the very gesture of representing everything except
itself, of abjecting everything other than itself as the (dumping) ground
of representation. To make reason shit, to prod the phallus toward self-
abjection, to push hyperbole towards abolition, would be to disrupt the
dominant operation by which only others become shit, by which only
others are obliged or forced to reenact compulsively the defining, shattering conditions of subjectivity itself.

Twentieth-century history has shown us how that operation can
become the most destructive paradigm of modernity as project, a pro-
jectile modernity that knows no other way to negotiate squander than
to turn it on the dispossessed that its heaven never learned to treasure.
Expenditure becomes a matter of efficient disposal, consigning others
to the dunghill, by way of the gas chamber: the anxiety of production
can lead to the mass-production of death. It is not only the self but
philosophical totality that can become a sanction for violence when
promoted to the status of an ethical ideal.

But if we believe, with Lyotard, that we "have paid a high enough
price" for that promotion, "for the nostalgia of the whole and the one,
for the reconciliation of the concept and the sensible, of the transparent and the communicable experience"—if we want, like Lyotard, "to
wage a war on totality" (*Postmodern Condition* 81–82)—then perhaps,
like Bataille, we must learn to play dirty. For it is not only sexuality,
as Bersani insists, but also the anguished experience of modernity that
is always already "inseparable from the experience of failure," that is

always "constituted as a kind of psychic shattering, as a threat to the stability and integrity of the self" (*Freudian Body* 60). As Lyotard puts it, "Modernity [which for Lyotard means postmodernity], in whatever age it appears, cannot exist without a shattering of belief, and without discovery of the 'lack of reality' of reality, together with the invention of other realities" (*Postmodern Condition* 77).

If, as Lyotard suggests, there is something strikingly masochistic about giving oneself over to this shattering postmodern sublime, perhaps we should privilege that masochism, not only in Lyotard's sense, as well as Bersani's, but also in Kaja Silverman's sense of "returning to the male body all the violence [and degradation] that it has historically directed elsewhere" (*Male Subjectivity* 9). Perhaps it is the Bataillean version of postmodernity as sacrificial modernity that allows both men and women access to (or perhaps men access to and women a reprieve from) this de-meaning *jouissance*, without all the hype of teleological narrativization, without all the projections and disavowals through which phallic identification is enabled.

3

Dysgraphia 1: Freud's Anxiety

Masculinity between Cloaca and Castration

It is necessary to find the subject as a lost object. More precisely
this lost object is the support of the subject and in many cases is a
more abject thing than you may care to consider.
—Jacques Lacan, "Of Structure as an Inmixing of Otherness"

What a rest to speak of bicycles and horns. Unfortunately, it is
not of them I have to speak, but of her who brought me into the
world, through the hole in her arse if my memory is correct.
—Samuel Beckett, *Molloy*[1]

Appearing with Ronald Reagan at a New York anti-abortion gathering, Peter Grace, chairman of H.R. Grace Co., declared: "Everybody who's for abortion was at one time themselves a feces. And
that includes all of you out there. You were once a feces."
—cited in the *Utne Reader* (March-April 1990)

Like Bataille, Freud was interested in the antithetical
sense of such primal words as *sacred*.[2] Freud also had a patient who dis-
played the symptoms of what Bataille calls an "identical attitude towards shit [and] gods" (*VE* 94), a patient who was struck, if not tormented, by "the identical nature . . . of God and excrement" (*VE* 102).
In "From the History of an Infantile Neurosis," Freud reports that this
patient, the obsessional neurotic "Wolf-Man," had in childhood been
plagued by "some blasphemous thoughts that used to come into his
head like an inspiration from the devil. He was obliged to think . . .
'God—shit.' . . . He was tormented by the obsession of having to think
of the Holy Trinity whenever he saw three heaps of horse-dung or
other excrement lying in the road" (*SE* 17:17).

The Wolf-Man's blasphemous boyhood inspiration "God—shit" collapses deification into defecation and so brings him close to Bataille's
notion that "the realm of sacred things is composed of the pure and the

impure" (*E* 121). In his desire to make reason shit, Bataille submits "the God of reason" (*AS* III:379) to a *Durchfall* similar to the one enacted in the Wolf-Man's obsession. Bataille exposes the expulsion of impurity, the logic of excluding filth, on which the self-construction of the God of reason depends, pointing back to the ambiguous nature of the divinity whose position reason comes to occupy.[3] If God is "only idealized capital"[4] or as Bataille puts it, "nothing more than hypostasized work" (*OC* 7:395; Richman 64), then to de-idealize God back into capital is only the first step in a sort of reverse alchemy—what Bersani calls "the corruptive power of . . . a carnal irony" (*Freudian Body* 9)—that would transform capital, the money form, the abstract universal equivalent, back into baser material still. This carnal irony or base materialism would turn God as idealized capital back into the excrement that money represents in the well-known Freudian symbology, in which an "ancient interest in faeces is transformed into the high valuation of *gold* and *money*" (*SE* 22:100). To make reason shit, then, would be to reopen that sacred grove or rectal grave where previously, in some archaic space of pre-oedipal economic history, the divine was defiled, where money was the heterological stuff of sacrifice, oblation, and play.

In *Reading Georges Bataille* Michèle Richman writes that Bataille's notion of *dépense* "challenges the opposition of rationality and irrationality and reopens to modern experience the equivalent of a sacred space of archaic expenditure. How the special nature of the sacred is determined is the underlying issue for an appreciation of heterogeneity" (43). Granted, the Wolf-Man was an obsessional neurotic, not a Bataillean heterological materialist. Nevertheless, the question of Freud's appreciation of a heterogeneity that can be designated as Bataillean allows us to examine not only his response to the Wolf-Man's divinely defiled vision but also the occlusions and foreclosures at work in Freud's own teleological narrativization, and normativization, of male sexuality—specifically, the disavowal of both maternal and feminine subjective agency.[5]

Beginning with the Wolf-Man, we can note in his collapse the conspicuous absence of any *grammatical* relationship between God and shit. There remains only a dash to signify that absence. Any number of verbs could be substituted for this dash, but the most likely candidate is *is,* the copula. At least, the copula was the most likely candidate for Freud, since in Freud's analysis the Wolf-Man's obsessive neurosis can be traced back to a scene of copulation, the primal scene of the parents copulating *a tergo,* which the Wolf-Man either actually witnessed or constructed by projecting a real scene of animals copulating back onto an imagined parental scenario.[6] In Freud's analysis, what the Wolf-Man thinks he has seen his parents engaged in is not vaginal intercourse from the rear but rather an act of anal penetration.

This misapprehension or displacement is a function of what Freud regards as the Wolf-Man's disavowal of castration. For Freud, castration is all the little boy sees when looking at female genitalia, not the presence of a vagina but the absence, or loss, of a penis. In his essay "Psychoanalysis and History" Dominick LaCapra formulates this disavowal in terms quite suggestive for my discussion thus far:

> The bizarre narrative of castration anxiety tells the story of fetishism. It begins with a nonevent, a disavowal of perception, a refusal to see what is there. For "in the beginning" the vagina is foreclosed—a derealized reality. It is replaced by another reality which is "perceived" as absent—something one "knows" should be there: the penis. . . . What is missing is the very phallus which the woman (the phantasmatic phallic mother) had "in the beginning" but lost through some misdeed—an obvious lesson for the boy himself. The fetish for Freud is itself the narcissistically invested surrogate for the phantasmatic lost totality—a totality that never existed and whose imaginary constitution requires a conversion of absence into loss on the basis of a nonperception. Yet with the appearance of the imaginary totality, the castration narrative becomes a variant of (or perhaps the prototype for) the greatest story ever told—the classical "apocalyptic" narrative (as well as the displaced narrative of speculative dialectics) in which a totality fully present at the origin is lost through a sinful fall only to be regained in a utopian future. (241–42)

In the case of Freud's speculation about the Wolf-Man's narrative, the disavowal of castration entails imagining the vagina as a "front-bottom," that is, as a forward extension of the posterior region. This particular extension, however, extends into Freudian theory itself, for as Freud writes in "Anxiety and Instinctual Life," any "interest in the vagina, which awakens later, is also essentially of anal-erotic origin. This is not to be wondered at, for the vagina itself, to borrow an apt phrase from Lou-Andreas Salomé, is 'taken on lease' from the rectum" (*SE* 22:101). The Wolf-Man, then, having disavowed castration by foreclosing on the vagina's lease from the rectum, can see his parents' copulation only as anal intercourse because for him—if not in certain ways for Freud himself—the anus seems to be the primordial site of all transactions.

For the Wolf-Man, "God—shit" signifies at once the recollection and the repression of this analized primal scene. What the Wolf-Man's obsession remarks is an episode in which "God" the Father has been "in the shit"—that is, in the mother's rectum. But this reading of the Wolf-Man's blasphemy does not quite allow the conjecture that the missing grammatical link between the signifiers *God* and *shit* is in fact the copula and not a preposition, for there is a difference between "God is shit" and "God in shit." In the latter case, God can always pull back out, whereas the former implies a certain inextricability. As long as the grammatical relationship is effaced, however, the matter remains undecidable. Thus we might say that although the Wolf-Man brings God and shit into close proximity or contiguity (recollection of the primal scene), the dash functions prophylactically to keep the two separate by holding their relationship in suspension (repression of the recollection).

As Stanley Fish has remarked, Freud withholds a certain portion of his relation of the Wolf-Man's story that he later produces as a missing piece ("Withholding" 935–38). This withheld bit of information is the conjecture that "the child finally interrupted his parents' intercourse by passing a stool, which gave him an excuse for screaming" (*SE* 17:80). In Freud's analysis what overdetermines the Wolf-Man's reaction to the memory of (perhaps) having viewed his parents' intercourse *a tergo* is his repressed "homosexual" desire to occupy the mother's "passive" position and hence to introduce his father's penis into his own rectum. For Freud, the child's spontaneous defecation not only interrupts the parents but indicates his own sexual excitation. Moreover, this significatory act of defecation, in which the Wolf-Man signs or autographs the primal scene, becomes a sort of auto-affection in which his own fecal column performs the same function that he ostensibly desires from his father's penis—that is, to fill up his rectum, if only for a passing moment.

This momentary identification of the father's penis with the son's column of feces opens up some complex questions. As we have seen, Freud's missing portion turns out to be the Wolf-Man's stool. This stool solidifies the copula as the missing grammatical link between God and shit in the Wolf-Man's blasphemous inspiration, for if the Wolf-Man had only witnessed the primal scene without making his own signal contribution, the preposition *in* might remain the most likely substitute for the effacing dash. The Wolf-Man sees "God" go "into the shit" and then come back out, unscathed, intact, its own proper self. In fact, when Freud writes of the patient that "during the coitus of the primal scene he had observed the penis disappear, that he had felt sympathy for his father on that account, and had rejoiced at the reappearance of what he thought had been lost" (*SE* 17:88), what Freud actually describes is a sort of specular *fort-da* game in which the reappearance of the father's penis is a moment of pure joy. At the moment of the

Wolf-Man's own defecation, however, when the identification between penis and fecal column is sealed, this *fort-da* becomes problematic: what goes in as penis comes out as turd. What is sent as spool returns as stool. God (as) the father's penis is not simply *in* shit from which it could eventually pull out again. God inextricably *is* the shit, and this abject identification opens up a deeply scatontological anxiety that no *fort-da* can ever completely assuage.

For Freud, the Wolf-Man's problem is that his "active" masculinity rebels against his desire to assume a "passive" feminine position in order to gain sexual satisfaction from his father.[7] Curiously enough, Freud seems to see the identification of the penis with feces as completely unproblematic, no threat of danger, no cause for alarm. Freud's calm is all the more curious considering that in his various writings on the subject of anxiety (to which I now turn), he consistently links that affect to castration, as well as to separation from the mother's body, but not to anal expulsion—this even though he repeatedly designates the act of defecation as a sort of prototype for both birth and castration.

Although Freud writes about anxiety in a number of places—*Beyond the Pleasure Principle, Inhibitions, Symptoms and Anxiety, Introductory Lectures on Psychoanalysis*—my focus is on "Anxiety and Instinctual Life" in the *New Introductory Lectures*. As Freud discusses it here, anxiety arises in response to a perceived threat or danger. Anxiety is real if the threat or danger is real. Neurotic anxiety, on the other hand, occurs when the perception of threat can no longer be aligned with an existing danger but can be traced back to an earlier situation perceived as threatening. In Freud's reading this earlier situation of anxiety is primarily the unpleasurable tension caused by the absence of the mother. For women, says Freud, this anxiety entails the fear of the loss of love. For men, on the other hand, the unpleasurable tension of the mother's absence is coupled with anxiety about the castration that the male child imagines as punishment against his desire for her presence. Thus in Freud's legend of masculinity both castration and separation from the mother, a separation related to birth, are interrelated occasions of anxiety. Freud writes:

> Fear of castration . . . finds no place in women, for though they have a castration complex they cannot have a fear of being castrated. Its place is taken in their sex by a fear of loss of love, which is evidently a later prolongation of the infant's anxiety if it finds its mother absent. You will realize how real a situation of danger is indicated by this anxiety. If a mother is absent or has withdrawn her love from her child, it is no longer sure of the satisfaction of its needs and is perhaps exposed to the most distressing feelings of tension. Do not

reject the idea that these determinants of anxiety may at bottom repeat the situation of the original anxiety at birth, which, to be sure, also represented a separation from the mother. . . . You may add the fear of castration to this series, for a loss of the male organ results in an inability to unite once more with the mother (or a substitute for her) in the sexual act. (*SE* 22:87)

I will not rehearse here the well-known arguments against Freud's phallocratic attribution to women of a castration complex and the concomitant penis envy. I will, however, note the distinction Freud makes between complex and anxiety. In *Inhibitions, Symptoms and Anxiety* Freud writes "though we can with certainty establish in [women] the presence of a castration *complex,* we can hardly speak with propriety of castration *anxiety* where castration has already taken place" (*SE* 20:123). For Freud, the absence in women of castration anxiety marks their "inability" to overcome the oedipus complex and to develop a strong superego, hence Freud's well-known opinion of women's "moral deficiency." In the essay entitled "Femininity" in the *New Introductory Lectures* he writes that since girls do not fear castration, they lack the "chief motive" that "leads boys to surmount the Oedipus complex." Since girls remain in the oedipus complex for an indeterminate length of time, and perhaps never completely demolish it, their superegos "cannot attain the strength and independence which give it its cultural significance, and feminists are not pleased when we point out to them the effects of this factor upon the average feminine character" (*SE* 22:129).[8]

The relationship between this discussion of, on the one hand, castration anxiety and Freud's view of femininity and, on the other, anal expenditure may not seem particularly clear. What might anal eroticism have to do with castration anxiety, and hence with the development of a superego that for Freud imbues the average masculine character with the strength and independence that ensure its cultural significance and that the "average feminine character" lacks?[9] What, in short, does anality signify—or refuse to signify? Freud is curiously silent, although not about anal eroticism; he has much to say on that subject, and in some ways one might agree with Irigaray that in Freud's theory we are caught up in "an anal symbolic from which there is no escape" (*SW* 75). Rather, Freud is tight-lipped about the relation that he himself seems to establish between anality and anxiety. Freud appears to establish or allude to this relation in the latter part of "Anxiety and Instinctual Life":

After a person's own faeces, his excrement, has lost its value for him, this instinctual interest derived from the anal source passes over on to objects that can be presented as *gifts*. And this is rightly so, for faeces were the first gift that an infant could make, something he could part with out of love for whoever was looking after him. After this, corresponding exactly to analogous changes of meaning that occur in linguistic development, this ancient interest in faeces is transformed into the high valuation of *gold* and *money* but also makes a contribution to the affective cathexis of *baby* and *penis*. It is a universal conviction among children, who long retain the cloaca theory, that babies are born from the bowel like a piece of faeces: defaecation is the model of the act of birth. But the penis too has its fore-runner in the column of faeces which fills and stimulates the mucous membrane of the bowel. When a child, unwillingly enough, comes to realize that there are human creatures who do not possess a penis, that organ appears to him as something detachable from the body and becomes unmistakably analogous to the excrement, which was the first piece of bodily material that had to be renounced. A great part of anal eroticism is thus carried over into a cathexis of the penis. (*SE* 22:100–101)[10]

This passage, with its heavy emphasis on birth and castration, on loss and separation (the loss of value, love, or objects), seems to have everything to do with the problem of anxiety as Freud has introduced it. Well before this passage, however, at the point in the lecture where he segues from anxiety to instinctual life, Freud attempts to make a clean break: he announces, "I feel sure you are rejoicing, Ladies and Gentlemen, at not having to listen any more about anxiety" (*SE* 22:84). And indeed, he never mentions the word again. Although everything about Freud's discussion of anal eroticism seems to relate it to those unpleasurably tense experiences that he designates as anxiety's locus, Freud apparently wants us to believe that we are no longer listening to a discourse about anxiety.

So what, to echo Lacan, does the analyst want? We may find a clue if we turn again to Freud's assertion in *Inhibitions, Symptoms and Anxiety* that "as soon as writing, which entails making a liquid flow out of a tube onto a piece of white paper, assumes the significance of copulation . . . writing [is] stopped because [it] represent[s] the performance of a forbidden sexual act" (*SE* 20:90). Here Freud seems anxious that writing, or indeed any process that entails making a liquid flow out onto a surface, assume the significance of copulation and so *not* assume the ostensible insignificance of other, more de-meaning bodily functions.[11] Freud's oedipalizing attempt to let all excorporation signify heterosexual copulation may help to account not only for the alignment of heterosexuality with significance (which I have shown to occur in Hegel as well) but also for the rigorous distinction Freud makes between (castration) anxiety and anal expenditure. Indeed, Freud clearly states that the stake of castration is nothing more or less than the loss of the means of copulating with the mother or her substitute. He also stresses castration anxiety, which women lack (even though they do possess a castration complex), as the means of forming a superego that guarantees strength, independence, and cultural significance (and here we might remember Bataille's definition of abjection as "the inability to assume with sufficient *strength* the imperative act of excluding abject things" [*OC* 2:217; emphasis added]). In the Freudian/oedipal teleology, then, a generalized anxiety about anal expenditure must be restricted to a specific anxiety about castration precisely so that the latter eventually can be assuaged through the significance of reproductive copulation—life's "highest fulfillment," as Hegel calls it. I consider this restriction to be an aspect of what Bersani has identified as "a certain trend to expel or bypass sexuality in psychoanalytic thought unless it has been teleologically narrativized" (*Freudian Body* 64). I also suggest that it is only the teleological promise of such significance that allows Freud to recognize the otherwise quite dangerous fungibility of the elements in the feces-penis-baby triad, a metaphoric unity that, without that promise, could quickly become the metonymic site of abject contamination or absolute loss. This is an appropriate point at which to examine how this promise/premise functions, how the conception of this triadic exchange system as metaphor (the realm of substitution) fortifies itself against the threat of loss or contamination it would represent as metonymy (the realm of contiguity).[12]

To equate the penis with feces initially seems to be a threatening proposition, for to do so is to recognize, as Freud says, that the penis, like the turd, can be detached from the body and lost. To identify the baby with feces also seems to be a risky business, for the baby, again like the turd, can then be irrecuperably expelled from the mother's body, with no promise of return. But we should remember that in the first instance, in the Wolf-Man's case at least, the turd does not correspond to just any penis but rather to that of the father: the Wolf-Man, says Freud, identifies the fecal column that is filling his rectum on the way out with the paternal penis that would fill the same space on the way in, thus recuperating the father's phallus from its disappearance and reemergence from the mother's rectum. In the second instance (baby = feces, as per the cloaca theory) there is also a repatriation, a recuperation of the phallus, for if this dyad is triangulated, if the baby is not only a turd but also a penis (or has a penis; here the distinction between "to be" and "to have" is none too clear), then there is in fact some hope of return, of getting back in, if not to the mother herself then at least to a substitute. And if something comes back out again, it will not be feces this time but rather another baby, preferably male. Happiness will abound, says Freud, "quite especially if the baby is a little boy who brings the longed-for penis with him" (*SE* 22:128). As Irigaray comments, "This boy child is the sign of the seed's immortality, of the fact that the properties of the sperm have won out over those of the ovum. Thus he guarantees the father's power to reproduce and represent himself, and to perpetuate his gender and his species. What is more, the son, as heir to the name, ensures that the patrimony will not be squandered" (*SW* 74).

Obviously, then, it is the Name of the Father that saves the penis-baby-feces triad from representing squander and expenditure or abject contamination. It is the phallus as symbolic guarantor of an abstract universal equivalence that keeps anality on the level of metaphorical substitution rather than metonymical contiguity, as in Lacan's comment that "the anal level is the locus of metaphor—one object for another, give the faeces in place of the phallus" (*FFC* 104). It is the phallus, or Name of the Father—which Lacan assumes as that which oblativity inevitably desires to bestow—that metaphorically prevents either the penis or the penised baby from being or ever having been irrecuperably or contiguously "in the shit." It is the phallus that grants to fecal matter a stabilizable value within a reproductive economy, provided that feces assume a certain phallomorphism that would allow their solidification into metaphor.

But here we confront again Irigaray's question of "what is in excess with respect to form" (*TS* 111). According to this same metaphoric paradigm, a baby born without a penis (or more accurately, with something that is not a penis) and who never develops the desire to be the phallus for someone who is attached to a penis—or even a baby born with a penis who never learns to value that appendage over all other bodily spaces—will remain only a piece of feces. We can see, then, how the phallus functions from the beginning to overdetermine both the *gendering* and the *sexing* of abjection as "the mode by which Others [women and queers] become shit" (Butler, *Gender Trouble* 134).

Not only others, however, but also mothers undergo this equation. After discussing the boy child as the sign of the seed's immortality, Irigaray goes on to consider the place of the woman in this restricted economy: "woman's job," she writes, "is to tend the seed man 'gives' her, to watch over the interests of this 'gift' deposited with her and return it to its owner in due course. The penis (stool), the sperm (seed-gift), the child (gift), all make up an anal symbolic from which there is no escape." Irigaray wonders whether it is really the penis and not the feces that "underpin . . . the system" and decides that it is the turd that remains "the standard of value." She writes that "woman's role seems to require only that she detach herself from the anal 'object': the gift-child, just as she is required to give up the 'fecal column' [penis] after coitus. Repeating, thus, her separation from the feces. . . . If the penis re-presents the fecal mass, she has always already been cut off from it" (*TS* 75).

This separation, however, this state of being "cut off," may be a more undecidable and anxious space within the phallic imaginary than Irigaray's analysis allows. In Irigaray's reading it is *"anal erotism's primacy over what is called genital sexuality"* (*TS* 74) that ensures that the phallus is undergirded by the feces, which somehow remain a stable, determining standard of value. Nonetheless, only the recuperative teleology of genital finality can finally grant a *retroactive* metaphorical stability to the feces-penis-baby triad. Without that enforced finality—*a compulsory heterosexuality subtending metaphoricity itself*—a purely or generally excremental economy would never provide even the briefest illusion of a solid, stable base. The phallus would never find in such a general economy either relative autonomy or sure footing against the threat of its own *Durchfall*.

It is therefore a mistake to argue, as does Irigaray, that anal eroticism retains an absolute primacy over phallocentric, heterosexual genital sexuality, that the feces can remain a stable standard of value. On the contrary, there is something quite undecidable and unstable about anality that phallogocentrism wants decided, wants to escape, occlude, repress, or secure. In Irigaray's description of the phallogocentric economy, the penis as fecal column or fecal mass is positioned as a stable center from which the woman is separated, detached, or cut off. Phallogocentrism does attempt to legitimate the male occupation of a central position from which women and others are culturally and politically marginalized. Nonetheless, insofar as it follows the logic of the *corps propre*, phallogocentrism must exclude the excremental as such and identify that devalued element with the feminine. Centering (on) the fecal thus entails an unavoidable contradiction. Moreover, the centering by which the feces-penis-baby triad is finally stabilized is perhaps only the effect of reversing a logically and chronologically prior state of affairs in which, for the infant, the mother's body occupied center stage. I refer to this crucial reversal, this founding denial of constitutive alterity, as *primontological:* it is primary or primordial to the establishment of a certain masculine ontology that thereafter depends on the rigorous maintenance of this reversal to remain ontological, to retain a masculine being, and to protect itself from the encroachment of a scatontological anxiety.

If, as I have suggested, this anxiety is a site of undecidability, we should ask just what is it that cannot be decided, that presents itself both as *refuse* and as a *refusal* to stabilize signification, to fix and maintain identity. If we return to Freud's formulation of anal eroticism in the long passage from "Anxiety and Instinctual Life" previously quoted, we find the assertion that "after a person's own faeces, his excrement, has lost its value for him, this instinctual interest . . . passes over on to objects that can be presented as *gifts*." Freud says this is all "rightly so, for the faeces were the first gift that an infant could make, something he could part with out of love for whoever was looking after him" (*SE* 22:100). It is important to stress here that for Freud the fecal gift's subsequent loss in erotic and affective value is purely a function of cultural inculcation; civilization, that is, must channel the incontinence of its discontents. As Freud points out in *Civilization and Its Discontents*, the infant must learn to devalue its own feces, which it initially regards without disgust. It learns this hard lesson by observing the negative value that the adult world places on its gift, deeming it "worthless, disgusting, abhorrent and abominable" (*SE* 21:100). In the "Femininity" essay Freud points out that "urine and faeces are the first gifts that children make to those who look after them, and controlling them is the first concession to which the instinctual life of children can be induced" (*SE* 22:104–5). In a footnote in *Three Essays on the Theory of Sexuality*, Freud writes,

> The first prohibition which a child comes across—the prohibition against getting pleasure from anal activity and its products—has a decisive effect on his whole development. This must be the first occasion on which the infant has a glimpse of an environment hostile to his instinctual impulses, on which he learns to separate his own entity from this alien one and on which he carries out the first "repression" of his possibilities for pleasure. From that time on, what is "anal" remains the symbol of everything that is to be repudiated and excluded from life. (*SE* 7:187)

This first concession, however, involves more than the renunciation of the blind somatic pleasure of releasing the body's products whenever and however; it also involves a lesson in exchange value. For excrement is not simply the first but in fact the *only* tangible or visible product that the infant can offer up in exchange for the love and nourishment it receives, and it must be a bitter concession indeed to learn that this precious gift, this alienated labor of love that the infant identifies as a part of its own body, elicits at best patient indifference and at worst disgust or even punishment.[13]

For Freud, moreover, the infant identifies the feces as more than just a part of its body that it offers as a gift—as Bataille puts it, "a part of oneself destined for open sacrifice" (*VE* 119). Freud also suggests that the infant identifies its own body in its entirety as a production of the mother's anus. It is the mother's anus that causes that body to appear. "It is a universal conviction among children," writes Freud, "that babies are born from the bowel like a piece of faeces: defaecation is the model of the act of birth" (*SE* 22:100). Again, one might expect Freud to stop here to consider the relation between this supposedly universal conviction and the loss of value that fecal matter undergoes on the infant's concession to sphincteral control. (I.e., how might the infant's perception of the negative value that the adult world places on its sacrificial fecal gift affect its conviction that it was born through the bowel, as was the "worthless, disgusting, abhorrent and abominable" substance that elicits such hostility?) In addition, if defecation is in fact the model of the act of birth, one might expect Freud to consider defecation's relation to anxiety, since he has already granted that "determinants of anxiety may at bottom repeat the situation of the original anxiety at birth" (*SE* 22:87). But he does neither. Instead, he moves immediately to the fecal column as a prototype for the penis and thus to a castration anxiety that can always be oedipally, narratively, teleologically, and heterosexually assuaged. We know how the rest of this story comes out.

But suppose we suspend this generalized anxiety of expenditure before it can be recuperated within a restricted castration anxiety that serves as the alibi for its own oedipal sublation. Suppose we suspend the construction of the phallus before it finds the ability to assume with sufficient strength the imperative act of excluding abject things. What we are left with is the unsublatable specter of what Kristeva calls the "anal penis"—that is, "the phallus with which infantile imagination provides the feminine sex" (*PH* 71). Since for Freud the infant perceives the feminine sex as castrated, the anal penis would be what is always already absent or missing, what was there before the castration supposed to have taken place. In Irigaray's description of Freud's phallocentric theory, this anal penis is somehow centered and granted priority, whereas the woman herself is detached and cut off. If, however, the mother's body is at any time perceived as originally occupying this center, then it may be the infant's own body—phantasmatically coded as anal penis, detachable part-object, sacrificial lump—that the infant perceives as cut off, lost, discarded. That is, if the mother is ever even dimly perceived as the original possessor or retainer of the anal penis that the infant identifies as its own body, then the infant could well figure itself as the result or effect of a defecation/castration, the phallic mother's loss or sacrifice of her own valued part-object. Moreover, since this speculative infant imagines the production of its own body as the mother's sacrificial loss, and since it has experienced defecation, its only mode of production prior to speech, similarly as loss, it may come to figure production itself as the potential site of loss and anything its body might visibly produce in the future (urine and semen, for example, but also mental images or "picture-thinking" via speech and writing) as potentially losable (visibility = divisibility = losability), as a potential site of sacrificial violence. These losable productions would have been produced from a source that is itself a lost product—detached, abjected, expelled, cut off. As Kristeva writes, "The abjection of self would be the culminating form of that experience of the subject to which it is revealed that all its objects are based merely on the inaugural *loss* that laid the foundations of its own being" (*PH* 5).

To my knowledge, Freud never considers the possible psychic consequences opened up by the anxious perception of this phantasmatically abject (pre)self-image. Rather, he quickly oedipalizes and hence expels them: a general anxiety about anal expenditure (abjection) becomes restricted or condensed into castration anxiety, which is sublatable and resolvable into significance (whereas the turd cannot otherwise be *aufgehoben*). As Elizabeth Grosz puts it, "Abjection . . . is the precondition of castration; castration is an attempt to cover over and expel it" ("The Body of Signification" 92–93). For Freud, after all, the subject of anxiety is always *le sujet supposé perdre*—the subject who is supposed to lose, or supposed to fear losing (which of course means that Freud's subject is, as Irigaray and many other feminists rightly charge, always male). This supposed subject of loss, however, is never supposed to have been a lost object in Freud's phallocentric scenario. If "the subject is already constituted as an object from before its birth" (Wilden 161), it is exactly this anterior constitution that the phallic subject anxiously wants to turn around. If, as Jacqueline Rose writes, "the Imaginary itself, through which the subject sets itself up as subject and the other as object, can be seen to contain a potential reversal [in which] the subject is constituted as object by the Other" (*Sexuality* 190), it is just this potential that must be guarded against if the phallic subject is to set itself straight. Such is the crux of what I call the *primontological reversal*, which desires to decide permanently that undecidable space between losing and being lost, between being the losing subject and having been the lost object, between producing and having been produced, between being the one who excludes and expels and being that other who is excluded, expelled, and abjected.

Irigaray argues that for Freud, maternal activity is always passive, decentered, marginalized, granted neither priority nor authority. In the primontological reversal this deauthorization of the maternal—the devaluation of the mother's role in reproduction, the silencing of the mother's speech and the suppression of her active desire—seems to be a necessary step toward the authorization of the phallus, just as the rigorous passivation and objectification of the mother's body (or, later, any female body) is necessary for the accession to, and maintenance of, an active phallic subjectivity. Thus, the primontological reversal may be one of the founding moments in that mode of masculine thinking that can imagine self-preservation only as the domination of an alterity figured as feminine. For the split subject, however (and all subjects are split), self-preservation as the domination of alterity must also be a form of self-domination: "I—mark(s) the division" (Derrida, *Glas* 64); "*Je est un autre*" (Rimbaud, "Letter" 304); "You are not yourself" (Barbara Kruger, in Mitchell, "An Interview" 441).[14] The phallic mode of subjectivity already contains, in the phantasmatic form of the anal penis, its own intolerable but perhaps constitutive contradiction: because it is figured as a penis, it is potentially a phallus with the corresponding power to generate meaning and value. Because it is figured as fecal, however, it can never be a phallus, can never generate meaning and value, can never be anything but powerless. Bersani's definition of phallocentrism—"not primarily the denial of power to women (although it has obviously also led to that, everywhere and at all times), but above all the denial of the value of powerlessness in both men and women" ("Rectum" 217)—deserves reemphasis here. Denied both power and the powerful attraction of its very lack of value, the anal penis is like a letter that can neither be kept nor sent away. Whereas the phallus must stand at the center to retain its significance, its power to generate meaning, the anal penis can neither stand up straight (it is insufficiently solid) nor remain centered—particularly if phallic subjectivity, obeying the logic of the *corps propre*, manages to assume with sufficient strength the imperative act of excluding abject things. If phallic subjectivity is to follow this imperative, then it must rigorously repress or expel the specter of the anal penis (perhaps, like Freud and Lacan, by forcing the feces to signify metaphorically). Moreover, since in the original phantasm it is the spectral mother who actively loses/produces the infant's body as shit, *any trace of maternal determination in the constitution of the phallic subject must also be vigorously repressed.*

Thus, to maintain itself within the primontological reversal, the phallic subject is charged with two related responsibilities: to keep itself clean and to fecalize, passivate, and objectify the (m)other. The latter process can take the form of the devaluation of the mother's role in reproduction. It can also result in masculine fantasies of symbolic self-paternity (such as, to cite but one example, the one Stephen Dedalus attempts to construct for himself in *Ulysses* by figuring Shakespeare as a guarantor of his own self-fashioning and thus holding his mother's insistent ghost at bay). As Harold Bloom asks in *The Anxiety of Influence,* "what strong maker desires the realization that he has failed to create himself?" (5). But with this galling realization of what Bloom calls "lack of priority" may come the unwanted recognition of what Lacan, following Merleau-Ponty, calls the "stain" of determination (*FFC* 74). This failure to self-create, then, is also a contaminating *Durchfall:* it is as if the mere recognition of prior maternal determination, the simple acknowledgment of active subjectivity on the part of the (m)other, were enough to shatter the hyperbolic self, plunging the phallus down the shithole. The nature of this plunge, however, indicates not only the antimaternal aspects of phallic self-constitution but a certain homophobia at work as well, a fear of the anus as phantasmatic origin in the former instance and as destination of desire or locus of pleasure (rather than of metaphor) in the latter. This involvement of matrophobia with homophobia—a fear, mixing phantasmatic memory with desire, of either having had or wanting to have contact with an anus—allows us to consider the anal penis as functioning within a devalued metonymic contiguity, whereas the notion of the phallomorphic turd functions within the realm of metaphorical substitution and hence signals the triumph of both rationality and exchange.

The anal penis, however, the penis that lapses and allows its production(s)—its origin and destination—to become visible, to be recognized, remains the specter that threatens to subvert that triumph. This threat looms whenever the phallic subject attempts to designate itself in a statement, whenever the split opens between the subject of the enunciation and the subject of the enounced, whenever "I— mark(s) the division" or the *Je* confronts itself as *un autre* (and it always does), whenever you are not yourself (and you never fully are). Such is the abject threat of metonymic contamination posed to phallic mastery by writing, by the (di)visibility and heterological materiality of semiotic production itself.

Freud's own writing is hardly immune to this anxious form of dysgraphia, this ambivalent disinclination and incitement to write. Did Freud not refer to his earliest productions as exercises in "dreckology"

(*CL* 290–301)?[15] Does he not attempt to redeem his logos from the dreck, and thereby keep the threat of the spectral mother at bay, by letting the normative, compulsory assumption of heterosexual copulative significance become the condition of possibility for any "liquid flow" onto a piece of white paper?

I submit that this dysgraphic anxiety about dreckology, about the rupture or *Durchfall* of phallic authority, haunts not only Freud but the whole enterprise of masculinist self-representation and disturbs its hyperbolic maintenance of identity and power. In the next two sections I continue to examine how and why the foreclosure of this anxiety depends on the denial of subjective agency to mothers and to women—an agency that, if granted, would phantasmatically turn the phallic subject into shit. Here I will simply allude to the third epigraph of this section, to Peter Grace's ludicrous confusion, itself born of an unconscious retention of the cloaca theory, between *fetus* and *feces*. Is it merely a coincidence that this graceless slip occurred at a political rally whose goal was to deny women choice?

An Impressive Caesura

> The abject has only one quality of the object—that of being opposed to the I. If the object, however, through its opposition, settles me within the fragile texture of a desire for meaning, which, as a matter of fact, makes me ceaselessly and infinitely homologous to it, what is abject, on the contrary, the jettisoned object, is radically excluded and draws me toward the place where meaning collapses.
>
> —Julia Kristeva, *Powers of Horror*

> In at one ear and incontinent out through the mouth, or the other ear, that's possible too. No sense in multiplying the occasions of error. Two holes and me in the middle, slightly choked. Or a single one, entrance and exit, where the words swarm and jostle like ants, hasty, indifferent, bringing nothing, taking nothing away, too light to leave a mark. I shall not say I again, ever again, it's too farcical.
>
> —Samuel Beckett, *The Unnameable*

At a certain point in *Inhibitions, Symptoms and Anxiety* Freud employs a curious metaphor: he refers to the act of birth as an "impressive caesura" (*SE* 20:138). Derived from classical prosody, the word *caesura* refers to a particular sort of break in a line of verse, and it interests me that Freud would liken childbirth to a formal scission or discontinuity within an equally formal signifying process, attributing a semiotic quality to the former and a somatic morphology to the latter.

It is not separation or interruption, however, but rather continuity that Freud stresses in his description of childbirth as caesura. Just as a caesura represents only a moment of disjunction within the ostensible unity of the poem, so for Freud the act of birth represents only a momentary break in the mother's unified and unceasing care for the infant. Freud writes that

> just as the mother originally satisfied all the needs of the foetus through the apparatus of her own body, so now, after its birth, she continues to do so, though partly by other means. There is much more continuity between intra-uterine life and earliest infancy than the impressive caesura of the act of birth would have us believe. What happens is that the child's biological situation as a foetus is replaced for it by a psychical object-relation to its mother. But we must not forget that during its intra-uterine life the mother was not an object for the foetus, and that at that time there were no objects at all. (*SE* 20:138)

The immediate context for Freud's discussion here is his disagreement with Otto Rank about the importance of birth trauma as a prototype for all later anxiety. As I already discussed, Freud is willing to admit that "determinants of anxiety may at bottom repeat the situation of the original anxiety at birth, which, to be sure, also represented a separation from the mother" (*SE* 22:87). Here, however, Freud seems to suggest that because the newly born infant does not yet perceive the mother as a separate object (in Lacan's terms, the infant is still in the Real), the continuity between the intrauterine and the immediately postpartum states undermines the notion that the infant experiences its own birth as a danger situation. Freud writes that the "'danger'. . . against which [the infant] wants to be safeguarded is that of non-satisfaction, of a *growing tension due to need*, against which it is helpless. . . . The situation of non-satisfaction in which the amounts of stimulation rise to an unpleasurable height without its being possible for them to be mastered psychically or discharged must be analogous for the infant to the experience of being born" (*SE* 22:137). In other words, Freud argues against Rank that the infant cannot immediately experience the act of birth as a trauma that would serve as the prototype for later anxiety but can only posit it as such by means of analogy. This analogy, moreover, can be posited only retroactively, after the infant has experienced the unpleasurable tension of the mother's absence as the loss of an object. Thus, the primal anxiety of birth, like the primal scene, is for Freud less important as an empirical event than as a psychic construction that receives its primacy, as well as its traumaticity, only through the process of *Nachträglichkeit,* "deferred action" or "retrodetermination."

Freud, however, never considers the possibly traumatic effects that the cloaca theory—the childbirth/evacuation confusion on whose universality among children he himself insists—might have on the retroactive construction of the primal anxiety of birth. As I have suggested, he never makes this consideration because to do so would disrupt his own construction of the (male) infant as the supposed subject of castration anxiety. This construction depends on the marginalization and objectification of the mother; it forecloses any perception the male infant might have had of the mother as a powerful figure in her own right—not an object that the infant/subject loses but rather a subject capable of losing the infant as object or expelling it as abject. Freud speaks often enough of the disavowal of castration, but he never recognizes that the hurried construction of the masculine subject as the subject of castration anxiety may itself be a disavowal of the more deeply anxious perception that not only is this subject constituted as an object from before its birth, but it may retroactively *reconstitute* itself as a particularly abject sort of object vis-à-vis the moment of birth as that moment is phantasmatically recoded through the cloaca theory.

We might speculate that if the infant at some point perceives itself as such an object—expelled, pinched off, dropped on the abject side of an impressive caesura—that perception might allow the figuration of the mother as the powerful subject who herself authorized that expulsion well *before* any paternal/oedipal prohibition. Even if she is thus figured as the once-phallic but now castrated mother, castration in this instance might betoken to the infant not her powerlessness but rather an even more incredible power than the anxious possession of a phallus could ever guarantee: the power to do without, to relinquish not the phallus but that anal penis which the infant identifies as its own body, the power to have had and yet to have sacrificed that valued partobject through her own agency, choice, and desire—through her own freedom if not through the incomprehensible *jouissance* of an ecstatic self-mutilation.

Faced with the terrifying implications of this power ("she could have held onto me if she had wanted, but she spit or shit me out, cut or pinched me off: I am worthless, abjected"), the male infant has sufficient reason to accept the more reassuring fiction of paternal prohibition—the Name of the Father as *nom du père* and *non du père*—as part of the bargain of his accession to the symbolic order of language, even though that bargain entails the assumption of castration anxiety and the renunciation of both the mother's body and the blind somatic pleasures of semiotic pulsion (i.e., the unsublimated activation of the oral and anal sphincters, the polymorphous perversity of disunified component drives). The "legal fiction" of paternity, as Stephen Dedalus calls it, might seem a more comforting version of the story than an alternative or *sub*version that grants subjective desire to the mother: the renunciation of the mother's body, and of certain pleasures of the infant's own, might seem a small price to pay for the repudiation of her power, her subjectivity, her desire. ("No, it wasn't her after all but him: she belongs to him. She had no choice in the matter. It's he who pulls the strings: it's we—he and eventually I, for after all, we're alike—who do the abjecting around here. All I have to do is renounce her and he'll let me keep what allows me to identify with him and what will eventually allow me to take his place. What a relief—I'm not an object but a subject. I'm not a piece of shit after all!")

In *Powers of Horror* Kristeva distinguishes between the corporeal territory of maternal authority and the symbolic order of paternal law. She suggests that maternal authority "is experienced first and above all . . . as sphincteral training" (*PH* 71). This authority "shapes the body into a *territory* . . . where the archaic power of mastery and neglect, of the differentiation of proper-clean and improper-dirty . . . is impressed and exerted." Kristeva refers to this "primal mapping of the body" as semiotic because "while being the precondition of language, it is dependent upon meaning, but in a way that is not that of *linguistic* signs nor of the *symbolic* order they found." Kristeva goes on to say that

> Maternal authority is . . . distinguished from paternal laws within which, with the phallic phase and acquisition of language, the destiny of man will take shape. If language, like culture, sets up a separation and . . . concatenates an order, it does so precisely by repressing maternal authority and [its] corporeal mapping. . . . It is then appropriate to ask what happens to such a repressed item when the legal, phallic, linguistic symbolic establishment does not carry out the separation in radical fashion—or else, more basically, when the speaking being attempts to think through its advent. . . . (*PH* 72)

I will continue to investigate what happens to the repression of maternal authority and its phantasmatic power not only when the speaking being attempts consciously to think through its advent but also when it attempts to speak or write about itself at all, when the anality that Kristeva contends is repressed with the acquisition of language is reactivated by the process of linguistic production.[16]

For the moment, however, I will simply reamplify the contention that the question of objectification and castration may initially cut both ways: anterior to the subject's fear of losing the object there may exist the fear of having been lost as such an object. This paradox or tension may be difficult to sustain or incompatible with a certain mode of psychic organization; in fact, I have suggested that Freud himself disavows entirely the question of being lost in favor of the question of losing. This disavowal constructs a certain (sort of) masculine subject and depends on a consistent objectification and devaluation, if not fecalization, of the mother—and, by extension, of femininity, regardless of the important fact that not all women are mothers and regardless of whether a particular masculine subject consciously equates the feminine, the maternal, and women (in other words, although these three terms are not naturally or essentially identical, it is nonetheless difficult to distinguish them when examining their historical devaluation in a patriarchal configuration that groups them together precisely to denigrate all three). Whether the inclination to objectify and abject the mother can be considered an inherent tendency in male infantile object relations and to what extent that tendency might obtain for female infants are problematic questions that I will not attempt to answer. I take it as more than a workable assumption, however, that this tendency receives support and legitimation from the existing system of gender relations, in which not only mothers but women of all races and classes have been objectified and denied the status of active desiring subjects. In other words, this tendency toward objectification may or may not be completely culturally constructed, but it is certainly culturally congealed and ossified in and by the existing system of gender relations.[17] This ossification, which Freud's oedipal theory of castration anxiety both reflects and enforces, decides and forecloses the paradoxical tension of losing/being lost in the form of a rigidly gendered subject/object polarity that is the hallmark of the sort of masculine thinking that can imagine self-preservation only as the domination of women, of the (m)other, of any alterity figured as feminine.

It is this ossification, or reification, that functions as the main obstacle to the egalitarian intersubjective relationships that Jessica Benjamin advocates in *The Bonds of Love: Psychoanalysis, Feminism, and the Problem of Domination*. Although here she never touches on the Kristevan theory of abjection that allows me the notion of productive anxiety, Benjamin's analysis, which follows more from the problem of recognition in Hegel's master-slave dialectic, also posits that the inability to sustain paradoxical tension results both in and from a rigidly gendered subject/object polarity that serves as a condition of possibility for male domination. Benjamin argues that "domination begins with the attempt to deny dependency" (53). She writes that "true independence means sustaining the essential tension of . . . contradictory impulses; that is, both asserting the self and recognizing the other [as an independent desiring subject]. Domination is the consequence of refusing this condition" (53). For Benjamin, this refusal—insofar as it can be traced back to oedipal and pre-oedipal relationships—entails the denial of any subjective agency or desire on the part of the mother and a consequent devaluation of whatever is culturally associated with the maternal, the feminine, and women (again these three terms are not, for Benjamin, naturally or essentially equated).

> The derogation of the female side of the [gender] polarity leads to a hardening of the opposition between male and female individuality as they are now constructed. The taboo on maternal sexual agency, the defensive mode of separation where the father is used to beat back the mother, the idealization of the father in identificatory love, and the confirmation that dependence and independence are mutually exclusive poles rather than a unified tension—all serve to devalue femininity. . . . The idealization of the father and the devaluation of the mother constitute a profound split that has infused the culture at large, and shaped our very notion of individuality. (114)

Benjamin rightly contends that the solution to this dilemma "must include a mother who is articulated as a sexual *subject*, one who expresses her own desire. . . . Under such conditions, the child's tendency to split the paradoxical elements of differentiation would not be reinforced by the gender arrangements" (114). According to Benjamin's analysis, an intervention into the current gender arrangements (based on the division of labor) that articulated women's subjectivity, independence, agency, and desire would necessarily also articulate those of the mother, and this lifting of the taboo on maternal sexual agency would in turn open a space for more justly intersubjective relationships within the public sphere. This intervention, that is, would drive a wedge between what Benjamin identifies as an infantile tendency "to split the paradoxical elements of differentiation" and the cultural reinforcement of that tendency in the current system of gender relations.

I want to focus on Benjamin's distinction between psychical tendency and social reinforcement as a way of offering some speculation about reification. The *Dictionary of Marxist Thought* defines reification as "the act (or result of the act) of transforming human properties, relations and actions into properties, relations and actions of man-produced things. . . . Also transformation of human beings into thing-like beings which do not behave in a human way but according to the laws of the thing-world.

Reification is a 'special' case of alienation, its most radical and widespread form characteristic of modern capitalist society" (411). Following this definition, albeit loosely, one might locate a reificatory tendency in the pre-oedipal and presymbolic stages of infancy—that is, in the imaginary itself. If reification in Marxist analysis is a special case of alienation, then so in psychoanalytical discourse are the mirror-stage and the separation from the mother; and if reification in Marxist analysis involves the mystified misrecognition of social relations as if they were relations between things, then mirror-stage infancy qua speechlessness could be described as a state of reification par excellence. The infant, as yet uninitiated into a language or symbolic order that could articulate its social relationship with both the mother and with its own specular image in the mirror, perceives those relationships as solely imaginary and objectile—that is, precisely as relations between things. Only the signifying practice of language is capable of disrupting this particular phantom objectivity, of providing a sustained mediation of these reified imaginary object relations; only language, that is, can articulate and locate these positions within the social and within history.[18] Language, however, conspicuously fails to dissolve reification to the extent that language is subtended by an already objectifying and hierarchizing patriarchal symbolic order that in its specific historical moment has itself been permeated by the instrumental rationality and commodity formalism of capitalist reification. Without attempting to assign historical priority to any of these three moments of reification—infantile (imaginary), patriarchal (symbolic), and capitalist (economic)—and without assuming that "always historicizing" would necessarily entail assigning that priority to the third, I can nonetheless stress how these reifications collude with and consolidate one another, each moment representing a tendency that the other two vigorously reinforce. As Goux suggests, the processes of oedipalization prime the subject for symbolic insertion into the reified capitalist relations of language and labor.

Of course, to use the one word *reification* to describe this priming— as if it designates a single process with both historical and (seemingly) transhistorical overdeterminations—is to disrupt the specificity of what reification means in orthodox Marxist analysis.[19] The point that needs underlining, however, is that although it may seem an ahistoricizing gesture to gather the objectifying tendencies of infancy, patriarchy, and capitalism under the rubric of "reification," one can nonetheless argue that these three instances seem, on a specific level of political intervention, to have a single element in common: the passivation of women into objects of exchange and the denial of their status as active, speaking, desiring subjects.

More important, this objectification, however it is historicized, remains a condition of possibility for the interpellation of a certain sort of masculine subject. Again, the point is not that men objectify women because that is just what men want to do: patriarchy must situate men as objectifiers so as to reproduce its own conditions of production. As Benjamin argues, what is at stake in the objectification of women, from the perspective of the patriarchal and capitalist status quo, is the production and maintenance of a fully rationalized and masculinized subject who views dependency, mutuality, and intersubjectivity only as dangerously irrational regressions into the maternal swamp of undifferentiation, who distances himself from a feminized nature only to better dominate it, and who views power only as something to wield, but never to yield or to share. This masculine subject— an armored ego, a full metal jacket—thus becomes the capable agent of a capitalism that exploits and deploys that subject's independence and autonomy in the name of dominating and monopolistic economic practices and the global expansion of the so-called free market. As Benjamin writes,

> the center of male domination lies . . . in the societal rationality which may or may not be defended by men. Male domination, as Weber said of rationalization, works through the hegemony of impersonal organization: of formal rules that refer to the hypothetical interaction of autonomous individuals; of instrumental knowledge founded in the subject's control of the object world; of the accumulation of profit, which bows neither to need nor tradition. It is this protean impersonality that makes it so elusive. (216)

But the capitalist deployment of masculinity through rationalized commodity formalism may also, for a certain individual male subject, be considered an extension and reinforcement of male infantile reification, for which, as we have seen, there is something other than economic independence and autonomy at stake in the objectification of women and the disavowal of maternal authority—namely, the avoidance of that self-abjection by which the masculine subject becomes the turd of his own fantasy. This leads back to that anxiety on the part of this masculine subject concerning a mode of recognition in and by which he is turned into shit. It is now apparent, however, that at the core of this anxiety is a fear of recognizing the woman's or (m)other's subjectivity and authority. Within the confines of a strictly gendered and hierarchical subject/object polarity, to grant subjectivity and authority to the feminine side of the equation is to objectify and deauthorize the masculine, thus accentuating not only the latter's lack of autonomy, its dependency and helplessness, but also its abjection, its inert and fecal passivity.

This anxiety plays its part in that protean impersonality that makes the center of male domination so elusive. The center will remain elusive, however, and perpetuate male domination, unless we recognize the way in which this anxiety is inscribed in textual production. In *Revolution in Poetic Language* Kristeva examines "the dialectical interplay between semiotic and symbolic dispositions," which for her comprise texts. For Kristeva, any text constitutes itself as a tension between corporeal, semiotic, or "genotextual" energies and drives and the societal, symbolic, or "phenotextual" containments and restraints that such semiotic pulsions tend, or even strive, to disrupt. As Leon S. Roudiez explains, discursive formations that "issue from societal, cultural, syntactical, and other grammatical constraints constitute the phenotext; they insure communication." On the other hand, it is often "the physical, material aspect of language . . . that signals the presence of the genotext" (5). Note the similarity between the semiotic-genotextual/symbolic-phenotextual dialectic and Kristeva's distinction between maternal authority and paternal law as it relates to the confrontation with abjection that for her, as we shall see, inheres in all literary production. The anxiety about the phantasmatic consequences of recognizing maternal authority, an anxiety that is ostensibly assuaged by the masculine assumption of authority vis-à-vis the reassuring fiction of paternal prohibition, may be covertly brought back into play whenever the masculine subject attempts to assert his own authorship—that is, by any process of production by which the subject attempts to accede to self-identity through representation, to produce himself as representation, to designate himself in a statement. Anterior to the oedipal drama of a Bloomian anxiety of influence in which the "strong maker" does battle with his paternal literary forebears, there lies a pre-oedipal anxiety of production, a dysgraphic anxiety of exfluence, in which the writer confronts both maternal authority and his own abjection in the vertigo of the blank white page. Kristeva writes:

> On close inspection, all literature is probably a version of the apocalypse that seems to me rooted, no matter what its socio-historical conditions might be, on the fragile border . . . where identities (subject/object, etc.) do not exist or only barely so—double, fuzzy, heterogeneous, animal, metamorphosed, altered, abject. . . . If "something maternal" happens to bear upon the uncertainty that I call abjection, it illuminates the literary scription of the essential struggle that a writer (man or woman) has to engage in with what he calls demonic only to call attention to it as the inseparable obverse of his

> very being, of the other (sex) that torments and possesses him. Does one write under any other condition than being possessed by abjection, in an indefinite catharsis? (*PH* 207–8)

There are obvious problems with Kristeva's formulation, not the least of which is the universalizing assertion that her vision of the abject writer obtains for either "man or woman" when her own models— Baudelaire, Lautréamont, Kafka, Joyce, Bataille, Céline—are all European men. Unlike Kristeva, I imagine that there may be others—possibly men but perhaps particularly women—who write or have written under conditions other than being possessed by abjection. Authors of slave narratives, for example, wrote under completely other conditions of being possessed.[20]

Nonetheless, despite apparent political insufficiencies, Kristeva's notion that, for a certain masculine authorial subject operating within the dominant fiction, a confrontation with abjection, and thus with maternal authority, lies at the heart of literary production remains a suggestive means of theoretical inquiry into the construction of that subject and the deployment of that subjectivity. One of the things this masculine authorial subject confronts in the indefinite catharsis of his attempt at producing a self-representation through writing is, again, the split between the subject of the enunciation and the subject of the enounced, between the "I" that speaks and the pronominal signifier *I* that is produced to designate that speaker. This split, ostensibly invisible or at least less explicit in speech, can be exacerbated by the physical, material aspect of language, and thus particularly by writing, in which the signifier *I* takes on the more readily discernible characteristics of an object (visibility, divisibility, losability). If even in speech "I expel *myself*, I spit *myself* out, I abject *myself*, within the same motion through which 'I' claim to establish *myself*" (*PH* 3), then writing only makes that abject expulsion more painfully apparent. When I produce a self-representation, I put my own abjection in writing, make a dirty deposit, put my body on the line. In keeping with the strictly gendered subject/object polarity that obtains in the dominant system of gender relations, my scripted, externalized, objectified *I* must accordingly be devalued as feminine. But I do not simply feminize (i.e., "castrate") myself. I do not, as a function of womb envy, simply give birth to myself. Nor do I, like a Bloomian strong maker, accede to a symbolic self-paternity. Rather, I dump myself on the abject side of my own impressive caesura and thus again come to face my being lost as my being shit, my own body as anal penis; I confront maternal authority and the terrifying corporeal mapping on which I phantasmatically imagine I was once, thanks to her, metonymically located. If various forms of reification come to my rescue, if they present themselves as means of repudiating maternal authority, beating back the mother and thus protecting myself from the abjection with which she threatens me, then perhaps I will be more than happy to *sign* myself *up*—to erect my identity on those reified premises, to maintain that erection whenever I attempt to sign myself, to write (to) myself, to deliver myself (as) a letter. I will gladly become the supposed subject of loss and will dutifully objectify the (m)other and organize my own desires accordingly whenever I am called on to do so, whenever I am hailed as the one who does so—that is, constantly.

But perhaps it is my own body, its corruptive power of carnal irony, that also threatens to intervene into this reassuring interpellation. If the devaluation of writing is a function of a repression of maternal authority carried out in the infantile interest of avoiding abjection, and in the phallocapitalistic interests of constructing a fully autonomous masculine subject assured of its own freedom and power, then the physical, material process of writing is always accompanied by the possibility of the reauthorization of the maternal, the reactivation of abjection, and the disruption of the boundaries of the phallic, hyperbolic self. Writing that reveals me also reveals to me at least the price, if not the impossibility, of attempting to accede to myself, to stabilize my identity, through coherent self-representation.

But if the split between the subject of the enunciation and the subject of the enounced can be aligned with Kristeva's distinction between symbolic and semiotic, or with Gallop's distinction between Body and body, could we not also align that split with the difference between the phallus and the penis vis-à-vis the question of the money shot? If, that is, it is when the penis allows its productions to become visible to the male gaze that it potentially lapses and falls short of the phallus, could we not suggest a certain split that, through deferred action, would reinforce itself by retroactively recoding, realigning, and reifying all the heterogeneous corporeal and linguistic splits that come before it, a split between the subject of the (invisible) orgasm and the subject of the (visible) ejaculation, a scission or caesura between coming and come stain, between vital inwardness and moribund exteriority in which the latter would mark the shameful excess of the former?[21] Just as the poem is the unity that sutures its own caesuras, phallic authority is finally that which attempts to suture the orgasm/ejaculation split by ensuring a unified and in(di)visible transmission, by channeling or teleologically narrativizing that potentially excessive flow toward "woman" misogynistically deployed as passive and objectified destination, receptacle, or reassuring surface. As a result of this process, these deployments become vertiginous scenes of writing, representational spaces for the assertion of a masculine authority; as Irigaray would put it, woman in phallogocentric specula(riza)tion becomes the silvered backing, or tain, of the mirror that, when functioning "properly"—that is, passively and objectively—returns to man not only his reassuring reflection but his identity, his subjectivity, his agency, his desire.

If woman as reflecting surface refuses to function properly, refuses a passive and objective mutism, if the scene of writing assumes a life of its own, then man's vision is clouded, his subjectivity (s)tained. Given the proper functioning of the mechanisms of reification, reflection, and reproduction, however, man must always direct toward and deflect onto woman his language, his writing, his substance, his gaze, and his death in order to protect his being, to avoid shaming himself, to keep himself from being lost, to keep his essence from "being in the picture," from "being (in the) shit." Such is the birth of a certain solid form to which all masculinized sexual and discursive externalizations are subjected and in which the masculinized subject is supposed to find assuagement for his anxieties about the production(s) of his body.

This reified form, however, is always threatened with a subversive "liquifecation" on two counts: whenever women assert their actively subjective desires and whenever the male body transgresses its culturally constructed sexual and discursive boundaries, overflows its systems of containment—whether through gay or queer sex or through a sheer discursive excess that splashes over the margins of compulsory heterosexuality, the compulsory in heterosexuality, as that compulsion is discursively maintained. The potential alignment of these instances of subversion indicates that a straight man's project of speaking his body is also potentially coaxial with feminist and queer politics that assert in their full conflictual plurality the active subjectivity of different women's and men's different desires. Although no project is completely immune from co-optation by dominant cultural forces, of behavior overdetermined by those forces—in certain forms both feminist and lesbian/gay identity politics are quite capable of maintaining and enforcing their own exclusions and hierarchies—the straight man's project is more than particularly susceptible to co-optation by a patriarchal status quo that rewards men for not speaking their bodies and for speaking against the bodies and embodied practices of others.

Before suggesting any possibly salutary political effects of this project, then, I must continue to consider the collusion between the cultural and intrapsychic forces of reification and reaction that work against it, the means that phallic authority possesses of assuaging its own anxieties, of reducing its own unpleasurable tensions, either by dominating things, by mastering the culturally congealed and gendered subject/object paradigm, or by attempting to get upstream of or beyond it.[22] This consideration entails yet another return to Freud.

Utter(ed) Dismemberment

> To restore silence is the role of objects.
>
> —Samuel Beckett, *Molloy*

> Whereby the silent allegiance of the one guarantees the auto-sufficiency, the auto-nomy of the other as long as no questioning of this mutism as a symptom—of historical repression—is required. But what if the "object" started speak? Which also means beginning to "see," etc. What disaggregation of the subject would that entail?
>
> —Luce Irigaray, *Speculum of the Other Woman*

> Shut up. Don't look at me. Don't you fucking look at me!
>
> —Frank to Dorothy, in David Lynch, *Blue Velvet*

As I have suggested, the dominant form that the disavowal of abjection takes for Freud is the positing of the masculine subject as the subject of castration anxiety, the subject always supposed to lose. Perhaps we need no further examples of what we might call the rush toward castration in Freud's narrative teleology. I reproduce, nonetheless, the following: "Anxiety appears as a reaction to the felt loss of the object; and *we are at once reminded* of the fact that castration anxiety, too, is a fear of being separated from a highly valued object, and that the earliest anxiety of all—the 'primal anxiety' of birth—is brought about on the occasion of a separation from the mother" (*SE* 20:137; emphasis added). Freud goes on, however, to say that "a moment's reflection takes us beyond this question of loss of object." The beyond to which we are then taken is a return to *Beyond the Pleasure Principle*, for beyond the question of object loss lies the infant's sense of danger, "of non-satisfaction, of a *growing tension due to need*, against which it is helpless" (*SE* 20:137). This feeling of helpless nonsatisfaction leads to an "unpleasurable" excitation that must be mastered psychically. What the loss of the mother as object and castration anxiety have in common, then, is "the economic disturbance caused by an accumulation of amounts of stimulation which require to be disposed of" (*SE* 20:137).

I have argued that the disturbance of which Freud speaks, as well as its disposal, always lies for Freud within the domain of a certain restricted economy and that there may be a more generally disturbing economy at work in his construction of masculine subjectivity than his theory of that construction can countenance. Nonetheless, Freud's formulation allows us to understand that when anxiety accrues from economic disturbances, these excessive stimulations must be mastered psychically if the subject is to remain within the dominant parameters of the pleasure principle. Although this psychic mastery may take the form of the domination of objects, as in the *fort-da* game, Freud sees such compulsively manipulative repetition as subtended by a much more powerful nostalgia, a conservative desire to return to a plenitude of absence, to that time when there was neither time nor space, when there were no objects at all—a state of quiescence and absolutely reduced tension that Freud identifies as death in *Beyond the Pleasure Principle* but that in *Inhibitions, Symptoms and Anxiety* he compares, as we have seen, to a *poem*.

In this poetic economy of death Freud figures the maternal body as a text in which all tension-producing caesuras are sutured: he feminizes and formalizes the textuality of death. To the extent that this formalization takes place in the name of Oedipus, it is not only textually but narratively performed in the name of a castration that is itself "a specialization of and a defense against a more general anxiety" (Boothby 148). Castration as narrative construct, as specialized defense, metaphorically forecloses on more general anxieties that correspond to the contaminating threat of metonymic contiguity. This nonnarrative shattering plunges the phallus back into a dependence on the maternal body as its phantasmatically cloacal origin, a priority that grants certain "powers of horror" to the (m)other and that reveals the rectum in yet another capacity as "the grave in which the masculine ideal . . . of proud subjectivity is buried" (Bersani, "Rectum" 222).[23] The phallic subject, the hyperbolic self that would psychically master unpleasurable tension, confronts that which "overflows mastery as the seat of its condition" (Derrida, *PC* 395). The "master," writes Irigaray, "is reminded that he is dependent on death. And on birth. On the material, uterine foundations of his mastery. Only if these be repressed can he enjoy sole ownership" (*TS* 127).

As I argue in a later chapter, Jacques Derrida has his own way of foreclosing on certain of these questions (his rather fastidious treatment of Bataille has already been noted). Nonetheless, Derrida's comments on castration in "The Purveyor of Truth," his critique of Lacan's seminar on Poe's "The Purloined Letter," are more than pertinent here. Derrida argues that, not only for Lacan, but for the discourse of psychoanalysis itself and the phallogocentric tradition of metaphysics that Derrida thinks lurks behind it, the "determination of the proper, of the law of the proper, of *economy* . . . leads back to castration as truth, to the figure of woman as the figure of castration *and* of truth" (*PC* 441). This truth of psychoanalysis, however, does not amount to "truth as essential dislocation and irreducible fragmentation," says Derrida.

> Castration-truth, on the contrary, is that which contracts itself . . . in order to bring the phallus, the signifier, the letter, or the fetish back into their *oikos*, their familiar dwelling, their proper place. In this sense castration-truth is the opposite of fragmentation, the very antidote for fragmentation; that which is missing from its place has in castration a fixed, central place, freed from all substitution. . . . The phallus, thanks to castration, always remains in its place. . . . In castration, the phallus is indivisible, and therefore indestructible, like the letter which *takes its place*. And this is why . . . the materiality of the letter as *indivisibility* is indispensable for this restricted economy, this circulation of the proper. (*PC* 441)

As Derrida makes clear throughout *The Post Card*—in which he writes, as he says, "for, against, with, and without psychoanalysis" (*PC* 5)— this restricted economy of the circulation of the proper is an economy not only of death but also of power. "Beyond the pleasure principle— power" (*PC* 405).

> The entire economy of the PP [pleasure principle] and its beyond is governed by relations of "mastery." One can envisage, then, a quasi-transcendental privilege of this drive for mastery, drive for power, drive for domination. . . . The latter denomination seems preferable: it marks more clearly the relation to the other, even in domination *over oneself*. . . . It is a question of a relation to oneself as a relation to the other, the auto-affection of a *fort:da* which gives, takes, sends and destines itself, distances and approaches itself by its own step, the other's. (*PC* 403)

Derrida refers to the broadest frame of this sending and receiving of oneself as other, a destining by which one hopes to be acquitted of a relationship to oneself as other, as "the postal system." What the postal system attempts to ensure, says Derrida, is that one's own letter reaches, or comes to rest on, its proper destination. Derrida's main thesis in *The Post Card* is that the letter can always not arrive at its destination. The point is not, he says, that it never arrives, but that the possibility of nonarrival, of not coming to rest—or perhaps of coming, but not to rest, arriving only to erase itself—inhabits and haunts the letter in the very structure of its sending. This demonically haunting possibility can be thought of as the letter's unrest, unpleasurable tension, or to let my own terminology intrude, productive anxiety, an anxiety about sending oneself a letter, producing oneself as an abject letter, that can always not arrive at its destination, always not come into its own. Derrida writes, "The master addresses to himself the text or the corpus of this simulated engagement [with himself] via the detour of an institutional telecommunication. He *writes himself, sends himself [s'envoie]:* but if the length of the detour can no longer be mastered, and rather than its length its structure, then the return to (one)self is never certain, and without return to sender the engagement is forgotten to the very extent that it becomes undeniable, unshakable" (*PC* 282–83).

Derrida aligns the postal system with Freud's notion of the death drive, which for Freud is not simply the organism's drive toward death but its attempt to ensure that it reaches death properly, that it dies its own death, achieves its own proper relationship to death. Derrida also argues that Freud, in writing *Beyond the Pleasure Principle,* in writing the *fort-da,* in fact plays *fort-da* with his own writing—that is, with himself. He sends himself his own name, sends himself (as) a legacy, sends himself (to himself as) the founder of the psychoanalytic movement. Ensuring his "letter" to the post, says Derrida, Freud tries to come into his own: writing (to) himself (as) his own proper death, Freud sends himself and finds/founds (himself as) psychoanalysis. This circulation of the letter remains for Derrida the truth of psychoanalysis, insofar as psychoanalysis attempts to establish itself as a discourse of truth, as it does for Derrida quite relentlessly in Lacan's seminar on Poe's "The Purloined Letter."

In that seminar Lacan insists on the (m)other's body, the space between the "legs" of the fireplace, as the letter's inevitable destination. Freud, as we have seen, posits the (m)other's body as (deathly) poetic text, womb and tomb, origin and finale, and the castration subject's relation not only to that text but to his own body, or at least to a significant or signifying portion thereof, as an always potentially anxious one. To master psychically the unpleasurable tension arising from this anxiety, the subject must assume a position of certainty in relation not only to the (m)other's body—and to his own productive body as material other—but also to significance itself, to the materiality of signification, the play of symbolic meaning and semiotic unmeaning that makes up textuality. The mastery of meaning becomes the meaning of mastery. It is not simply that the subject must decide what things mean or where letters should go in order better to dominate them; it is that the very acts of deciding and dominating are in a sense coterminous, inextricable, always already caught up in culturally reinforced devaluations. The word *decide*, after all, derives from the Latin *decidere*, "to cut off." Thus the one who decides matters is the one who cuts or pinches off some bit of deciduous matter, who expels or otherwise assumes with sufficient strength the imperative act of excluding abject things. Undecidability, then, implies an ambiguous and unpleasurably tense relation to deciduous materiality, to cutting. The one who is indecisive, who does not make the cut, confronts the abject.

It is with the matter of abjection foregrounded that I want to explore in more specific detail two of the most discussed but perhaps still indecisive moments in psychoanalytic discourse—the *fort-da* and the mirror stage. Such a turn may by this point seem rather late if not unwelcome, but I make it to continue to investigate a speech, a gesture, and a gaze that seek masterfully and decisively to turn the other into shit, that attempt to turn the unpleasurable or shattering tension of "a relation to oneself as a relation to the other" into a calm and coherent but still quite shitty relationship in which only the other is fecalized.

The details of the *fort-da* game are by now familiar:

> The child had a wooden reel with a piece of string tied round it. . . . What he did was to hold the reel by the string and very skillfully throw it over the edge of his curtained cot, so that it disappeared into it, at the same time uttering his expressive "o-o-o-o" [which Freud interprets as representing the German word *fort*, "gone"]. He then pulled the reel out of the cot again by the string and hailed its reappearance with a joyful "*da*" ["there"]. This, then, was the complete game—disappearance and return. (*SE* 18:15)

Here, however, we might recall an earlier instance of disappearance and return in Freud's writing, namely, the moment in the Wolf-Man case history when Freud's patient discloses that "during the coitus of the primal scene [a coitus that the Wolf-Man misrecognizes as anal intercourse] he had observed the penis disappear, that he had felt sympathy for his father on that account, and had rejoiced at the reappearance of what he thought had been lost" (*SE* 17:88). I recall this passage to suggest that, even though there is no direct reference to feces or phallus in the description of the *fort-da* proper, the account still seems to be caught up here in an inescapably anal symbolic that calls into question the bid towards phallic mastery that the game ostensibly inaugurates.

Two aspects of Freud's description come into prominence here. The first is Freud's assertion that the *fort-da* is "related to the child's great cultural achievement—the instinctual renunciation (that is, the renunciation of instinctual satisfaction) which he had made in allowing his mother to go away without protesting. He compensated himself for this, as it were, by himself staging the disappearance and return of the objects within his reach" (*SE* 18:15). If we compare this assertion with Freud's claim in "Femininity" that "urine and faeces are the first gifts that children make to those who look after them, and controlling them is the first concession to which the instinctual life of children can be induced" (*SE* 22:104–5), we might well wonder which instinctual renunciation or concession Freud considers to be the child's foremost cultural achievement—that of the mother, which he designates as "great," or that of urine and feces, to which he awards the privilege of being "first." In any case, these two instances of instinctual renunciation seem to be related for Freud. At the very least, they both involve a certain culturally reinforced lesson in exchange value. One generally does not learn to allow something or someone—one's gift or one's mother—to go away without an according devaluation, without psychically divesting the object of the importance one had previously attached thereto and, importantly, without a consequent *re*valuation, an elevation of one's own status in reward for having learned to make such nice distinctions. In other words, the masculinized subject will eventually learn the most rewarding role to play, how to be a "good boy" in a culture that treats "bad girls" like shit.

This lesson is already inscribed in the *fort-da*, which subjects women—or at least the mother as the object of a representational game—to the same treatment. This treatment, as well as another curious link between Freud's deployment of the *fort-da* and his maneuvers in "Femininity," becomes readable in the second prominent aspect of his description in *Beyond the Pleasure Principle*. As we have seen, Freud explains the *fort-da* as a response to the mother's absence. Freud writes, "one gets the impression that the child turned his experience into a game from another motive. At the outset he was in a *passive* situation—he was overpowered by the experience; but, by repeating it, unpleasurable though it was, as a game, he took on an *active* part. These efforts might be put down to an instinct for mastery that was acting independently of whether the memory was in itself pleasurable or not" (*SE* 18:16). Beyond the question of the subject's manipulation of a representational object, then, the ontological stakes of the *fort-da* involve the subject's movement from passivity to activity, from dependence to independence, from an inert objectivity to subjectivity. This movement can be thought to take place within the parameters of what I have called the primontological reversal, the main function of which is to assuage or contain a predominantly scatontological anxiety—the infant's putative fear that it may actually be the anal penis that the phallic mother decided to do without. Within a hierarchically gendered system of binary opposition, the movement toward a completely active and independent male mastery can tip the scales of value only toward the utter passivation of the "(m)other woman." The "wave of passivity" that patriarchy washes over the feminine robs the (m)other woman of any power of decision and locates her as the decided thing, the space of deciduous matter.

The phrase "wave of passivity" comes from Freud's essay entitled "Femininity." For Freud, this wave is what "opens the way to the turn toward femininity" (*SE* 22:130). It is this wave that a girl with a "powerful masculinity complex" attempts to avoid: "the girl refuses, as it were, to recognize the unwelcome fact [of her 'castration'] and, definitely rebellious, even exaggerates her previous masculinity, clings to her clitoridal activity and takes refuge in an identification with her phallic mother or her father" (*SE* 22:129–30). Irigaray, in her essay on Freud in *Speculum of the Other Woman*, examines Freud's metaphor of a passivating wave to question "the precedence given to the active/passive polarity in the Freudian representation of the sexual economy" (91). Irigaray highlights Freud's contention in "The Infantile Genital Organization" that "the active/passive opposition dominates the pregenital sadistic-anal organization, during which there is still no question of male and female" (*SE* 19:145). She wonders "why this opposition continues so insistently to shape the masculine/feminine polarity, to the point of providing its 'psychological meaning.'" Irigaray concludes that "the wave of passivity would therefore coincide with a *redistribution of anal instincts* . . . with activity and passivity being attributed to man and woman respectively" (*SW* 92).

Freud did issue warnings (even if he himself did not fully heed them) against simply or naturally attributing activity and passivity to man and woman, respectively; we should note again his suspicion (however wavering) that such an attribution is culturally enforced. Nonetheless, since the active/passive polarity seems to dominate the *fort-da* and to choreograph its movement as well, we could characterize both it and the culturally enforced attribution as being subtended by a redistribution of anal "instincts"—a redistribution that is equiprimordial with a doubly marked instinctual concession that is itself, insofar as it is caught up in the game that it motivates, an accession to representational and linguistic mastery. The "little master," when he lets go of his reel and lets out his *fort,* also sends out a wave of passivity toward the (m)other, a wave that will henceforth always be intricated with his throw, his shoot, his sending, and his deliverance. When, in the mirror stage and in the symbolic order, he (mis)recognizes that it is (to) himself that he sends, that representation and language inscribe him in a relation to himself as to an other, it will be this same wave of passivity, by which he had attempted to master the (m)other woman's powers of decision, that now threatens him with engulfment—whenever representation becomes divisively undecidable, the object refuses play the game (by beginning to speak, to see), or the refuse itself returns in a way that threatens the prophylactic boundaries of the game's proper rules.

In the *fort-da* the rules of the game are subtended by a poetic economy of death, an economy that, as Irigaray's speculation suggests, also involves a certain anal redistribution. The "master" does not want to die, however, nor, if he plays by the rules, does he allow himself to be turned into shit. Rather, he calms himself, reduces his tensions, assuages himself of anxiety, not by becoming inertly passive himself but by acceding to a certain state of activity, of authority, of sending. From this authorized position the postmaster relentlessly sends toward the other the wave of passivity from which he himself is supposedly protected and from which he attempts to remain forever upstream. Beyond the streams of the pleasure principle lies not death but, as Derrida stresses, power; instead of actually dying, the master attempts to assume the powerful position of death itself, "the absolute master" (Lacan, *FFC* 27). It is indeed only death that can put itself in the position to master what Irigaray calls "the work of death" (*SW* 55). It is only death that can escape dependence on a relationship to death, that can perpetuate and produce itself as death in a purely self-identical transmission, without becoming or being contaminated by the dead thing that it produces. For death never dies. Blanchot defines it succinctly as "the impossibility of dying" (*Gaze of Orpheus* 55). Working on the vulnerability of bodies but never compelled to have one of its own, death would be the ultimate, invulnerable subject position, the deadly a(r)mour of the most proper *corps propre*, a clean machine in search of the killable other. For although "death itself" never dies, it remains, itself, deadly: it produces death without remains.

The relevant question, then, is not the Heideggerian one concerning the ontic/ontological difference between "Being" and beings but the more material one of the difference between "being-death" and being dead, which also concerns the difference between being the one supposed to lose and being lost, Being and being (in the) shit. What needs to be asked is the question concerning the difference between the absolute master's tense recognition of the rest of the world and his calm vision of a world at absolute rest.

There is no mention of the *fort-da* in Irigaray's discussion of the ac-

tive/passive polarity and the gendered way it redistributes anal instincts. Nor, to my knowledge, are there any discussions of anality in
Irigaray's treatments of the *fort-da*.[24] Nevertheless, she has much to say
about anality in relation to the economy of death that subtends this
game of activation/passivation, disappearance and return. She writes,
for example, that "the anal instincts . . . are sex-blind, according to
Freud."

> However, anal erotism . . . is possessive, narcissistic, constantly react-
> ing offensively or defensively to the demands of [the] other; it is ag-
> gressive toward the "object" that it tortures systematically whenev-
> er possible, that it would like to eliminate when its needs have been
> served or when its strength no longer relies on dominating and pos-
> sessing the object: for anal erotism deals in death. . . . It is always at
> war in order to have things, and have more things, and take things
> from others; in order to accumulate and build up capital, losing noth-
> ing. In this relentless, exhausting, anxious "activity," in this merci-
> less struggle for appropriation, for property, for the promotion and
> defense of territory, how can a minimum of repose, security, self-
> preservation, be guaranteed? They will be ensured by *the status as-
> signed to woman in warfare*. Instinctual warfare. . . . [For women] are
> havens of refuge and safety. They represent the total reduction of in-
> stinctual arousal. Therefore, the re-assurance of death. Soft, calm,
> painless. Swooning contentedly in the mother's womb. Welcome,
> relaxation, rest for the warrior. (*SW* 94)

Irigaray views anality as a death-dealing distribution that sadistically
subtends and reinforces a phallic sexual economy. She seems not to
recognize what Kristeva stresses as the subversive quality of a nonsublimated and nonphallomorphic anality that semiotically disrupts the
boundaries of the patriarchal symbolic. Nor, perhaps, would she accede
to Bersani's radical suggestion that "if the rectum is the grave in which
the masculine ideal (an ideal shared—differently—by men *and* wom-
en) of proud subjectivity is buried, then it should be celebrated for its
very potential for death" ("Rectum" 222). Nonetheless, Irigaray's speculation allows us to see how most commentary on the *fort-da* tends to
lose sight of the redistributive anality of, and the status assigned to
woman in, the instinctual warfare that this economic game wages.
Such, as I have indicated, is the case with Freud, who despite his insistence on the importance of anality in instinctual life, is conspicuously
picky about when and where he will trundle out such matters.[25]

The details of the mirror stage, like those of the *fort-da*, are also familiar. In Lacanian psychoanalysis the mirror stage is that moment in
the infant's life—sometime between six and eighteen months—when

it first (mis)recognizes its own image in a mirror. This moment is simultaneously one of jubilation and alienation, jubilation because the infant recognizes itself and alienation because it does so only in another scene, the scene of the other, sees itself only by seeing itself as another. Moreover, the infant, having had no particular or discrete body image until then, sees in the mirror a totalized and coherent *corps propre* that retroactively posits the fantasy of a *corps morcelé*, or fragmented body (i.e., it is only after having seen itself as the former that the infant imagines itself as having been the latter). Thus the mirror stage is for Lacan a moment that constitutes the subject by initiating it in a certain movement. Lacan writes that "the *mirror stage* is a drama whose internal thrust is precipitated from insufficiency to anticipation—and which manufactures for the subject, caught up in the lure of spatial identification, the succession of phantasies that extends from a fragmented body-image to a form of its totality that I shall call orthopaedic—and lastly, to the assumption of the armour of an alienating identity, which will mark with its rigid structure the subject's entire mental development" (*É* 4).

What functions of mastery, of sending, and of the poetic economy of death are reflected in the mirror stage? If there is a relation between the mirror stage and the *fort-da* (and Freud provides such a relation in a footnote in *Beyond the Pleasure Principle*),[26] how might the active/passive polarity and its predominantly anal redistribution be caught up in the lure of spatial identification? If, that is, the mirror stage inaugurates a movement from a phantasmatically fragmented insufficiency to the anticipation of imaginary totality, how might there also be reflected here a movement from passivity to activity, from the scattered object(s) the infant fears it has been to the coherent subject it wants to be? And what fantasy of absolute mastery, of being-death, might be inscribed in the rigidly structured assumption of a subjective armor, a self-alienating identity that protects itself from self-contamination precisely by alienating itself, but only in a certain way—by spitting itself out, but at the other, by sending itself out through the agency of its own gaze, but in the aggressive if not deadly form of a wave of passivity aimed like a bullet (ultimate condensation of liquid into solid) at the body of the other?

A look, in other words, that kills. Such might be the paradigmatic instance of the poetic economy of death as that economy is channeled through what Lacan calls the seer's "shoot," a sort of ocular money shot with the biggest payoff of all: the total erasure of the mirror's (s)tain, the calm assurance of a spotless self-reflection, rest, as Irigaray says, for the warrior. But how does this specular absolution come to be foiled, and what is the status assigned to woman in this tin-soldier's warfare? In *Speculum of the Other Woman,* in a section of "Blind Spot of an Old Dream of Symmetry" called *"Idealization, What Is One's Own,"* Irigaray writes:

> In this war, other *stores* will also be set up: the permanence of the booty and treasure. If what you want to get hold of, keep, accumulate, is perishable; if it can be taken away from you; if one look, for example, can change its value, then the toil and the war will be relentless and endless. Therefore, in place of the feces—decomposed/decomposable matter that is taken from you and that is subject to being appreciated by an other eye—will be substituted the *image* (*SW* 95).

Irigaray argues that imaginary substitution metaphorically ensures the eye's recovery and mastery of anal eroticism and its product. The mirror's idealization of the fecal mass serves as the frame for all "fetishistic representations, including femininity." In "And If, Taking the Eye of a Man Recently Dead," Irigaray asserts that this framing founds the subject's reflective existence and that this founding works like a tain, "the backing of a mirror that has been introjected . . . and is thus beyond perception" unless "speculative activity itself is suspended" (*SW* 181). Irigaray writes that, within the boundaries of unsuspended speculative activity, in which "the 'I' exists over and above the day-to-day material of perception," the subject "will be required to trace himself *a path, a way,* which he *freely decides* to follow, as opposed to letting himself be swamped (by those images), in a flood of dreams or even of doubts in which he can neither swim nor wade. Much less think. Since the ground threatens every minute to shake the present certainties of the subject, *it must not be allowed any power of specularization*" (*SW* 181).

For Irigaray it is woman that functions as the ground of phallogocentric self-reflection. She is there as the condition of possibility for reflection even when the subject thinks he is looking only at himself, and it is thus only himself that he sees even when he thinks he is simply looking at her. In this "hommosexuality," woman thus becomes the silvered backing of the mirror that allows the masculinized subject to see himself clearly, to (re)produce himself cleanly, to idealize his own proper self-reproduction. Her status becomes the crucial question in the male subject's movement from the unpleasurable tension of a fragmented passivity to the absolute reduction of an actively armored totality. When Irigaray designates this movement as a path or a way, she also indicates that proper route toward death along which the subject attempts to trace himself, arrogating to himself alone the power of free decision.

If he loses himself along the way, however, if the ground pulls itself out from under him, this missionary of speculation becomes swamped by images that resist his control, flooded by asymmetrical dreams, engulfed in a torrent of unframed femininity that, according to the specific terms of Irigaray's analysis, is also a river of shit. The purpose of the "woman-tained" mirror is to prevent a *male-stained* self-reflection, to prevent a change in value, to idealize the male's excremental product and ensure the masculine mastery of anal eroticism, which is also mastery of the work of death. The function of the proper way or path, the routing or sending by which the subject attempts to gain mastery over death's work, is not only to keep the subject from being castrated, or dying too soon, but also to keep him from the contamination of an impure expenditure, from crapping out, shooting his wad. Woman, again, is for Irigaray the repository, the safety-deposit box of the subject's speculation, his guarantee of self-certainty, provided that she stays in her place, beneath him, in the frame. Woman is his assurance not only that he is always looking only at himself while looking (down) at her but also that the best part of himself, his essence, remains securely in(di)visible either in the stock exchange of her womb or across the reassuring surface of her body. If she steps outside the frame and no longer gives him himself back, however, then there is no longer a guaranteed return but only the threat of abjection. "The phallus," as Linda Williams puts it, "is left staring at its own reflection" (*Hard Core* 54). In this botched money shot, the subject can only stand before the mirror with his essence on his face.

This threat of abjection is present not only when woman steps out of a frame that in her case is the feminine masquerade but also whenever production/representation threatens to overrun its enframing, whenever the represented—the woman, the (m)other, the image, the reel—decides to assume a life of its own. The other's life, speech, vision, and desire are what is at stake and what must be repressed in the subject's bid for the mastery of the work of death, which is a question of controlling the production of representation. Although it is always a question of misogyny, domination, and power, it can also be a question of writing—of seeing, speaking, tracing (oneself as) the other, of being seen, spoken, or traced by the other—which is why the master must never allow his being to be "appreciated by another eye" (*SW* 95), why the other must not be allowed any power of specularization. ("Don't you look at me," says Frank in *Blue Velvet*.)

In the essay "Of the Gaze as *objet petit a*" in *The Four Fundamental*

Concepts, Lacan characterizes this difference between seeing and being seen as a split between the eye and the gaze. Lacan sums up that split or difference with the following sentence: "I see only from one point, but in my existence I am looked at from all sides" (*FFC* 72). Noting here the active construction of the first clause in this sentence opposed to the passive construction of the second, we might conjecture that certain polarities, reversals, and redistributions are at work in the split between eye and gaze that would align it with other splits that have come under discussion here: between the subject of the enounced and the subject of the enunciation, between the subject of the orgasm and the subject of the ejaculation, between being-death and being dead. In Lacan the eye ("I") represents the Cartesian subject of certainty, or consciousness as transparent self-identity, whereas the gaze represents the occlusion of that transparency to the extent that the "I" is given over as the object of another's decisive vision. Here, with reference to Catherine Barkley's fear of rain in Hemingway's *Farewell to Arms,* we might say that the subject is afraid of the gaze—sometimes he sees himself dead in it.

In *it*—that is, in the picture insofar as "picture" would refer to the realm of the other's vision ("in the scopic the gaze is outside, I am looked at, that is to say, I am a picture" [*FFC* 106])—the subject no longer sees himself seeing himself but rather sees himself being seen, and not as active subject but rather as a pictorial object that can be taken and "is subject to being appreciated by an other eye"—which is the language that Irigaray uses to describe "the place of the feces" (*SW* 95). Lacan himself is hardly unaware of this messy metaphoricity vis-à-vis the split between eye and gaze, nor of what the "I" fears about being caught up in the lure of spatial identification, this "matter of the visible" in which "everything is a trap" (*FFC* 93). If the split marks the difference between seeing from one point and being seen from all sides, the latter precedes the former, thus "marking the pre-existence to the seen [and to the seer] of a given-to-be-seen" (*FFC* 74). For Lacan, it is this anteriority of the other to the one that turns the "point" from which the seer sees to that as which he is seen. This reversal changes the point to a "stain." Lacan writes, "If the function of the stain is recognized in its autonomy and identified with that of the gaze, we can seek its track, its thread, its trace, at every stage of the constitution of the world, in the scopic field. We will then realize that the function of the stain and of the gaze is both that which governs the gaze most secretly and that which always escapes from the grasp of the form of vision [eye or 'I'] that is satisfied with itself in imagining itself as consciousness" (*FFC* 74). The "I," that is, can sustain itself, satisfy itself in imagining itself as consciousness, only by foreclosing on the preexisting function of the stain. But the subject cannot sustain itself in representation without staining itself, because the representation of which subjectivity is an effect—for the subject is an effect not only of the signifier but of the materiality of signification—is also unavoidably "that which turns me into a picture" (*FFC* 105), that process by which "I situate myself in the picture as stain" (*FFC* 98).

Lacan foregrounds the divisible, heterological materiality of this situation when he writes, "The authenticity of what emerges in painting is diminished in us human beings by the fact that we have to get our colours where they're to be found, that is to say, in the shit. . . . The creator will never participate in anything other than the creation of a small dirty deposit, a succession of small dirty deposits juxtaposed" (*FFC* 117). What is repressed, then, is the knowledge that the creator cannot participate in his creation without placing his being in the shit, that insofar as he gives himself over to representation and to the other's gaze, he pointedly stains himself and becomes caught up in a metoynmic succession of small dirty deposits. This repressed knowledge gives rise to the anxiety of production, the creator's vertiginous, dysgraphic, scatontological anxiety when confronting any blank white page, any reflecting surface in which he can see himself as something other. To assuage this anxiety, to avoid being stained, to keep being from being framed, the tricks would be (1) to attempt to stay out of the picture altogether, either by imagining oneself as the immaculate origin of representation or by withdrawing not only from representation but from subjectivity itself, paddling upstream toward some more primordially "ownmost" origin where not the "I" but some essence of thinking Being imagines it has eluded representation altogether, has escaped being narrowed to a merely subjective point vulnerable to representational staining, or (2) to make woman the object of the gaze, to position woman as the tain of a mirror that, to the extent that she remains in place, will always compliantly give back to the subjective or metasubjective "I" an unstained reflection of its own desire. Without woman as the representational guarantee of proper speculation (the lack in its place, the truth of castration), the "I" can participate in its own self-production only as a shattering, self-contaminating sacrificial crisis.

But this crisis is not castration. The most shattering, most critical vision is not that of the loss of the penis, or even blindness as the pure and simple absence of the phallic "I"—at least, not for my money. Rather, and as Bataille knew, it is the nonnarrative story of the eye as enucleated object, the "I" that comes out, that *plops* out like an egg, a turd, a testicle: a globular "I" that in its utter(ed) dismemberment, its own lugubrious self-objectification, excretes itself, comes oozing out of its own dark orifice.[27] The restricted and oedipocentric economy of specular reflection that keeps the lack in its place, the woman positioned or pinioned as the tain of the mirror and the truth of castration, also keeps and sustains the "I" in a supposedly unstained position—safely screwed into its own head. If woman steps out of the frame, however, if representation overruns its margins, if the bodily in masculinity is encountered in all its rectal gravity, the specular mode by which others become shit is disrupted. The subject of speculation can no longer give himself a good, clean kiss in the mirror. He can only return (as) his own soiled letter, a dark wave of passivity washing back on itself in an excruciatingly impure expenditure, a money shot that is not one, that can return to itself only by coming into itself, saturating the abyss of its emptied-out socket.

4

Dysgraphia 2: Deconstruction and the Fear of Mere Writing

Heidegger's *Durchfall*

> I apologize for having to revert to this lewd orifice, 'tis my muse
> will have it so. Perhaps it is less to be thought as [an]
> eyesore . . . than as the symbol of those passed over in silence, a
> distinction due perhaps to its centrality and its air of being a link
> between me and the other excrement. We underestimate this lit-
> tle hole, it seems to me, we call it the arsehole and affect to de-
> spise it. But is it not rather the true portal of our being[?]
>
> —Samuel Beckett, *Molloy*

> To think Being itself explicitly requires us to relinquish Being as
> the ground of beings in favor of the giving that prevails concealed
> in unconcealment, that is, in favor of the It gives. As the gift of
> this It gives, Being belongs to giving. As a gift, Being is not ex-
> pelled from giving. Being, presencing is transmuted. As allowing-
> to-presence, it belongs to unconcealing; as the gift of unconceal-
> ing it is retained in the giving.
>
> —Martin Heidegger, *On Time and Being*

> There is no production here.
>
> —Martin Heidegger, *On Time and Being*

Bertolt Brecht once referred to Georg Lukács and other antimodernist adherents of the critical dogma of socialist realism as "enemies of production." Aesthetic production in particular, said Brecht, "makes them uncomfortable. You never know where you are with production; production is the unforeseeable. You never know what's going to come out. And they themselves don't want to produce. They want to play the *apparatchik* and exercise control over other people" (Benjamin, *Aesthetics* 97).

At some remove from Brecht, Martin Heidegger extensively critiques both metaphysics and modern technology as instances of a will to power that forgets the question of Being precisely in order to exercise control. For Heidegger, however, this control is exercised less over other people than over the destiny of a particular people, the German *Volk*, who, caught up in the modern metaphysics of technology, were thus closed off from their "ownmost" ontologically disclosive capacity (a capacity Heidegger for a while believed could be reopened by National Socialism—at least until the Nazis who Heidegger imagined were Greek "presencers" turned out to be Roman imperialists).[1]

Although the stakes of Heidegger's critique are remote from those of Lukács (despite certain similarities, about which see Lucien Goldmann), Heidegger also can be considered an enemy of production, or rather an enemy of what Michael E. Zimmerman calls "productionist metaphysics," the "metaphysical conception that 'to be' means to be produced, caused, or created" (*Heidegger's Confrontation* 224). Production made Heidegger profoundly uncomfortable, and my concern here is to reinscribe Heidegger's discomfort with and enmity to production in terms of the masculinist anxieties I have examined thus far. The juxtaposition of citations from Heidegger and Beckett at the beginning of this chapter does not indicate an affinity between the philosopher and the writer—far from it—but rather my desire to collapse fundamental ontology into what Bersani calls a "Beckettian consciousness" that would bring "the corruptive power of . . . carnal irony" (*Freudian Body* 9) to bear on Heideggerian thought. This corruptively carnal ironization of Heidegger may reveal the more actively abjecting dimensions of his philosophical and political affiliations, what Lyotard calls "an abjection essential to Heidegger's 'politics'" (*Heidegger and "the Jews"* 64).[2] Beyond that, it may also suggest that the "It gives" (*es gibt*) of Jacques Derrida's critical engagement with Heidegger retains more than it disseminates, protects more than it produces. This protective retention, in turn, has consequences not only for Derrida's own sexual politics but also for his particular take on the so-called repression of writing—a take in which, as I will show, the question of what might be called "mere writing" tends to get left behind.

Since I will argue that Derrida seems to want what might be called a Heideggerianism "without nostalgia" (*SP* 159), I might begin by asking how nostalgia is inscribed in Heidegger. In *Prophets of Extremity* Allan Meghill characterizes the notion of crisis that underlies modernist and postmodernist art, literature, and thought as "the belief that all continuity ha[s] been lost and that in consequence new and unexpected possibilities ha[ve], for good or ill, been opened up" (114). The alternative "for good or ill" allows Meghill to posit that the notion of crisis engenders a "desire for cultural regeneration [that] could lead in two opposing directions. On the one hand, it could lead to an enthusiastic embrace of the new; on the other, to an attempt to revitalize the old. In other words . . . the response to crisis could lean in an 'imaginative,' or alternately in a 'nostalgic' direction" (114). In Meghill's reading Heidegger "embraces the nostalgic side . . . constantly looking back to a mode of thinking that allegedly lies hidden in that dim period preceding the emergence of Greek philosophy" (115). Heidegger's works, writes Meghill,

> are pervaded by a metaphoric of "going back," of "return to origins." Heidegger perpetually wants to go back, to return, to go home again, to some earlier, more primal, more immediate, less articulate, but definitely more authentic state or condition. In short, we find in Heidegger a persistently nostalgic orientation. If we take the word *nostalgia* in its original Greek sense of homesickness (*nostos*, return home; *algos*, pain) rather than in its more attenuated contemporary sense, we can see how [Heidegger's] notion of *Unheimlichkeit* is one expression of this. (119)

Unheimlichkeit—"uncanniness" or "not-being-at-home" [*das Nichtzu-hause-sein*]—is for Heidegger related to a certain state of anxiety. In *Being and Time* Heidegger privileges anxiety as the mode of Being-in-the-world that allows *Dasein* to experience the sheer uncanniness of its lostness in the "they." Anxiety thus pulls *Dasein* out that lostness, that tranquility, and frees it for the more primordial resoluteness and authenticity of its *Sein zum Tode*—its Being toward a death that "reveals itself as that *possibility which is one's ownmost, which is non-relational, and which is not to be outstripped*" (*BT* 232). Original anxiety, says Heidegger, "makes manifest in Dasein its *Being towards* its ownmost potentiality-for-Being—that is, its *Being-free for* the freedom of choosing itself and taking hold of itself" (*BT* 232).

This emphasis on a decisive freedom in which *Dasein* takes hold of itself seems to gather Heidegger's anxiety into the domain of castration. Indeed, Ned Lukacher has spoken quite rightly of Heidegger's pervasive "separation anxiety" ("Writing on Ashes" 3–4).[3] I have shown how in Freud a privileged form of separation anxiety (castration) serves to paper over another, more abjectly productive mode that cannot be addressed as such, that remains unthought. How, then, might Heidegger's privileged mode of original anxiety be reinscribed? What does it cover over? If Heidegger wants anxiety to prod *Dasein* back toward some dim and less uncanny time before the emergence of modern representational thinking and, before that, of Greek philosophy—before the emergence of a metaphysics he did not consider sufficiently "primordial," did not consider "metaphysical enough"[4]—what other, more material "emergence," or emergence of material otherness, does he also want to place *Dasein* back behind? If this step back, this return to the "back behind," reveals an opening that is, as Heidegger says in his *Discourse on Thinking*, "beyond the distinction between activity and passivity" (*DT* 68), how might that opening be related to the lewd orifice that Beckett's Molloy designates as the true portal of our being? Back behind what other configurations and redistributions of the anality that for Freud subtends the active/passive polarity might the analgesic of Heidegger's *nostos* want to insert itself? How is Heidegger's nostalgic desire to link with what Ferry and Renaut call "the headwaters upstream of modernity" (*Heidegger and Modernity* 70) deployed against a notion of modernity as crisis, as wasteland, as "deformation and decay," "the darkening of the world, the flight of the gods, the destruction of the earth, the transformation of men into a mass," "emasculation of the spirit, the disintegration, wasting away, repression, and misinterpretation of the spirit" (Heidegger, *IM* 38, 45)? How do these specific figurations (which date from 1935) of modernity as an emasculating misinterpretation that transforms men into a mass relate to a more general male modernist anxiety in which, as Andreas Huyssen puts it, "male fears of woman and the bourgeois fear of the masses become indistinguishable" (*After the Great Divide* 52)? How is Heidegger's thought a reactionary deployment not only against his own formulation of the crisis of modernity but also against that related sacrificial crisis or self-division (by) which the representational subject produces (himself) in his vertiginous confrontation with the blank white page? Finally, insofar as these desires and deployments are implicated with the political affiliation with National Socialism that Heidegger once blithely referred to as his "big blunder" (Ferry and Renaut 68), how might that blunder and all that it entails be read as a defense against a decidedly unprivileged anxiety about an even more primordial *Durchfall?*

For Heidegger, the big blunder not only of his own affiliation but of National Socialism itself—of whose "inner truth and greatness" Heidegger was still convinced not only in 1935 (*IM* 199) but in 1953 (the revision of the 1935 text, which lets the troubling assertion stand forth) and even as late as 1966, when Heidegger still "did not in any way question the possibility of a 'good' National Socialism" (Ferry and Renaut 70)—might be considered rather small potatoes in comparison with the series of world-historical errancies and degradations by which man has forgotten the question of Being, the ontic/ontological difference between Being and beings, and the "event of appropriation" (*Er-*

eignis) that makes that difference possible and to which the difference belongs.[5] This forgetting, which for Heidegger has darkened the world and transformed men into a mass, enacts itself in two decisive historical moments: metaphysics (as Platonic, categorical, conceptual thinking), and modernity (as Cartesian, humanist, representational, and finally technological or calculative thinking). Characterized by Heidegger as moments of lapse, falling-off, degradation, decay, and emasculation, both productionist metaphysics and technological modernity bring about what Heidegger considers a woefully impoverished relation among thought, language, and representation, with representation (*Vorstellung* as degraded *technē*) posing a threat to the more originary Being-disclosive *poiēsis* of language and thought. Representation is what indicates for Heidegger modern man's forgetfulness of the question of Being, the reduction of *Dasein* into *hypokeimenon*, the *subjectum*, or merely subjective identity.

The problem, however, does not originally concern representation as picture-thinking but rather language: the degradations of metaphysics and modernity are for Heidegger the results of linguistic errancies in which the words used to let Being "shine" or "jut forth" lose their disclosive power. Thus, in *An Introduction to Metaphysics* Heidegger describes his project (as well the historical destiny of the German *Volk* under National Socialism) as the "attempt to regain the unimpaired strength of language and words; for words and language are not wrappings in which things are packed for the commerce of those who write and speak. It is in words and language that things first come into being and are" (*IM* 13). Alternatively, as he more famously puts it in the "Letter on Humanism," "Language is the house of Being" (*BW* 193).

For Heidegger, then, the way to track the history of the forgetting of Being is to examine what Being has been called. In pre-Socratic (Parminidean and Heraclitean) Greek philosophy, Heidegger says, Being was originally referred to as *physis*. Terry Eagleton, in his chapter on Heidegger in *The Ideology of the Aesthetic,* gathers the various meanings that Heidegger suggests for *physis* in *An Introduction to Metaphysics* and writes that for Heidegger, *physis* "originally meant a 'standing forth' or 'coming to stand,' that which unfolds, blossoms or arises. Being is a kind of 'jutting forth,' and this uprightness or 'erect standing there' is a permanent one, an unfolding which will never fall down." Noting the rather obviously phallic overtones of these meanings, Eagleton wryly comments, "It would seem that this oldest of all stand-bys is indeed always ready-to-hand" (313). According to Heidegger, however, Plato and the Socratics transformed this originary jutting-forth of Being as *physis*, and "in the end the word *idea, eido[s], . . .* came to the fore as the decisive and predominant name for being (*physis*). Since then the interpretation of being as idea has dominated all Western thinking throughout the history of its transformations down to the present day" (*IM* 180).

What is important in relation to the question of representation is that this transformation of *physis* to *eidos* also entails the reduction of appearing—which Heidegger calls "the very essence of being" (*IM* 101)—to mere appearance and the concomitant degeneration of vision into "mere optics" (*IM* 61). Heidegger writes that "the word *idea* means that which is seen in the visible, the aspect it offers. What is offered is the appearance, *eidos*, of what confronts us. The appearance of a thing is that wherein . . . it . . . places itself before [*vor-stellt*] us and as such stands before us" (*IM* 180–81). Heidegger then goes on to consider the difference between *physis* and *eidos* in regard to an ambiguity inherent in appearing itself:

> *Physis* is the emerging power, the standing-there-in-itself, stability. *Idea*, appearance as what is seen, is a determination of the stable insofar and only insofar as it encounters vision. But *physis* as emerging power is by the same token an appearing. Except that the appearing is ambiguous. Appearing means first: that which gathers itself, which brings-itself-to-stand in its togetherness and so stands. But second it means: that which, already standing-there, presents a front, a surface, offers an appearance to be looked at. (*IM* 182)

If we follow Eagleton in recognizing the markedly phallic overtones of Heidegger's description of Being as *physis*, and further, if we note the contrast between the activity that Heidegger grants to *physis* (emerging, gathering, bringing itself to stand) and the apparent passivity of *eidos*, which presents itself as surface to be looked at, subject to another's gaze, could we not suggest that there is something conspicuously *urethral* about Heidegger's appearing/appearance ambiguity, his insistence on that which remains concealed in the unconcealing? With Heidegger are we not again at least in the proximity of a phallus/penis split in which the latter's mere appearance would mark the ejaculatory-cum-excremental degradation of the former's in(di)visibly orgasmic appearing?[6] Is the anxiety papered over by Heidegger's privileged original anxiety qua *Unheimlichkeit* thus less about the metaphysical transformation of *physis* into *eidos* than the all-too-physical conversion of *physis* into feces, his apprehension less about the forgetfulness of Being than about the deeper-seated suspicion that, as Beckett's Molloy suggests, a certain lewd orifice may be that Being's true portal? And if here we strategically recall Molloy's cloacally confused memory of being born through his mother's anus, could we not suggest a certain fear of the spectral mother at work in Heidegger's discourse as well? Can we not detect what I have called the primontological reversal—a desire to beat back maternal sexual agency and to repress all trace of maternal determination in the construction of male subjectivity—underlying and motivating fundamental ontology itself? Do not such considerations suggest that Heidegger's attempt to get back behind subjectivity—as Habermas puts it, to get *"behind* or *above* real history . . . with the help of an operation we might call 'abstraction via essentialization'"* ("Work and Weltanschauung" 449)—might be intricated with an attempt to get back behind "productionist metaphysics" as both maternal determination and male corporeal productivity?

This carnally ironic interpretation of what Edith Wyschogrod refers to as Heidegger's "repristinization" (*Spirit in Ashes* 200) receives some support from *An Introduction to Metaphysics,* where Heidegger laments not only the degradation of *physis* to *eidos* but also the fact that "this basic Greek word for the essent [*physis*] is customarily translated as 'nature.'"

> This derives from the Latin translation, *natura,* which properly means "to be born," "birth." But with this Latin translation the original meaning of the Greek word *physis* is thrust aside, the actual philosophical force of the Greek word is destroyed. This is true not only of the Latin translation of *this* word but of all other Roman translations of the Greek philosophical language. What happened in this translation from the Greek into the Latin is not accidental and harmless; it marks the first stage in the process by which we cut ourselves off and alienated ourselves from the original essence of Greek philosophy. (*IM* 13)

In the separation anxiety that unconceals itself here, the difference between *physis* and *natura* emerges not so much as that between Being and beings but as that between Being and being (of woman) born, as if Heidegger does not want the essent to bear the mark of that materially productive process. Thus, although he notes that *"physis* as emergence can be observed . . . in the coming forth of man and animal from the womb," he insists that *"physis,* the realm of that which arises, is not synonymous with these phenomena" (*IM* 14). More than anything, then, Heidegger does not want Being to be observed, to be looked at. He wants to avoid having Being be cut off not from the mother's body but from that more originary and essential source that he variously names but finally designates as *Ereignis,* the event of appropriation. He does not want to let the appearing of fundamental ontology's original essence be seen, be contaminated by subjection to the merely ideational appearance he considers to be the watermark of metaphysics and modernity. As Lyotard remarks, "it will be a question of making understood that the unveiled is never the truth . . . but that the truth is the unveiling, and that the forgotten of thought as metaphysics (and physics) cannot be presented. . . . One betrays the Absolute by representing it on the stage of the presentable, in accordance with form and concept" (*Heiddeger and "the Jews"* 60).

This speculation about Heidegger's anxiety of production renders problematic the status of the difference on which Heideggerian thought is said to insist. One wonders what, if anything, Heideggerian difference has to do with the word *difference* as it is generally deployed in current radical discursive practice, wherein the term refers to heterogeneities of race, class, gender, ethnicity, and sexual orientation that are recognized, insisted on, celebrated.[7] In Heidegger's thought difference always amounts to the same thing: the ontic/ontological difference between Being and beings. As Richard Rorty points out in *Contingency, Irony, Solidarity*, whatever else a Heidegger essay purports to question—such as, say, the difference between *poiēsis* and *technē*—it always boils down to this one issue (121). To recognize this difference, however, is not in Heidegger's case to celebrate or even tolerate sexual, cultural, and material differences as such; to the contrary, it is to arrive at and dwell within that stainless and ever-more primordial event that is prior to their production. In *Identity and Difference*, for example, Heidegger writes, "We speak of the *difference* between Being and beings. The step back goes from what is unthought, from the difference as such, into what gives us thought" (*ID* 50). In *Poetry, Language, Thought* Heidegger writes: "The word difference is now removed from its usual and customary usage. What it now names is not a species concept for various kinds of differences. It exists only as this single difference. It is unique. . . . The dif-ference does not mediate after the fact by binding together world and things through a mean added on to them. Being the mean, it first determines world and things in their presence, i.e., in their being toward one another, whose unity it carries out" (*PLT* 202).

What we need to interrogate here is Heidegger's step back from a difference that itself already seems to be a fastidious withdrawal from social, historical, sexual, or racial differences ("real history," as Habermas puts it). We need to question his denunciation of a Hegelian mediation after the fact—after *what* fact, if not that of a specific difference to be mediated?—and his concomitant privileging of a first determination, a repristinized unity carried out presumably before that fact.

Mark C. Taylor tries to put the best face on this by arguing that Heidegger's difference "is not the Hegelian mean [*Mitte*] that mediates identity and difference by securing the *identity* of identity and difference. The delivery *of* difference is also the delivery *from* every form of all-inclusive identity that negates, reduces, absorbs, or swallows up otherness. As 'the threshold' of identity and difference, *dif-ference* is neither identical nor different. This distinctive *Unter-Schied* is what Heidegger labels 'the same' [*das Selbe*]" (*Altarity* 44). But if for Heidegger "the same is not merely identical" because "in the merely identical, the difference disappears" (*ID* 45), then *the* difference is not mere difference (material difference) but rather a "same" in which material differences disappear, a unity that precedes not only the difference between difference and identity but also any Hegelian identity of identity and difference. In other words, Heidegger still makes differences disappear, only in the name not of identity but rather of some essence preceding and more primordial than identity. *All* identity, even Hegelian absolute identity, is for Heidegger only mere identity, metaphysical or merely subjective identity that, by falling short of or forgetting the unified essencing of Being as *physis*, as *Ereignis*, is not sufficiently metaphysical or primordial. As Ferry and Renaut put it, "speaking of Dasein as a 'subject' is to substantialize it, thus to think of it in the mode of a thing" (44). But Being rescues *Dasein* from such substantial thingness. Being is delivered from what Taylor calls an "all-inclusive identity that negates, reduces, absorbs, or swallows up otherness," because in Being—the pure movement of temporality in which, as in the Freudian prenativity, there are no objects, no things at all, the pure emergence of a *physis* that is radically and prophylactically nonsynonymous with *natura* as "being born"—there is no otherness to negate, reduce, absorb, or swallow up. Quoting Heidegger extensively, Taylor writes: "The 'sameness' (*Selbigkeit*) with which Heidegger tries to pass beyond Western philosophy 'approaches [*herkommt*] from further back than the kind of identity defined by metaphysics in terms of Being as a characteristic of Being' [*ID* 28]. . . . By taking a 'step back' (*Schritt zurück*) from the ontotheological tradition, Heidegger attempts 'to return to' (*zurückgehen*) that which is 'prior to thought' [*DT* 83]" (*Altarity* 44).

In Heidegger, then, *the* difference is delivered from an identity that is only a characteristic of Being, an identity that is not sufficiently the same. Ultimately, *the* difference is delivered from differences and returned to a same that is prior to thought. Heidegger's attempt to return to what is prior to degraded thought, however, to "step back out of metaphysics into its essential nature" (*ID* 51), is also and perhaps even primarily an attempt to return to what is prior to the spatializing and objectifying *technē* of modern picture-thinking: "How can such an entry come about? By our moving away from the attitude of representational thinking" (*ID* 32). Heidegger then, like Hegel, also has his problems with *Vorstellung*. But whereas Hegel at least recognizes the material, corporeal differences inscribed in representation—if only to identify them as stages in the narrative of self-consciousness, if only to attempt to work through those differences in the name of an absolute *Aufhebung* whose enucleated blind spot comes to be a pee stain—Heidegger just wants to get upstream of the whole "dripping mass." The high-water mark of the Hegelian system is Reason, and Bataille, to use Denis Hollier's words again, wants to make Reason shit. Can Being be similarly prodded? "Prior to" and further upstream than Hegelian Reason and its utter(ed) dismemberments, further back even than Freud's *fort-da*, Lacan's mirror stage, and their always potentially messy redistributions of the active/passive polarity, is Being an even more originary, even more primordial effacement of the inextricably scatontological production of representation itself?

Heidegger certainly wants to keep Being out of the picture, to withdraw from representation, to turn his face from the metaphysical mirror of production. This aversion to *Vorstellung* in its specifically modern or technological permutations is spectacularly evident in the essay "The Age of the World Picture." There Heidegger begins by posing the question of the essence of modern science: "only the essential," he says, "is aimed at here" (*QCT* 118). The essence of modern science, says Heidegger, is research, and the essence of research in modern science is representational calculation: "To set up an experiment means to represent or conceive [*vorstellen*] the conditions under which a specific series of motions can be made susceptible of being followed in its necessary progression, i.e., of being controlled in advance by calculation" (*QCT* 121). For Heidegger, however, this precontrolling and objectifying calculation delimits not only that research but also the researcher himself—setting him up, enframing him, narrowing him to the point of the "mere subjective experience" (*QCT* 116) characteristic of modern rational or calculative individualism: "We first arrive at science as research when the Being of whatever is, is sought in such objectiveness. This objectifying of whatever is, is accomplished in a setting-before, a representing, that aims at bringing each particular being before it in such a way that man who calculates can be sure, and that means be certain, of that being. We first arrive at science as research when and only when truth has been transformed into the certainty of representation" (*QCT* 127).

For Heidegger, the moment or movement of modernity is equiprimordial with the transformation of the truth of the world into the certainty of representation, in other words, when the world becomes picture. The danger is not so much to the world as to the essence of *Dasein*, which "lets itself be put at the *disposal* of representation" (*QCT* 126; emphasis added). Not only does the world become representation, but the subject becomes the subject *of* representation: "That the world becomes picture is one and the same event with the event of man's becoming *subjectum* in the midst of that which is" (*QCT* 132). If *Vorstellung* means "to set before," then the subject not only sets the world before himself as representation but also sets himself before that representation as *its* subject, its effect (all of which, of course, bears an uncanny resemblance to Lacan's notion of the constitution of the subject as an effect of its own representation in the mirror stage): "Therewith man sets himself up as the setting in which whatever is must set itself forth, must present itself, i.e., become picture. Man becomes the representative of that which is, in the sense of that which has the character of object" (*QCT* 132). As Heidegger maintains in one of the appendices to the essay, however,

> Where anything that is has become the object of representing, it first incurs in a certain manner a loss of Being. This loss is adequately perceived, if but vaguely and unclearly, and is compensated for with corresponding swiftness through the fact that we impart value to the object and to that which is, interpreted as object, and that we take the measure of whatever is, solely in keeping with the criterion of value, and make of values themselves the goal of all activity. Since the latter is understood as culture, values become cultural values, and these, in turn, become the very expression of highest purposes of creativity, in the service of man's making himself secure as *subjectum*. From here it is only a step to making values into objects in themselves. Value is the objectification of needs as goals, wrought by a representing self-establishing within the world as picture. (*QCT* 142)

Here Heidegger seems to be critiquing the security of subjectivity, if not the subjective armor of the mirror stage itself. Since this security entails for Heidegger a certain loss of Being, however, he is actually asserting that a subjectivity that representationally establishes itself within the world as picture simply is not secure enough: it has narrowed itself down to a treacherous point, technically secured itself from the poetic call of Being, of the "It gives," wherein its most authentic security groundlessly and ecstatically lies. What Heidegger is lamenting, then, is that, within the darkening of the world represented by modernity, the expression of what man considers to be the highest purposes of creativity has been corrupted to the expression of a mere subjectivity caught up in the lure of spatial identification and merely cultural values. For Heidegger, a mere subject is one who allows himself to be put in the picture, who lets himself be put at the disposal of representation, who forgets the question of Being and allows his in(di)visible essence to be narrowed to a di(vi)sible point, a point that by virtue of the processes of metaphysics, representation, and merely cultural valuation (not to mention the maternally overdetermined processes of *natura*) always threatens to become a stain. Here again, Heidegger exhibits his own anxiety about the fall of *physis* into *eidos*, of active appearing into merely passive appearance.

What we might say, then, in the name of carnal irony, is that for Heidegger, as well as for Hegel, to be in the picture is finally to be in the shit. Hegel, it may be recalled, not only excrementalizes (specifically, urinizes) picture-thinking; he also, in what I have argued is a related gesture, fecalizes the Jews. Heidegger, of course, never descends to the material specificity of Hegel's language, but this fastidiousness on Heidegger's part hardly exculpates him either from displaced abjection, that "mode by which Others become shit," or from the historically specific fascist deployment of that mode. To exercise that mode— as does a Hegel historically but in this instance not quite ideologically remote from the fascist terror—one must first recognize the existence of both of these merely heterogeneous forms. Heidegger, for the most part, would prefer to stay upstream of the whole question, dwelling in the *poiēsis* of an imageless truth, not only prior to metaphysics and degraded thought but also removed from ever having to think about degrading alterity itself: a very careful "rest for the warrior" (Irigaray, *SW* 94). Thus, in his more-metaphysical-than-metaphysical quest for a properly presubjective, pre-representational homeland that he privileges as a realm uncontaminated by *natura, Vorstellung,* and the mere subjectivities that are their pointed effects, Heidegger joined up with the Nazis, who wanted and tried to bring about a world purged of those mere beings who happened to be (born) Jews. Auschwitz was a horror for Heidegger not because of the extermination of millions of beings but because it, like industrialized agriculture, was just another modern form of *technē* that forgot the question of Being.[8] Those who attempt to exculpate Heidegger from charges of anti-Semitism on the grounds that he argued against certain biologist *forms* of anti-Semitism seem to believe that biologism itself accounts for and exhausts the possibilities of racism.[9] Those who suggest that Heidegger's silence about Auschwitz is "a silence we haven't yet learned to read"[10] may themselves be unable to read that silence as a text of collusion pure and simple. The case for Heidegger's non-anti-Semitism is about as strong as that for Joyce's Hegelian Mr. Deasy, who in the "Nestor" section of *Ulysses* blithely announces that Ireland never persecuted the Jews because "she never let them in" (*U* 2:446).

Of course, the specific record, if not of Heidegger's own anti-Semitism then at least of his opportunistic exploitation of anti-Semitism, speaks clearly enough; one only has to consider the "Baumgarten Report," a 1933 letter that Heidegger "destined" to the organization of Nazi professors at Gottingen "to warn them about the university's proposal to name Eduard Baumgarten to the chair of professor" (Ferry and Renaut 25). In this sending, which did in fact reach its destination, Heidegger accuses Baumgarten, a family friend, of being not only "liberal-democratic" but also "considerably Americanized," as well as "closely linked to the Jew Frankel." As Ferry and Renaut comment, "Is it really necessary to explain that . . . the reference to 'the Jew Frankel' betrays the hand of a vulgar anti-Semite" (26)?

> Is it really credible that a sensible and responsible person who joined the national Socialist Party in 1933 could do so without at least "concealing" the anti-Semitic "component" and by being so naïve or blind as to imagine it "possible to separate the racism from the movement"? Who—above all, what intellectual who is in principle an attentive analyst of ideas and texts—could imagine that racism in the Germany of 1933 was merely one aspect of Nazism, one not consubstantially bound up with it and its constitutive principles? (24)

Who indeed? But here we might note the way Heidegger's attack on Baumgarten links being "Jewized," as Ferry and Renaut put it, with being "Americanized." Allan Stoekl argues that for Heidegger, as well as for such French protofascists as Dandieu and Aron, America became a "metonym for a modernism gone wrong." Commenting on "Heidegger's excoriations throughout the 1930s of 'Americanism,'" Stoekl writes that Heidegger's anti-Americanism "serves exactly the same function that anti-Semitism serves elsewhere . . . in Nazi propaganda: the Americans, like the Jews, are the promoters and carriers of cosmopolitanism (the neglect of healthy natural and psychological strength), the destruction of spiritual values, the blind hyper-production of useless junk, the speculation that inevitably ends in collapse" ("Truman's Apotheosis" 190). I follow Stoekl here not to stand up for the United States. Rather, I am interested in the specific language of a Heideggerian anti-Americanism that functions in much the same way as not only anti-Semitism but also misogyny in other arenas of fascist male discourse. In *An Introduction to Metaphysics*, for example, Heidegger refers to America and Russia as the "great pincers" between which

Germany, "in its ruinous blindness forever on the point of cutting its own throat," lies "squeezed" (*IM* 37). These metaphors of enucleated blindness and a bloody laceration might suggest that for Heidegger, the great squeezing pincers of the United States and Russia constitute the two sides of some immense *vagina dentata* and that he is afraid of what will happen to the German jutting forth when, to trope Irigaray, these two lips speak together.

Also conspicuous in this regard is Heidegger's characterization of Americanism as "flood" (Ferry and Renaut 67–68). Heidegger insists that America and Russia are the same. Klaus Theweleit, in *Women, Floods, Bodies, History,* volume 1 of *Male Fantasies,* analyzes the writings of the proto-Nazi *Freikorps* soldiers and finds in their language a relentless figuring of Bolshevism as a horrifying, inundating, and above all, *feminizing* "red flood." Theweleit argues that this fear of "succumbing to fluidity" (238) is constitutive for the class of men he designates as "fascist male warriors." This constitutive dread, says Theweleit, is not only of feminine sexuality and maternal physicality ("In childbirth, too, streams of water and blood—red floods—are released before the baby is delivered" [232]) but also of the productive fluidities of these men's own bodies. "The flood," writes Theweleit, "is abstract enough to allow processes of extreme diversity to be subsumed under its image. All they need have in common is some transgression of boundaries. Whether the boundaries belong to a country, a body, decency or tradition, their transgression must unearth something that has been forbidden" (232–33). Theweleit continues:

> Most dangerous of all, though, are the floods within oneself. . . . The "gigantic, filthy-red wave" that breaks over [the fascist male warrior] has really sloshed up inside him. He threatens "to drown" within himself. . . . The flood is close at hand . . . either in oneself or on the outside. The men seem to relate every actual or imminent flood directly to themselves, each one to his own body. The terrain of their rage is always at the same time their own body; this feeling is found in every single utterance associated with the "Red Flood." (233)

I bring in Theweleit here not to suggest that any male writer who evinces a horror of floods or figures as a flood something to which he stands opposed is automatically a misogynist fascist warrior (although I leave open the possibility that such figuration never transcends psychosexual and political meanings). Nor do I think that the simple instance of such figuration in Heidegger is by itself enough to link him to the *Freikorps* mentality Theweleit explores. Yet that instance is hardly isolable from other historical correspondences: Heidegger's appropriations of the masculinist elements in the thought of Ernst Jünger, one of the main subjects of Theweleit's study;[11] the specific rhetoric of his glowing tribute to the *Freikorps* member Schlageter;[12] and the salient fact that he gave "30 June 1934"—Hitler's Night of the Long Knives, when Nazism purged itself of the Röhm *Freikorps* faction that comprised the core of the SA—as the date of his recognition of his error concerning his support of National Socialism.[13] To some, these correspondences may seem reductive, too empirical, too easy, too readable. Certainly, as Lyotard puts it, "thought exceeds its contexts" (*Heidegger and "the Jews"* 59). This excess is not a transcendence, however; taken together with the enmity to production, representation, and embodiment that I have argued Heidegger's rhetoric discloses, these historico-discursive contexts help to suggest a productive anxiety that I believe Heidegger and the *Freikorps* did share—but of course, not only them. In her introduction to *Male Fantasies* Barbara Ehrenreich writes that "Theweleit does not push, but he certainly leaves open the path from the 'inhuman impulse' of fascism to the most banal sexism" (1:xv). Here, without pushing, one could also suggest a path from the inhuman impulse of fascism to the most exalted philosophy, a philosophical and psychosexual path, perhaps a "country path," from the anxious rector of Freiburg to the inhumanly tightened rectums of the men of the *Freikorps*.[14]

In "On the Essence of Truth" Heidegger writes, "Our thinking apparently remains on the path of metaphysics. Nevertheless, in its decisive steps . . . it accomplishes a change in the questioning that belongs to the overcoming of metaphysics" (*BW* 140–41). One might grant Heidegger's thinking that accomplishment. In regard to the question of productive anxiety and its relation to the real history of male domination, however, the real history of what Theweleit calls "murdering-production," Heidegger's thought, however disposed toward metaphysics, remains resolutely on the path of hegemonic masculinity and accomplishes no real change in any questioning that would belong to its overcoming.[15]

Derrida's Hold on Heidegger

"Hold" in our language means protective heed.
—Martin Heidegger, "Letter on Humanism"

Only by appropriating or holding on to Heidegger can Derrida demolish the historicity of this hold. But for this to occur, the addressee of Derrida's address must not only be held but held back, subjected to a withdrawal or concealment, so that he can be inscribed into his own problematic of how Being is both disclosed and withdrawn at the same time. Given the "holding back" which occurs as Derrida lays "hold" of Heidegger, it is certain that the letter, dispatch, or postcard "sent" to Heidegger will miss its address, and hence Heidegger's philosophy, in being missed, will fail to reach its "destiny," which is the philosophical afterlife it lays claim to in deconstruction.

—Herman Rapaport, *Heidegger and Derrida*

This matter is best disposed of from a great height—over water.

—Vandamm to Leonard, speaking about Eve, in Alfred Hitchcock, *North by Northwest*

What, then, after all, of the remain(s), today, for us, for a reading that produces rather than protects, here, now, of a Derrida? Here, now that Derrida can apparently only protectively reread but not productively release a Heidegger who, even then, would not necessarily need to be "rammed down the shithole."[16] If, as Barbara Johnson puts it in her introduction to Derrida's *Dissemination*, "a deconstructive reading does not point out the flaws or weaknesses or stupidities of an author, but the *necessity* with which what he *does* see is systematically related to what he does *not* see" (xv), might it not be that Derrida's retention of Heidegger renders him unable to see or speak a body—productive, male, and Jewish—that Heidegger himself could never have seen or spoken and would have preferred to abject?[17] There is, as Derrida would doubtless say, no simple answer to this question. The fact, however, that I choose this particular point in my discussion to segue into the problematic of Derrida's relationship to Heidegger should not serve as the high sign that I intend to implicate Derrida in Heidegger's "big blunder," exploiting Heidegger's affiliation with Nazism (not to mention the de Man revelations) to make some "we-knew-it-all-along" case for deconstruction as a crypto-fascistic discourse.[18] Deconstruction is anything but a fascist discourse; Derrida is anything but a fascist and has given us a nonfascist way of reading Heidegger. Nonetheless, the preceding discussion should indicate why I consider Derrida's presently quite tenacious hold on Heidegger to be problematic. In what follows I argue that Heidegger's anxiety about the production(s) of male bodies is, surprisingly enough, at work in places in Derrida's writing as well and that this anxiety allows us to reread not only Derrida's writing about the repression of writing but also the gender-political insufficiencies of deconstruction.[19] At issue is not some directive to Derrida to stop reading Heideggerian texts; moreover, my carnally ironic juxtaposition of epigraphs notwithstanding, I am not commanding that Derrida expel Heidegger, simply let him drop. Specific stakes and consequences arise from Derrida's refusal to let Heidegger go, however, and these are what I want to read.

In *Contingency, Irony, Solidarity* Richard Rorty suggests that "Derrida's earlier work can be read as . . . the project of going deeper than Heidegger went, in quest of the same sort of thing Heidegger wanted: words which express the conditions of possibility of all previous theory . . . words which get us 'beyond' metaphysics" (123).[20] As I have shown, the words with which Heidegger wanted to get beyond an apparently still-too-physical metaphysics, his tickets back behind the source of the metaphysical/technological flood, are Being and a difference that ends up being "the Same." In Derrida's earlier work it is of course the nonword, nonconcept *différance* (differing/deferring) that expresses the conditions of possibility for differences as such: "What we note as differance will thus be the movement of play that 'produces' (and not by something that is simply an activity) these differences, these effects of difference. This does not mean that the differance which produces differences is before them in a simple and in itself unmodified and indifferent present. Differance is the nonfull, nonsimple 'origin'; it is the structured and differing origin of differences" (*SP* 141). Elsewhere Derrida writes, "Doesn't . . . differance refer us beyond the history of Being, beyond our language as well, and beyond everything that can be named by it?" (*SP* 157).

Perhaps the repetition of *beyond* in the latter quotation calls into question the deployment of *before* in the former. Derrida says that *différance* produces differences, but this does not mean, he says, that *différance* exists before differences as some simple, unmodified, indifferent present that would in turn produce them. But Derrida means not that *différance* is *not* before differences but only that it is not before them as presence. At the same time, Derrida seems not to mean that *différance* is not beyond that presence and beyond the history of Being determined as presence. In other words, the playful movement of *différance* produces, and is more original than, the mere presence that—as a subjectively conscious identity that imagines itself only as the self-presence of consciousness, as identity—also imagines itself as the simple, full, self-present origin of differences. This origin and the seeming immediacy of its presence are in fact derived. *Différance* as the nonsimple, nonfull origin of differences is beyond the history of Being determined immediately as presence. But is it not by the same gesture also beyond differences as well, so that, despite certain appearances, Derridean *différance*, like Heideggerian difference, risks ending up being pretty much "the same"? Such is Peter Dews's assertion in *Logics of Disintegration:*

> In Derrida's work, *differance* cannot be defined through its opposition-
> al relation to identity, since it is considered to be the "nonoriginary
> origin" of presence and identity, and as such cannot be *dependent*
> upon them for its determination. But, if *differance* does not stand in
> opposition to presence and identity, then neither can it differ from
> them. However, if it were to be maintained that *differance* differs from
> identity, then by this very token it can *not* differ absolutely, since all
> determinate differences are internal to *differance*. Absolute difference,
> in other words, which is what Derrida must understand by a *differ-
> ance* which is the "possibility of conceptuality," and thus of determi-
> nation, necessarily collapses into absolute identity. (26–27)

If, that is, Derrida rightly argues for what Dews calls "an essential *logical priority* of non-identity over identity" (27)—a priority similar to that
which Lacan stresses by positing the subject as an effect of the signifier—Derrida sets his own Heideggerianism to work by making that
priority essential, by letting *différance* refer us to a transcendental beyond, to a priority even more prior (but finally less material) than the
priority of nonidentity to identity.

Thus, despite certain appearances of his having drifted downstream
of Heidegger, has Derrida actually attempted to get even farther up,
deeper in than Heidegger went but in search of the same thingless
thing that Heidegger wanted, back behind Heidegger's nostalgia for
the proper name and thus back beyond, before, and behind not only
the history but also the question of a Being that always stands in risk
of being determined as presence? If this is the case, could we not characterize Derrida's relationship to Heidegger less as an expenditure
without reserve than as a giving that retains more than it expels?
Could we not also inquire about the consequences, particularly for
his notion of writing, of Derrida's withholding of Heidegger, his inability or refusal to relinquish or expend without reservation that
particular theoretical object?

We should at least note the fierceness of Derrida's retention and the
specificity of its terms. In "Differance," for example, Derrida fully implicates Heidegger in nostalgia for the proper name, but he asks whether "differance finds its place within the spread of the ontic-ontological
difference, as it is conceived, as the 'epoch' conceives itself within it,
and particularly 'across' the Heideggerian meditation which cannot be
gotten around." He concludes that "there is no simple answer to such
a question" (*SP* 153). In "*Geschlecht* II: Heidegger's Hand" Derrida charges Heidegger with a logocentric "devaluation of writing" (citing Heideg-

ger's evaluation of Socrates as "the purest thinker of the West" because he "wrote nothing") but then goes on to say, "I never 'criticize' Heidegger without recalling that that can be done from other places in his own text" (189)—with the implication that such criticism can be done *only* from those places. In "The Ends of Man" Derrida charges Heidegger with being caught up in the metaphysics he thought he had overcome and implicates Being with the metaphysics of presence and proximity. Nevertheless, he writes, "Any questioning of humanism that does not first catch up with the archeological radicalness of the questions sketched by Heidegger . . . any metahumanist position that does not place itself within the opening of these questions remains historically regional, periodic, and peripheral, juridically secondary and dependent" (*MP* 128). Of course, one could argue against Derrida that there have been some quite radical questionings of humanism—feminist, queer, Marxist, psychoanalytic, and postcolonial critiques, for examples—that *have* "gotten around" the Heideggerian meditation, that have not placed themselves within Heidegger's opening. Moreover, just as one might ask what Heideggerian difference has to do with difference as it is deployed in these other questionings, one might also ask what Heideggerian metahumanism—in which "humanism is opposed because it does not set the *humanitas* of man high enough" (Heidegger, *BW* 210)—has to do with critiques of humanism that recognize the supposedly universal humanist subject as Eurocentric, white, middle-class, and heterosexually male. Finally, one could also note how closely the adjectives Derrida uses to describe a non-Heideggerian posthumanism resemble the logocentric descriptions and devaluations of writing with which Derrida himself has made us so familiar. Indeed, what words would be the opposites of "regional, periodic, peripheral, secondary, and dependent" if not "universal, timeless, central, originary, and autonomous"—the standard phallogocentric calling cards of pure self-presence, if not of Eurocentric humanism itself?

Derrida, for whatever reason, still chooses to retain himself within the Heideggerian opening and to retain Heidegger within his own. This retention helps to underwrite Derrida's relationship to sexual difference and to certain aspects of psychoanalysis as well.[21] After all, Heidegger is hardly known for his engagement with either sexuality, the body, or the texts of Freud. Indeed, psychoanalysis itself may have figured abjectly for Heidegger, for when he finally got around to reading Freud in 1958, the experience "disgusted" him and "made him literally feel ill."[22] This rather telling reaction on Heidegger's part casts a somewhat different light on Derrida's assertion, in the interview with Christie McDonald called "Choreographies," that Heidegger's reluctance to speak about either sexual difference or psychoanalysis was "neither negligence nor omission" (*EO* 179–80). This interview, along with such pieces as "Women in the Beehive" and the two *Geschlecht* essays, can be read as part of Derrida's effort not only to articulate his relationship to feminism but also, in a related gesture, to rescue Heidegger from the charge that his sexual neutrality reinscribes phallogocentrism, that his silence on sexual difference might be attributed to anything so vulgar as mere "omission, repression, denial, foreclosure, [or] even the unthought" (*"Geschlecht"* 129). In "Choreographies" Derrida describes Heidegger's conception of *Dasein* as sexually neuter and goes on to say that this "originary and powerful" asexual neutrality

> does not signify in this instance the absence of sexuality—one could call it the instinct, desire or even the libido—but the absence of any mark belonging to one of the two sexes. Not that the *Dasein* does not ontically or in fact belong to a sex; not that it is deprived of sexuality; but the *Dasein* as *Dasein* does not carry with it the mark of this opposition (or alternative) between the two sexes. Insofar as these marks are opposable and binary, they are not existential structures. Nor do they allude in this respect to any primitive or subsequent bisexuality. Such an allusion would fall once again into anatomical, biological or anthropological determinations. And the *Dasein*, in the structures and "power" that are originary to it, would come "prior" to these determinations. (*EO* 180)

Derrida is dancing as fast as he can in this choreography. Although he admits that he has put the word *prior* in quotation marks because "it has no [merely?] literal, chronological, historical or logical meaning," he goes on to suggest that because Heidegger's analytic of *Dasein* "subjected all the concepts of traditional Western philosophy to a radical elucidation and interpretation," we should have an idea of "what stakes were involved in a neutralization that fell back this side of both sexual difference and its binary marking, if not this side of sexuality itself" (*EO* 180)—as if the notion of a side of sexuality did not reinscribe itself in a binary difference against some other side. What is most conspicuous in Derrida's formulation of *Dasein*'s sexual neutrality, however, and all the more conspicuous for the way Derrida seems to privilege it, is the fact that it is precisely the *mark* of sexuality and of sexual difference that both Heidegger and Derrida want to see effaced. Derrida is careful to point out that, for Heidegger, *Dasein*'s "powerful and originary a-sexual neutrality" is the absence not of instinct, desire, or libido but rather of the mark, the "binary marking" of sexual difference. Although Derrida's target here seems to be binary opposition (indeed, the strongest part of his argument in this interview is against the rigidification of sexual difference[s] into two opposable "options"), it is still the mark, the inscription, the *trace*, that Derrida devalues, wants to get back behind. In fact, the Derrida who made his own mark by attacking the phonocentric privilege granted to speech over writing here approaches the materiality of the sexual mark only to fall back into the vague and invisible register of the *voice:* "I would like to be-lieve in the multiplicity of sexually marked voices. I would like to be-lieve in the masses, this indeterminable number of blended voices, this mobile of non-identified sexual marks whose choreography can car-ry, divide, multiply the body of each 'individual,' whether he be clas-sified as 'man' or 'woman'" (184). Although there is much to admire, or desire, in this utopia of sexual undecidability (which seems, how-ever, to be less a dance troupe of moving bodies than an angelically noncorporeal choir), there still seems to be a withdrawal or effacement that leaves little room for the material specificity of any productive bodily mark.

What emerges, then, in Derrida's defense of Heidegger's neutral si-lence on sexual difference is a conception of a sexuality that has no body—and a sexuality without a body might be compared to a Being that is not a mere being. This bodiless sexuality leaves no marks of difference behind it—or rather, perhaps, it leaves no marks from its behind: it can speak of only certain "Ends of Man." For it is not only sexual difference but all bodily functions that the analytic of *Dasein* disavows, particularly that involvement of sexuality with excremen-tal functions on which Freud generally insists (even if he restricts that general insistence). *Dasein* is allowed to have instinct, desire, even li-bido, but not to have a body, which helps to explain how concepts such as "desire" can become so disembodied as to be voided of any content. Still less is *Dasein* allowed to have, say, an anus, which in a carnally ironic way helps to explain why any objectifying or spatializing *technē* is out of the question for *Dasein* (and here the difference between hav-ing no content to void and no means of voiding mere content amounts to the same thing: the effacement of production). As Beckett's Molloy suggests, however, the lewd orifice may be the portal of our being af-ter all. Alternatively, as Freud has it, "The Early Christian Father's '*in-ter urinas et faeces nascimur*' [between urine and feces are we born] clings to sexual life and cannot be detached from it in spite of every effort at idealization" (*SE* 7:31).

Heidegger's project, despite its critique of the Platonic *eidos*, is nothing if not an effort at idealization, at repristinization, and one wonders how Freud's insistence not only on sexual etiology but on the way the ex-cremental clings to human sexual life may have figured in Heidegger's disgust on finally confronting psychoanalysis. In any case, Heidegger's reaction to Freud renders problematic the following effortless assertion, or assertion of effortlessness, from Derrida in *The Post Card:* "there are a thousand ways to settle affairs with Freud and Heidegger, between Freud and Heidegger. No matter, for it is done by itself, without one having to take the slightest initiative" (357). One might say that this operation is done by itself only when there is no matter, only when certain matters are excluded from consideration. Although Derrida criticizes "opportunistic assimilations," he also suggests that one should "avoid the decrees of incompatibility or of heterogeneity, of untranslatableness, between 'Freud' and 'Heidegger' [for] these decrees are always accompanied by a hierarchizing judgment" (*PC* 357). Thus, despite the fundamental incompatibility between the two thinkers that Heidegger (or perhaps Heidegger's body) registers, Derrida argues here against heterogeneity, attempting an effortless appropriation in which the difference between Freud and Heidegger is reduced to the same thing, in which the Freudian death-drive and the Heideggerian being-toward-death are, if not identical, at least identically indentured to the metaphysics of the proper.

> And if this alleged propriety . . . this notion of the immanence of death in life, if this familiar domesticity of death were nothing but a consoling belief? . . . And if the authenticity proper to *Dasein* as *Sein zum Tode* . . . were but the lure of a proximity, of a self-presence (Da) of the proper, even if in a form which would no longer be that of the subject, of consciousness, of the person, of man, of living substance? And if it were precisely the *poem*, the poetic itself, this death which is immanent and proper to life? A great narrative poem, the only story that one always tells oneself, that one addresses to oneself, the poetic of the proper as reconciliation, consolation, serenity? (*PC* 363)

Ned Lukacher suggests that such passages from *The Post Card* indicate "Derrida's strategic appropriation of Freud as the figure through whom Derrida is better able to think his own 'correspondence' to Heidegger" and that they make explicit "the strategic role that Freud has always played for Derrida in triangulating his own relation to Heidegger" ("Writing on Ashes" 129). At the risk of making a hierarchizing judgment, I again suggest that in Derrida's strategic correspondence with Heidegger certain matters from Freud must be left out if the letter is to reach its dest(a)ination. I have suggested that Derrida's retention of Heidegger is coterminous with his own devaluations of the marks of sexual difference and of the "regional, periodic, peripheral, secondary, and dependent" characteristics that according to Derrida have been logocentrically attributed to writing. How, then, does Derrida's hold on Heidegger—which I read as being in structural solidarity with Heidegger's own effacement of the question of bodily production—figure not only into Derrida's unease with a certain psychoanalysis but also into his theory of a phallogocentric repression of writing?

I do not intend an extensive rehearsal of that theory. Simply put, for Derrida the word *writing* refers to all that is not speech, and speech is what properly guarantees the speaking subject's proximity to itself: speech is the very breath of Being determined as pure self-presence, and writing is what always already disrupts that determination. As Derrida writes in *Of Grammatology*, "What writing itself . . . betrays, is life. It menaces at once the breath, the spirit, and history as the spirit's relationship with itself. It is their end, their finitude, their paralysis. Cutting breath short, sterilizing or immobilizing spiritual creation in the repetition of the letter . . . [writing] is the principle of death and of difference in the becoming of being" (25).

What interests me here, however, is not as much what writing is for Derrida as what it is not. Just as writing is not presence, is not the speech that guarantees self-presence, so writing also appears not to be what Derrida calls "writing in the narrow sense" (*OG* 167). In fact, it seems to be anything but such a narrowly sensual appearance. In "Differance," for example, Derrida writes of "a sort of inscription *prior* to writing, a protowriting without a present origin" (*SP* 146; emphasis added). In *A World of Difference* Barbara Johnson comments that in Derrida "'speech' stands for the privilege accorded to meaning as immediacy, unity, identity, truth, and presence, while 'writing' stands for the devalued functions of distance, difference, dissimulation, and deferment." Johnson also writes, however, that "deconstruction *both* appears to grant to writing the priority traditionally assigned to speech *and* redefines 'writing' as *differance* (difference/deferment) so that it can no longer simply mean 'marks on a page'" (13). Also writing about the appearance of a priority granted to a writing that somehow never simply or merely appears, Gayatri Spivak, in her introduction to *Of Grammatology*, writes that for Derrida, the name *writing*, or *archi-écriture*, in its broadest sense refers to what Derrida calls "trace-structure." Spivak says that "trace-structure, everything always already inhabited by the track of something that is not itself, questions presence-structure. . . . This presence of the trace and trace of the presence Derrida names 'archi-écriture'" (*OG* lxix). Spivak, however, who like Derrida is at pains to avoid the charge of naïve empiricism, goes on to point out that "the name 'writing' is given here to an entire structure of investigation, not merely to 'writing in the narrow sense,' graphic notation on tangible material" (lxix).

One might wonder what else besides a resistance to empiricism motivates this Derridean lift-off, this devaluation of the function of "mere" writing in the narrow sense, which is to say, the graphic, tangible, and material sense. For can it be anything but the unsublatable materiality of writing that makes it threatening to Being determined as pure self-presence? If, as Lacan has it, subjectivity is that which passes through the defiles of signification, the materiality of signification is what ensures that those defiles are narrow—perhaps, as with Hegel, as narrow as a urethra—and that there is always something about them of *defilement*. By insisting that the name "writing" does not refer to "mere" writing in the narrow sense, by pointing to this difference between Writing and writing, does Derrida not reproduce once again the Heideggerian ontic/ontological difference between Being and mere beings, between appearing and mere appearance, and efface the abject corporeality of the signifier? Is not the recourse to the notion of the "mere" one of the marks of this somatophobic repression, particularly considering the proximity of the word *mere* both to *la mère* and to *merde?* To note this proximity is not simply to make a translinguistic pun at maternity's expense: as I have attempted to show, the anxieties about *la mère* as the *site* for the production of the body and about *merde* as the disturbing sight of one of the body's productions inhabit the very heart of the fear of "mere" writing. Without the relation of writing to the abject production(s) of the body, writing itself would have never been subjected to a repression.

Derrida himself is hardly unaware of this abject relation. In "Freud and the Scene of Writing," for example, Derrida quickly refers to and then leaves behind the notion of "the body of the written trace . . . as servile matter or excrement" (*WD* 197). In a brief footnote in *Positions* he makes a fleeting reference to "what Freud says about the well-known relationship mother/matter" and then goes on to speak of a "written concatenation, a play of substitution of differential marks that relate matter also to writing, to the remainder, to death, to the phallus, to excrement, to the infant, to semen, etc., or at least to everything in this that is not subject to the *relève* [Hegelian *Aufhebung*]" (106). Finally, in *Dissemination*, in his discussion of the problem of Hegel's prefaces, Derrida asks:

> But if something were to remain of the prolegemenon once inscribed and interwoven, something that would not allow itself to be sublated in the course of the philosophical presentation, would that some-

thing necessarily take the form of that which *falls away?* And what about such a fall? Couldn't it be read otherwise than as the excrement of philosophical essentiality—not in order to sublate it back into the latter, of course, but in order to learn to take it differently into account? (11)

My point, then, is certainly *not* that Derrida is not cognizant of these matters—his cognizance is nothing less than a condition of possibility for everything I have said thus far. But whereas I want to read "that which falls away" precisely as "the excrement of philosophical essentiality" in order to account for it differently than Derrida has done—in order, that is, to interrogate the construction of hegemonic masculinity and its abjection of the (m)other—Derrida introduces such abject materiality only and finally to subject it to a certain marginalization that is itself indentured to a Heideggerian distinction between writing in the narrow sense and writing as *archi-écriture.* This distinction not only serves to secure the latter from simply meaning the former; it may also regulate the substitutive play of these abjectly differential marks, establishing a certain discrete autonomy between them in their concatenation. Derrida, that is, uses a certain amount of discretion when it comes to excretions and secretions.[23]

To examine this discretion more closely, I return to the question of Derrida's relationship to psychoanalysis. Although Derrida insists that "despite appearances, the deconstruction of logocentrism is not a psychoanalysis of philosophy" (*WD* 196), he has also suggested, in what is probably a lesser-known proclamation, that "there is always something sexual at stake in the resistance to deconstruction" ("Women in the Beehive" 196). These two statements engage each other in an anxious contradiction, the former disavowing any role for psychoanalysis in the project of deconstruction, and the latter, with its emphasis on resistance and/of sexuality, indicating the extent to which deconstruction can be considered indentured to psychoanalytically motivated inquiry. Commenting on the first statement, Stephen Melville writes that "'appearances' here [in Derrida] are persistent and, in the end, constitutive; they cannot be simply or finally put aside, and psychoanalysis has become one of the most insistent references in Derrida's writing" (*Philosophy beside Itself* 85). Obviously I concur with Melville. But I argue that Freud's writing is constitutive for Derrida not in the end but in the beginning.

Speech and Phenomena is near that beginning, published at the same time (1967) as "Freud and the Scene of Writing" but foreclosing on any reference to Freud within its own scene (I am referring here to the main essay on Husserl and not to the appended essay "Differance," which does mention Freud). Freud, in fact, stands to *Speech and Phenomena* as Derrida says Nietzsche does to *Beyond the Pleasure Principle*, that is, as an insistently present absence, a disavowed debt. There is no direct reference to Freud in the title essay of *Speech and Phenomena*, and the only indirect reference is negative: "In the last analysis, what is at stake is indeed the privilege of the actual present, the now. This conflict . . . is between philosophy, which is always a philosophy of presence, and a meditation on nonpresence—which is not perforce . . . a theory of nonpresence *qua* unconsciousness" (*SP* 63). This is only to insist again that deconstruction, as a meditation on nonpresence, is not a psychoanalysis of philosophy. If there is always something sexual at stake in the resistance to deconstruction, however, then there is also something sexual at stake in the privilege philosophy grants to the actual present. Derrida will grant that a theory of nonpresence qua unconsciousness is a condition of possibility for deconstruction as a meditation on nonpresence. If *The Post Card* is any indication, however, Derrida places Nietzsche not only before but beyond Freud, taking the will to power as the true "beyond" of *Beyond the Pleasure Principle*. In a sense, then, the will to power would also be beyond whatever sexuality seems to be generally at stake in Freud. Both "the strong appeal of powerlessness" ("Rectum" 217) that Bersani posits as inherent to sexuality, however, and the excre-mentality that Freud says clings to sexual life despite all efforts at idealization must cling to the will to power as well; indeed, a will to power and a will to idealization might be considered much the same gesture.[24] To what extent, then, does Derrida's Heideggerian appropriation of Freud constitute an effort at idealization, repristinization, an attempt to shake off these clinging matters?

In *Speech and Phenomena* Derrida's task is to examine Husserl's hierarchical distinction between "expression" (*Ausdruck*) and "indication" (*Anzeichen*) as opposing modalities of signification. For Husserl, says Derrida, expression is a matter of pure intention. Expressions are "signs which 'want to say,' which 'mean'" (*SP* 32). "Ex-pression is exteriorization," but it is a significatory mode of exteriorization in which everything comes out as intended, that is, ideally. Expression "imparts to a certain outside a sense which is first found in a certain inside. . . . [But] the outside is neither nature, nor the world, nor a real exterior relative to consciousness. . . . The meaning intends an outside which is that of an ideal ob-ject" (32). Thus, writes Derrida,

> Expression is a voluntary exteriorization; it is meant, conscious through and through, and intentional. There is no expression with-

out the intention of a subject animating the sign. . . . In indication [on the other hand] the animation has two limits: the body of the sign, which is not merely a breath, and that which is indicated, an existence in the world. In expression the intention is absolutely explicit because it animates a voice which may remain entirely internal and because the expressed is a meaning, that is, an ideality "existing" nowhere in the world. (33)

Expressive meaning, that is, means only what it means to mean. There can be no involuntary or unintentional expression (there cannot, for instance, be any "nocturnal expressions"). Moreover, expression carries out this dry dream of "voluntaristic metaphysics" (34) all by itself, without any outside assistance. Indicative signs, however, depend on an externality that is really out there: they depend on "the body of the sign" to indicate and on an "existence in the world" to be indicated. Expression forecloses on that dependence. Expressive meaning "would isolate the concentrated purity of its *ex-pressiveness* just at that moment when the relation to a certain outside is suspended" (22). The suspension of the relation to an outside is the reduction of indication, and here Derrida is quite clear about what is thereby reduced:

Everything that escapes the pure spiritual intention, the pure animation by *Geist*, that is the will, is excluded from meaning and thus from expression. What is excluded is, for example, facial expressions, gestures, the whole of the body, and the mundane register, in a word, the whole of the visible and spatial as such. As such: that is, insofar as they are not worked over by *Geist*, by the will. . . . The opposition between body and soul is not only at the center of this doctrine of signification, it is confirmed by it; and, as has always been at bottom the case in philosophy, it depends upon an interpretation of language. Visibility and spatiality as such could only destroy the self-presence of will and spiritual animation which opens up discourse. *They are literally the death of that self-presence.* (35)

The notion that visibility and spatiality as such literalize or materialize the death of expressive self-presence allows Derrida to suggest that "indicative language" is simply "another name for the relation with death" (40). Husserl's reduction of indication, then, not only involves the exclusion of facial expressions (recall Bataille's messy evolutionary theories here), gestures, and the whole of the body; in its broadest sense the reduction of indication is the reduction of the relation with death. Expression, then, would be that which masters or escapes—or imagines itself as having mastered or escaped—the relation with death. The fact that only death itself escapes a relation to death indicates that being-death is the paradigm for expression's mastery of indication.

This language is familiar for good reason. If we can say that expression's reduction of indication, and hence of the relation with death, actually reduces an unpleasurable tension arising from a feeling of dependence or helpless passivity in relation to an exteriority outside of conscious, intentional control—the masterfully independent escape of the mundane register of the mere—then Derrida's debt to *Beyond the Pleasure Principle* becomes obvious. Freud's distinction between pleasure and unpleasure, his analysis of the way the former attempts to reduce the latter, and his conjecture that this attempted reduction is carried out in the interests of escaping an improper, unintentional, premature, and involuntary relation with death all serve as conditions of possibility for Derrida's critique of Husserl and his deployment of expression and indication in *Speech and Phenomena*. Derrida's debt to Freud, and to Freud's hypothesis that the child presents himself with his own independent mastery through the repetitive manipulation of the spool in the *fort-da* game, becomes apparent, for example, when Derrida discloses how expressive mastery as self-presence constructs itself through the pure intention of an idealizing repetition: "The presence-of-the-present," he writes, "is derived from repetition and not the reverse" (*SP* 52).

> But this ideality, which is but another name for the permanence of the same and the possibility of its repetition, *does not exist* in the world, and it does not come from another world; it depends entirely on the possibility of acts of repetition. It is constituted by this possibility. Its "being" is proportionate to the power of repetition; absolute ideality is the correlate of a possibility of indefinite repetition. It could therefore be said that being is determined by Husserl as ideality, that is, as repetition. . . . And this determination of being as ideality is properly a *valuation*, an ethico-theoretical act that revives the decision that founded philosophy in its Platonic form. (52–53)

Ideality effects itself, presents itself with itself, by virtue of repetition. Repetition in turn enacts itself through re-presentation. If repetition initially *depends* on the presentation and re-presentation of an object, it becomes independent of both the object and of representation by coming, instead, to be dependent only and entirely on its own acts of repetition. The idealized act of repetition forgets or effaces the representation of the object and thereby establishes itself as an ideality that forgets or effaces its origin in representation.

If, however, Derrida seems to be launching a critique of ideality in the name, so to speak, of the mundane register of represented objects—visibility and spatiality as such, the whole of the body, or perhaps even that bodily hole through which all mere beings are materialized—this appearance is finally deceptive. For when Derrida asserts this ideality to be a valuation that revives the decision that founds philosophy in its Platonic form, he discloses his own Heideggerian desire to get the jump on the ethico-theoretical determination of value. He critiques ideality, I submit, not so much for having forgotten its origin in repetition/representation but rather for having had repetition/representation as its nonoriginary origin in the first place. For Derrida, as for Heidegger, an ideality that is no more than an effect of representation is not ideal enough. If Derrida wants to interrupt "the circulation that transforms into an origin what is actually an after-effect of meaning" (*D* 21), it is in order to get back behind that circulation rather than to inscribe the mere aftereffect differently. Thus Derrida's Heideggerian destruction of metaphysics—to the extent that it remains Heideggerian, to the extent that Derrida *repeats* Heidegger (a repetition no longer dependent on the history of the empirical object and thus immune from any splash caused by that object's blunderous *Durchfall?*)—cannot be thought as being carried out in the name of something resembling a materialism (base, heterological, or historical). Despite certain appearances of Derrida's floating downstream toward the materiality of, say, mere writing in the narrow sense, his most fundamental gesture is to jump back upstream of the ideality that had imagined itself as the pure and prophylactically secured source of that materiality. Derrida sends himself down the river, to be sure, and at times he even gets his letter dirty and wet, but he does so only in the "Heideggerian *hope*" (*SP* 159) of finally being able to shake off those murky, troubled waters. As Drucilla Cornell puts it, "Deconstruction reminds us that we might yet fly away; it may not be our fate to forever 'sink into the same old shit'" (*Beyond Accomodation* 202).[25]

In *Of Grammatology* Derrida writes about two Hegels, one who was "the last philosopher of the book" and another who was "the first thinker of writing" (26). In my discussion of Hegel I tried to show how one Hegel had a problem with the other vis-à-vis the question of "the status of representation in language" (*SP* 49) and offered a pissy interpretation of that problematic. We might also speak of two Freuds, one who domesticates his discoveries and another who enables a critique of all domestication, one who consolidates gendered identities and another who exposes the tenuous fragility of all consolidation, one of Oedipus and castration and another who insists on a certain excrementality that clings to sexual life despite all efforts at idealization (with Oedipus and castration as the ideally heterosexualizing efforts within psychoanalysis itself). If one Freud forgets the other by failing, say, to recognize the anal redistribution subtending and subverting the inauguration of mastery in the *fort-da* (and the status of woman in this warfare), then Derrida's forgetting of Freud, and of the insistent and clinging excrementality of the Freudian corpus, raises Freud's own forgetting to the second power: Derrida, establishing his distance from the one Freud, redoubles the somatophobic, dysgraphic gesture by which that one Freud forgot the other. If I go on to speak here of two Derridas (and in the next chapter, of two Joyces, "paternal" as opposed to "risky"), it is only to indicate and return to that split that I argue haunts all hegemonically masculinized writing and that all such writing attempts to conceal, refuses to see—a split between the intentional and expressive auto-affection of orgasm and the always excrementalizable (di)visibility indicated by ejaculation.

Auto-affection is one of the major tropes of *Speech and Phenomena,* where Derrida begins to make the connections between the solitary voice and the solitary vice of masturbation, which he will handle further regarding Rousseau in "That Dangerous Supplement" in *Of Grammatology.* Derrida links expression with an auto-affective voice, with "A Voice That Keeps Silence," that "does not risk death in the body of a signifier that is given over to the world and the visibility of space" (*SP* 77–78), with "the absolute silence of self-relationship" (69), and to a "solitary discourse" in which the subject "manifests nothing to himself" (48). He writes that in expression

> this immediate repetition is a reproduction of pure auto-affection without the help of anything external. This possibility of reproduction . . . *gives itself out* as the phenomenon of a mastery or limitless power over the signifier. . . . Ideally, in the teleological essence of speech, it would then be possible for the signifier to be in absolute proximity to the signified aimed at in intuition and governing the meaning. The signifier would become perfectly diaphanous due to the absolute proximity to the signified. This proximity is broken when, instead of hearing myself speak, I see myself write or gesture. (80)

This purely diaphanous, auto-affective self-proximity is broken by seeing rather than by hearing because "in phenomenological interiority, hearing oneself and seeing oneself are two radically different orders of self-relation" (76). What subtends this masculine phenomenological interiority, however, is that for the male, hearing or feeling oneself come and seeing oneself ejaculate are two radically different orders of self-relation, and Derrida to a great extent occludes the specific corporeality of this sub-tension by dematerializing it into a polemic of language against itself. To be sure, this sub-tension always involves "the status of representation in language"; the culturally determined status of representation in language helps to make the whole question of what comes out of the male body problematic. Early on in *Speech and Phenomena*, however, Derrida writes the following: "It is at the price of this war of language against itself that the sense and question of its origin will be thinkable. This war is obviously not one war among others. A polemic for the possibility of sense and world, it takes place in this *difference*, which . . . cannot reside in the world but only in language, in the transcendental disquietude of language" (14). In this remark Derrida forecloses in advance on a consideration of the material effects of the disquietude he describes. He exchanges the closure of the transcendental signified for the endlessly differing/deferring opening of a transcendental unrest but remains transcendental just the same. From the vantage of a Heideggerian/linguistic *polemos* that is not merely one war among others, Derrida considers the problem of the status of representation in language in a way that cannot adequately consider the status of others in this linguistic warfare, the fact that there are both casualties and causalities that lie outside the text.[26]

Derrida writes that in speech, "the subject does not have to pass forth beyond himself to be immediately [auto-]affected by his expressive activity. My words are 'alive' because they seem not to leave me: not to fall outside me, outside my breath, at a visible distance; not to cease to belong to me, to be at my disposition 'without further props'" (*SP* 76). Derrida puts "without further props" in quotation marks to indicate that the notion of no further or prior props is illusory—representation always comes first, immediacy is derived. As I have shown, however, Irigary is more insistently specific than Derrida about what or who props up masculine phenomenological speculative interiority. Here I might also establish a greater specificity by suggesting that the proximity that keeps words alive in speech as auto-affective expression functions in much the same way as the proximity of masculinity to itself established in the money shots of hard-core porn. In those compulsively repetitive choreographies the actress's task is precisely to prop up masculinity and assuage masculine anxiety by preventing a change in value, keeping the externalized semen alive, keeping what falls outside from becoming mere moribund exteriority, from turning into the same old shit. Positioned as hyperfetishized surface and receptacle, the actress's body, breasts, voice, mouth, and facial expressions are deployed to stage an appearance that assures the male actor and viewer that the appearing of masculine essence is not just squirting out into the void—which is certainly where that essence would end up if the surface were to suddenly withdraw from the frame and thus open up the abyss. Secured within that frame, she lets him see (express) himself while looking at (indicating) something other (it/her, writing/surface) and lets him think that he is looking at (indicating) something other while seeing (expressing) only himself.

One of the questions, then, of a carnally ironic and heterologically materialist deconstruction—one that attempts to stay downstream of metaphysics, neither withdrawing from representation nor withdrawn from that withdrawal—would be whether the money shot might be posited as a sort of ludicrously paradigmatic instance of modernity itself as a crisis in the frame of masculinist reference, the male modernist "scene of writing" par excellence. How, for instance, might this question allow us to reinscribe Heidegger's anxiety about modernity as the Being-forgetful age of the world picture—an anguish about appearance, representation, and technology that, still within the history of a metaphysics bent on keeping the essential invisible, emerges precisely during the first century when that essence can be put at the disposal of a techno-representational apparatus, can be subjected to another's gaze through photographic, cinematographic, and now videographic mass production? Is the hegemonic male anxiety about modernity represented here by Heidegger inextricable from an anxiety of production exacerbated not only by mechanical reproduction, and the corresponding loss of the aura, but by social, cultural, and political movements by which women and others attempt to step outside the Euro-phallogocentric frame? After all, does Derrida not give modernity the auto-affective name of an archmasturbator by referring to it as "The Age of Rousseau?" And is not part of Rousseau's supplementary "problem" the fact that "it is at the moment when the mother disappears that substitution becomes possible and necessary," so that "the play of maternal presence or absence [fort-da], this alteration of perception and imagination must correspond to an organization of space" (OG 152–53; my interpolation)? Do we not see here again a figuration of modernity as an unpleasurable tension, an anguished dependence, corresponding on the one hand to a disappearance of the mother that we might also refer to as a disenframing of the feminine and thus on the other to a felt need for an increasingly masterful psychic organization of a maternally coded space? Does not Rousseau's Emile lament the "evil" fact that "'women have ceased [fort] to be mothers, they do not and will not return [da] to their duty,'" thus figuring modernity as, in Derrida's words, "a certain absence . . . of a certain sort of mother" (OG 152)?

Here I would like to recall Irigaray's discussion of the anal redistribution subtending the active/passive polarity, to remember Irigaray's speculation about the abject status of woman-as-(m)other in this redistribution, and to consider two references to that polarity in Derrida. In "Differance," for example, Derrida writes:

> Here in the usage of our language we must consider that the ending -*ance* is undecided between active and passive. And we shall see why what is designated by "differance" is neither simply active nor simply passive, that it announces or rather recalls something like the middle voice, that it speaks of an operation which is not an operation, which cannot be thought of either as a passion or as an action of a subject upon an object, as starting from an agent or from a patient, or on the basis of, or in view of, any of these *terms*. But philosophy has perhaps commenced by distributing the middle voice, expressing a certain intransitive-ness, into the active and passive voice, and has itself been constituted in this repression. (*SP* 137)

Irigaray would certainly agree that philosophy commences and constitutes itself by virtue of a repression that redistributes into active and passive what Derrida here calls the middle voice. In addition, Kristeva would have little trouble accepting the middle voice as related to a semiotic or genotextual articulation of the abject. What remains conspicuous in Derrida's formulation, however, is its disembodiment of both that voice and its redistribution, the way it voids them of any content, particularly that to which Irigaray has drawn our attention. This disembodiment becomes even more conspicuous in "That Dangerous Supplement," where Derrida writes, "To speak of the writing of Rousseau is to try to recognize what *escapes* these categories of passivity and activity" (*OG* 150; emphasis added).

But what are the terms of this escape for Derrida, particularly in regard to the connection he draws between writing and masturbation as dangerously supplementary operations? Derrida writes, "it is a question of the imaginary. The supplement [of masturbation] that 'cheats' maternal 'nature' operates as writing, and as writing it is dangerous to life. This danger is that of the image. Just as writing opens the crisis of the living speech in terms of its 'image,' its painting or its representation, so onanism announces the ruin of vitality in terms of imaginary seductions" (151). Derrida then goes on to quote Rousseau: "'This vice, which shame and timidity find so convenient, possesses . . . a great attraction for lively imaginations—that of being able to dispose of the whole sex as they desire . . .'" (151). Again, Derrida's formulation is nothing less than a condition of possibility for the entire theory of productive anxiety I have been attempting to produce here. Throughout his discussion of the relation of Rousseau's writing to his onanism, however, Derrida retains his proximity to the latter only as a question of imaginary seductions without also raising the question of imaginary—that is, divisibilized—secretions. Figuring masturbation only as an indulgence in a supplementary chain of mental substitutions, as the auto-affective activity of "summoning absent beauties" (153), Derrida escapes the question of the merely passive remains of that activity. The "danger" is not only that of the beautiful image; the "ruin" is not only in terms of imaginary seductions. The "irremediable loss" that the male "vital substance" undergoes involves its own transformation into a divisible image that then corresponds to that of the "whole sex" that is to be disposed of. Thus, for the masterfully active masturbator/writer, disposing of the whole sex and disposing of the visible, passive trace of one's own activity become the same imaginary problematic, an erasure of difference that is the function of anxiety about the status of woman in the production(s) of the male body, a fear of being put at the disposal of the merely other.

It seems, however, that these matters are exorbitant to Derrida's method. Outside of one reference to an "irremediable loss of the vital substance" (*OG* 151), a reckoning with sperm fluid, as Irigaray puts it, remains in suspension; there is in Derrida's expression of masturbation no specific indication of semen, of any passively material residue left behind by the auto-affective act. Just as he tidied up the impure expenditure of Bataille's apish anus, so too here Derrida seems to want to avoid getting anything of Rousseau's on him: the bodily in Rousseau is what deconstruction never touched. It is not so much that Derrida cannot handle abjection; rather, the moribund exteriority of visibilized semen does not answer to Derrida's description of the purely mental supplement, adds itself onto nothing, does not make up for any lack. This is why Derrida, faced with the abject operation of writing, prefers *différance* as a bottomless "operation which is not an operation." This is why for Derrida mere writing in the narrow sense can be only "one of the representatives of a the trace in general" but not "the trace itself," because *"The trace itself does not exist"* (167). Again, a certain question of gender politics, of the mark of sexual difference, is being foreclosed here. Furthermore, again despite certain appearances, my reading of this foreclosure is not contradicted by *Dissemination*, where Derrida does indicate semen quite heavily, as for example when he writes:

> Writing and speech have thus become two different species, or values, of the trace. One, writing is a lost trace, a nonviable seed, everything in sperm that overflows wastefully, a force wandering out-

side the domain of life, incapable of engendering anything, of pick-
ing itself up, of regenerating itself. On the opposite side, living speech
makes its capital bear fruit and does not divert its seminal potency
toward indulgence in pleasures without paternity. In its seminar, in
its seminary, it is in conformity with the law. (152)

At the same time, however, Derrida excuses himself from considering
the status of woman or of the (m)other within or without this law: "It
is all about father and sons, about bastards unaided by an public assistance, about glorious, legitimate sons, about inheritance, sperm, ste-
rility. Nothing is said of the mother, but this will not be held against
us" (143). In fact, what Derrida does have to say goes by way of appropriation: "As for 'feminine sexuality' . . . dissemination reads, if one
looks closely, as a sort of womb" (49 n.47). Could we not read a sort
of womb envy in this speculation that looks closely but not at itself,
an envy of the womb not for its reproductive capacities, but rather—
and quite conspicuously in regard to the material question of dissemination—for the capacity of that sex which is not one for a *jouissance*
without visibilized or perceptible remains? Perhaps this is less womb
envy than clitoris envy, after all. Surely many must have it.

What, then, does Derrida want? In "Differance" he writes, "we must
think through, without contradiction, or at least without granting any
pertinence to such contradiction, what is perceptible and imperceptible about the trace. The 'matinal trace' of difference is lost in an irretrievable invisibility" (*SP* 157). What I have been attempting here is
to grant a greater pertinence to this contradiction between the perceptible and the imperceptible, to sully the quite pure expenditure of an
infinitely irretrievable invisibility by focusing on the clinging visibility
of corporeal production, and to suggest that the repression of this visibility, vis-à-vis the mastery of representation in writing, might have
some bearing on the question of the politics of gender. Derrida, insofar as he repeats and retains Heidegger, appears to want to get upstream
of these matters, upstream of mere writing and the mere subjectivity
that remains as its effect. His recourse to contradiction without contradiction takes place in the midst of one of the more pronounced instances in "Differance" of his repetition/retention of Heidegger. If contradiction is a site of anxiety, if abjection is above all ambiguity, can
contradiction without contradiction be read as an anxiety without
anxiety, an abjection without the abject? Heidegger's desire to get to
that pointless point prior to metaphysics and modernity can be read
as a function of a reactionary nostalgia. Derrida, on the other hand,
wants a Heideggerianism without nostalgia (and thus, presumably,
without the political liability of Heidegger's blunderous *Durchfall* into

fascism). As Rorty contends, however, Heidegger's thought "is nostalgic or nothing" (*Contigency* 122). Does this mean that Derrida wants nothing? What would it mean to want nothing? Being irretrievably invisible, after all, what could a desire without desire look like? Lacan addresses similar questions when he writes, "What does *not wanting to desire* mean? The whole of analytic experience . . . shows us that not to want to desire and to desire are the same thing. To desire involves a defensive phase that makes it identical with not wanting to desire. Not wanting to desire is wanting not to desire" (*FFC* 235).

It is exactly this defensive phase that I have been attempting to examine here by theorizing a masculine anxiety of production. My thinking about this anxiety was first prodded by, among other things, this quotation from Lacan: "Ask the writer about the anxiety that he experiences when faced by the blank sheet of paper, and he will tell you who *is* the turd of his phantasy" (*É* 315). If in attempting to trace just who the turd of this fantasy thinks he is, to suggest the extent of his phantasmatic domain and the nature of its consequences, I bring this chapter to a close by giving the last word to Lacan, perhaps this will not be held against me: "Who does not know from experience that it is possible not to want to ejaculate? . . . Who does not know that one may not wish to think?—the entire universal college of professors is there as evidence" (*FFC* 234).

5

Not a Nice Production: Anal Joyce

A Phallus Playing Dead

Liquidation, liquefaction, of both feminine and masculine, in the flow of style, halting at no one identity—whether personal, ideological, or sexual—but knowing them all. . . . Sick, Joyce? Or esoteric? Or post-modern? Questions that inevitably pose themselves, however non-normative our reading might desire to be. Personally, I would reply that, even in their most abstruse [details], his symptom and his obscurity bring into relief the objects of post-modernism's critical interrogation: identification, representation.
—Julia Kristeva, "Joyce 'the Gracehopper'"

The danger is in the neatness of identifications.
—Samuel Beckett, *Our Exagmination round His Factification for the Incamination of Work in Progress*

Whence it is a slopperish matter, given the wet and low visibility (since in this scherzarade of one's thousand one nightinesses that sword of certainty which would indentifide the body never falls) to idendifine the individuone.
—James Joyce, *Finnegans Wake*

In *Powers of Horror* Kristeva writes of abjection as that "which modernity has learned to repress, dodge, or fake" (26). H. G. Wells, in an early review of Joyce's *Portrait of the Artist as a Young Man*, makes his famous complaint about Joyce's "cloacal obsession" and writes that Joyce "would bring back into the general picture of life aspects which modern drainage and modern decorum have taken out of ordinary intercourse and conversation."[1] Joyce privately concurred with Wells's assessment.[2] Moreover, this cloacal obsession, which disturbed not only Wells's sense of modern decorum but Ezra Pound's "gallic preference for Phallus" (*Pound/Joyce* 158), was one that Joyce never relinquished.[3] From the beginning of his career, Joyce was well aware that this obsession bore an integral relation to his own writing practice: as early as 1905, in a letter to Grant Richards concerning *Dubliners*, Joyce wrote of "the special odour of corruption which, I hope, floats over my stories" (*SL* 22).[4]

This corruptive Joycean hope is radically different from the Heideggerian hope to which Derrida refers at the end of "Differance." It also problematicizes Derrida's assertion that Joyce is "perhaps the most Hegelian of modern novelists" (*WD* 154).[5] As my previous discussion of Hegel suggests, Derrida's characterization is fundamentally incompatible with an appreciation of Joyce as perhaps the most abjection-friendly of modern novelists, who brings back into the general picture the general economy of writing itself, mobilizing the abjection that other male modernists—particularly those who embraced or leaned toward fascism—managed not only to repress, dodge, or fake but also and mostly to displace onto others.[6] As Joyce's contemporary Adrienne Monnier puts it, using language that adumbrates Bataille's and Kristeva's and that helps to mark Joyce as a precondition of much poststructuralist discourse, Joyce "chooses . . . that which has been sacrificed, shamed, cut off, mistreated—that which nobody had ever dared to present as it really was, that which had always been regarded as outside of the law, outside of love. Nothing to him appears useless or unworthy."[7] Joyce's writing situates itself in the abject space between identity and representation, desire and its satisfaction, anxiety and its assuagement, disrupting the masculine subject's assumption of a deadly symbolic mastery and revealing the way one version of hope might be subverted by another. To cite a beginning:

> There was no hope for him this time: it was the third stroke. Night after night I had passed the house (it was vacation time) and studied the lighted square of window: and night after night I had found it lighted in the same way, faintly and evenly. If he was dead, I thought, I would see the reflection of candles on the darkened blind for I knew that two candles must be set at the head of a corpse. He had often said to me: *I am not long for this world,* and I had thought his words idle. Now I knew they were true. Every night as I gazed up at the window I said softly to myself the word *paralysis*. It had always sounded strangely in my ears, like the word *gnomon* in the Euclid and the word *simony* in the Catechism. But now it sounded to me like the name of some maleficent and sinful being. It filled me with fear, and yet I longed to be nearer to it and to look upon its deadly work. (*DB* 9)

In her essay "Joyce: The (R)use of Writing" Hélène Cixous examines the opening of "The Sisters" to reveal the way it adumbrates the most subversive qualities of Joyce's later writing. She writes of a "plural hero" (perhaps a reference to HCE as the "Here Comes Everybody" of *Finnegans Wake*) and suggests that the first paragraph of *Dubliners* is a "scene of the decentering of the subject" in which "we shall grasp the first manifestation of the slide from One to the plural, from the disquieting plural of One, slipped between the narrator and the I subject, between the one and the other, between master of diction and master of interdiction" (16–17). To understand how the mastery of (inter)diction is subverted by the slip and slide of this passage, we can begin with the ambiguity of its last three words, "its deadly work." What does the pronoun refer to here? One has to trace backward through a series of neuter pronouns to arrive at a (possible) referent in the famous word *paralysis*, the trope that Joyce, in his own bid toward symbolic mastery, wanted to deploy against the homeostasis of Dublin: "I call the series *Dubliners* to betray the soul of that hemiplegia or paralysis which many consider a city" (*SL* 22). Does "deadly work" refer only to the state of paralysis, however, or even the word *paralysis?* What is deadly about the work of that word, and more important, for whom?

The motivation behind the deployment of the word *paralysis*—the effort, as Cixous writes, "to produce an effect of mastery" (19)—may initially be the same for Joyce as it is for his narrator in "The Sisters." Arguably, both utter the word in the attempt to gain mastery over the scene that is the object of their gaze, the scene that represents paralysis itself. For Joyce, that scene is Dublin, whereas for the narrator it is ostensibly the lighted square of the dying priest's window. Neither of these "texts" stays paralyzed, however, and Joyce's writing, even its most "scrupulous meanness" (*SL* 83), finally refuses the position of symbolic mastery and calls it radically into question. Similarly, the narrator's bid toward mastering the scene of the priest's dying by enouncing the word *paralysis* is disrupted, as I will show, by the very enunciation of that word. I submit that "its deadly work" refers not so much to the word *paralysis* as to the scene of its writing, that the deadly work is not paralysis but signification itself. What the narrator attempts to master here is his own enunciation of paralysis, the split between the subject of the enunciation and the paralyzed subject of the statement.

Cixous writes, "'*Its deadly work*': Thus it is the name which kills: the empire of the signifier which will subsequently be extended to the point of producing *Finnegans Wake*, infinitely mocking the conscientious control of the scriptor" (28). In "The Sisters" the narrator occupies the position of the scriptor whose conscious/conscientious control is mocked. The scene over which he desires control is the lighted square of the dying priest's window, which the narrator studies, in a sort of compulsive repetition, night after night. The figure who lies behind that window, Father Flynn, is marginalized from the symbolic order of which he—as priest, as Father—should be able to stand as guarantor. Not only dying but imbued with an aura of physical and spiritual corruption, Father Flynn is associated with simony, the selling of ecclesiastical offices; moreover, Joyce intended his paralysis to suggest general paresis, a syphilitic disorder of the central nervous system.[8] "There was something gone wrong with him"(*DB* 18); "There was something queer . . . there was something uncanny about him" (*DB* 9–10). The priest, in short, is abject, and the narrator's relationship to him is accordingly ambivalent. Although the narrator has a great deal of respect for this educator and symbol of authority who has told him stories about Napoleon and taught him "to pronounce Latin properly" (*DB* 13), he is both disturbed by and yet strangely drawn to the priest's corrupt corporeality, particularly his spittle-moist and snuff-stained mouth.

I will return to this disturbing orifice. For the moment, however, it is interesting to note the conspicuously liquidified terms with which the description of Flynn's snuff-taking calls attention to his lapsed and abject condition:

> It was always I who emptied the packet into his black snuff-box for his hands trembled too much to allow him to do this without *spilling* half the snuff about the floor. Even as he raised his large trembling hand to his nose little clouds of smoke *dribbled* through his fingers over the front of his coat. It may have been these constant *showers* of snuff which gave his ancient priestly garments their green faded look for the red handkerchief, blackened, as it always was, with the snuff-*stains* of a week, with which he tried to brush away the *fallen* grains, was quite inefficacious. (*DB* 12; emphasis added)

For the narrator, the name of the priest's abject condition, paralysis, takes on the deadly character of some maleficent and sinful being that he fears and yet to which he longs to be nearer. This mixture of loathing and desire adumbrates the devalued realms of didactic and pornographic art from which Stephen Dedalus, in *A Portrait*, will want to retreat, moving instead into the ideal stasis of purely esthetic emotion (a stasis that ironically resembles paralysis). Like Stephen, the narrator of "The Sisters" maintains his distance from his own improper desire for proximity. Using Lacan's distinction between the sign and the signifier—the sign "represents something for someone," whereas the signifier "is that which represents the subject for another signifier" (*FFC* 207)—we can say that the narrator positions between the abjection that the priest signifies and himself the scene of the lighted window, which he hopes will finally become the sign of the priest's death. Until the window does become a sign of death, however—until the narrator sees the reflection of two candles on the darkened blind—this scene remains rather a signifier of the priest's continual dying. That is, the scene remains a signifier that indicates a perpetual relation to death rather than a sign that expresses some (dead) thing for someone. The narrator, insofar as he desires that this signifier finally be converted into a sign, desires the priest's death. He wants to convert meaning into being, wants the still-living priest who continues to mean death to finally be dead. As Cixous writes, adopting the narrator's voice, "I cannot see him because he is not dead, because he is going to die. If he were dead I could see him; when he is dead, I shall see him: I want him to die so that I can see him; I want him to die" ("Joyce" 25).

Cixous's formulation suggests the extent to which a murderous will to mastery is implicated with the scopic drive, the will to see, to position another subject as the object of one's gaze, and to keep one's own subjectivity out of the general picture. In *James Joyce and the Politics of Desire* Suzette A. Henke suggests that "the vocabulary of prettiness and tidiness" that Father Flynn's sisters later use to describe his "beautiful corpse" "reduces the priest to an aesthetic object" and "allows them to admire the priest as a safely crystallized visual spectacle in a non-threatening, photographic tableau" (16). This crystallization into visual spectacle has already occurred in the story's first paragraph. Indeed, the scene of the lighted window that the narrator repetitively studies takes on the quality of a nearly photographic stasis, or to use Barthes's terms from *Camera Lucida*, a *studium*, the photographic field that one invests with one's "sovereign consciousness" (26). When the narrator gazes up at this *studium* and says the word *paralysis* softly to himself, he intends the word not simply as a caption registering the priest's condition. Rather, he issues the word as command. He orders the signifying scene to become a sign, attempts to make that which means paralysis be paralyzed, to paralyze in a sign the signifying movement of paralysis itself.

Such effort on the narrator's part is deadly work indeed, and he registers a guilty but liberatory pleasure once the dirty work is done: "I felt even annoyed at discovering in myself a sensation of freedom as if I had been freed from something by his death" (*DB* 12). It is, however, the narrator's own production of this "name that kills" that brings him closer to his own abjection and makes the work of signification deadly and dirty for him as well. To bend Barthes's terminology a bit, the soft enunciation of the word *paralysis* is the *punctum*—"sting, speck, cut, little hole" (*Camera Lucida* 27)—that rises out of the *studium*, pricks the narrator and disrupts his sovereign gaze. The *punctum* disturbs the sovereign, intentional, voluntaristic metaphysics of the *studium* as sign. It punctuates the narrator, draws him into that metonymic chain in which the signifier fails to resolve itself into a sign but continues to represent the subject for another signifier.

Only here the *punctum* rises not out of the *studium* but rather out of the "little hole" of the narrator's own mouth. He says the word softly, and its strange sound reminds him of *gnomon* and *simony*, two words whose murmuring, mellifluent semiotic qualities contrast with the harsh cacophony of the symbolic systems that contain them, Euclidian geometry and the Roman Catholic Catechism. That the narrator associates not the meaning but the sound of these words with sinful maleficence perhaps indicates an anxiety less about their meaning than about the way in which such soft murmuring language issues forth. Since "Stephen Dedalus" is also the name of a being who considers himself sinful and maleficent, we might note here Stephen's nightmarishly excremental vision in *A Portrait* of a hell filled with goatish creatures who "moved in slow circles, circling closer and closer to enclose, to enclose, soft language issuing from their lips, their long swishing tails besmeared with stale shite, thrusting upwards their terrific faces" (138). Later I examine more fully Stephen's vision, which is arguably a bad dream not only for Stephen but also for a high-modernist practice that stakes its ontology on diamondtine linguistic precision, on what Pound called the "clear hard prose" and "clarity of outline" (*Pound/Joyce* 27) of Joyce's writing in *Dubliners*. Here I note that the narrator of "The Sisters" also has a disturbing vision of a talking head:

> In the dark of my room I imagined that I saw again the heavy grey face of the paralytic. I drew the blankets over my head and tried to think of Christmas. But the grey face still followed me. It murmured; and I understood that it desired to confess something. I felt my soul receding into some pleasant and vicious region; and there again I found it waiting for me. It began to confess to me in a murmuring voice and I wondered why it smiled continually and why the lips were so moist with spittle. But then I remembered that it had died of paralysis and I felt that I too was smiling feebly as if to absolve the simoniac of his sin. (*DB* 11)

Here the narrator is haunted by the moist, murmuring, signifying mouth of the paralytic. It is exactly the priest's soft language, this brown-stained but continually smiling mouth, as well as his own feebly smiling implication in the priest's abjection, that the anxious narrator wants to paralyze with his killing word. He notes that when the priest smiled, "he used to uncover his big discoloured teeth and let his tongue lie upon his lower lip—a habit which had made me feel uneasy in the beginning of our acquaintance before I knew him well" (*DB* 13). We can perhaps better understand the root of the narrator's initial unease at this spectacle when we read Cixous's cryptic description of the priest's tongue as "a phallus playing dead" ("Joyce" 30). This phallus playing dead signifies death, indicates a relation to death, and does so in the form of a moist, inert object protruding from a corrupt orifice, assuming the phantasmatic shape of a fecal phallus, or to use Kristeva's term again, an "anal penis" (*PH* 71). And if the discolored teeth of this *anus dentata* were to bite down and sever that abject/object from its source? Here we might recall the two definitions of a *gnomon*, both "what is left of a parallelogram when a similar parallelogram containing one of its corners is removed" and "the name for the pointer on a sundial" (Gifford, *Joyce Annotated* 29). These definitions conflated, *gnomon* signifies a missing or mutilated pointer. In Joyce's passage, however, this sense of mutilation, of castration, is joined with or even overdetermined by an anxiety about "soft" language, about a malefi-cent/mellifluent collapse of oral and anal excorporation, which is articulated in both Stephen Dedalus's and the narrator's dreams. It is this anxiety of production, which is also an anxiety about his relation to death, his mastery of the work of death, that the narrator of "The Sisters" attempts to assuage in his compulsively repetitive enunciation or expression of the word *paralysis*—a repetition that enacts a murderous will to mastery and that is accompanied by the deployment of a relentlessly scopic drive. The narrator, that is, attempts to paralyze masterfully that which inscribes the possibility of his own paralysis. But the very act of enunciation calls this mastery into question, bringing the narrator into contact with his body's own abjection, its utter(ed) dismemberment, a dismemberment in which the uttered phantasmatically becomes a turd.

Kristeva asserts that "the anal penis is also the phallus with which infantile imagination provides the feminine sex" (*PH* 71). For an appreciation of Joyce's own fetishistic celebrations of the anal penis and his ample provisions of it to the feminine sex, one need look no further than the famous 1909 correspondence with Nora, the letters he and (presumably) she used as masturbatory aids during a period of separation. There, for example, Joyce writes: "Fuck me if you can squatting in the closet, with your clothes up, grunting like a young sow doing her dung, and a big fat dirty snaking thing coming slowly out of your backside" (*SL* 190); and "It must be a fearfully lecherous thing to see a girl with her clothes up frigging furiously at her cunt, to see her pretty white drawers pulled open behind and her bum sticking out and a fat brown thing stuck half-way out of her hole" (*SL* 191). Joyce was erotically invested in a quite literal and hopelessly non-Heideggerian materiality of the letter. For Joyce, *la mère* and *le merde* were both integral aspects of his appreciation of mere writing, of more writing; his hopes for the letter's destination were utterly dependent on its excess, its staining, its excess as staining, its being stained by the excess of the other: "Write the dirty words big and underline them and kiss them and hold them for a moment to your sweet hot cunt, darling, and also pull up your dress a moment and hold them under your dear little farting bum. Do *more* if you wish and send the letter then to me, my darling brown-arsed fuckbird" (*SL* 186). Also, in regard to the collapse of oral and anal excorporation that haunts his characters and erotically energizes his writing, we can note that Joyce uses the same word, *spluttering*, to describe both "the heavenly exciting filthy words" (*SL* 186) that he fondly remembers coming out of Nora's mouth and the "fat dirty farts" that he longed to hear "gush" from her "hole" (*SL* 185).

"Sick, Joyce?" Obviously, Joyce's abject/erotic enthusiasms can be aligned with such indications of his personal misogyny as his youthful announcement to his brother Stanislaus that "Woman is an animal that micturates once a day, defecates once a week, menstruates once a month, and parturates once a year."[9] Joyce can well be considered one of those infantile pornographers to whom Benoîte Groult refers as "old children who never left the pee-peedoodoo stage" ("Night Porters" 73). Joyce even exhibits a penchant for what the porn industry will later call the money shot: "The smallest things give me a great cockstand—a whorish movement of your mouth, a little brown stain on the seat of your white drawers, a sudden dirty word spluttered out by your wet lips, a sudden immodest noise made by you behind and then a bad smell slowly curling up out of your backside. At such moments I feel mad to do it in some filthy way . . . to fuck between your two rosy-tipped bubbies, to come on your face and squirt it over your hot cheeks and eyes, to stick it up between the cheeks of your rump and bugger you" (*SL* 184). This passage, however, follows a somewhat unorthodox trajectory, again collapsing orality and anality, whorish movements and brown stains, spluttering words and curling smells, all leading up to a blinding ejaculation destined to leave Nora bereft of any powers of speculation, allowing her only "to cluse her eyes and aiopen her oath and see what spice I may send her" (*FW* 165.4–5). This spatial delivery is then temporally followed by anal intercourse, however, as if to suggest that the money shot is not, at least in this case, the end of this spicy letter's story or the closure of its desire, a suggestion that contradicts the standard conceits of mainstream male pornography.

This is of course an overly generous reading on my part. Even if we argue that, to quote Karen Lawrence, "Joyce's texts unmask male anxieties of women's power" ("Joyce and Feminism" 241), we should not pretend that this unmasking is not also, inevitably, a reproduction of those very anxieties: "As Joyce's own dreams and letters attest, to expose the workings of male paranoia, desire, guilt, and ambivalence in one's fiction, is not necessarily to free one from the same feelings. Contending that Joyce exposes the workings of ideology and desire and subverts conventions is not the same as claiming that he completely transcends his own time. On the other hand, his scepticism of order, system, and style led to a radical critique of phallogocentrism" (242). Of course, a radical critique of phallogocentrism or patriarchy is not necessarily a conscientiously feminist project. As Frances Restuccia puts it in *Joyce and the Law of the Father*, Joyce's art may be "ultimately anti-patriarchal" (13), but Joyce himself remains "a fetishist, not a feminist" (175). The point here, however, is less Joyce's conscious attitudes than what Kristeva calls "a knowledge perhaps ignorant of itself as such but nonetheless assuredly at work, [of] the details of identification's mechanism" ("Gracehopper" 168).

My point in discussing so extensively Joyce's dirty correspondence with Nora, then, is that only the preeminently phallic mode of identificatory coherence that Joyce's writing constantly questions and struggles against would have allowed his writing to have left the "pee-pee-doodoo" stage, to have relinquished its fetishistic cloacal obsession. A subjectivity that retains a transgressive investment in the anal penis and provides it to the feminine sex may by that very gesture indicate, at least provisionally, a desire to let the desire of the other speak, to figure the other's body as an active site of production rather than as a mute and masterable object. If an investment in the slippery anal penis over and against the solidity of the phallus is what helps make possible "the slide from One to the plural" that Cixous says Joyce's first story signals, we might note that the story's title is not, after all, a masculine singular—"The Priest"—but rather a feminine plural—"The Sisters." Perhaps it is not only the (still-) signifying priest that the narrator wants to paralyze when, near the end of the story, surrounded by chattering women whose speech he considers tedious and garrulous, he holds fast to his own *studium*, his own hypostasized vision of the priest as a dead thing: "I knew that the old priest was lying still in his coffin as we had seen him, solemn and truculent in death, an idle chalice on his breast" (*DB* 18). Every *studium* has its *punctum*, however: "Eliza resumed:—Wide-awake and laughing-like to himself. . . . So then, of course, when they saw that, that made them think that there was something gone wrong with him"(*DB* 18).

So here the story ends with the narrator's final attempt to immobilize signification being disrupted by the endlessly punctuated/ing resumption of a feminine discourse, riddled with ellipses, a resuming that exhumes, bringing the priest's abjection quite disturbingly back to life. The text will not stay read. Paralysis will not stay paralyzed. The narrator's bid toward absolute mastery fades in the gaps of the speech of another who will not let being be.[10]

The Only Foolscap Available: Shem's Inkenstink

> In other words we must write dangerously: everything is inclined to flux and change nowadays and modern literature, to be valid, must express that flux.
>
> —Joyce, in Power, *Conversations with James Joyce*

> Yet is no body present here which was not there before. Only is order othered.
>
> —Joyce, *Finnegans Wake*

Joyce could only with great difficulty be considered an enemy of production in the sense intended by Brecht. Production, both in the Brechtian sense and in the sense I have been elaborating here, did not seem to make Joyce in any way uncomfortable; he did not seem at all afraid of what might come out. If there is a productive anxiety in or about the body of Joyce's writing, it must lie in what that writing interrogates, opens up, and works through.

Nowhere is that interrogative opening more evident than in that perpetually lapsing piece of "litteringture" (*FW* 570.18) called *Finnegans Wake*, a text that never ceases to insist on collapsing the distinction between "letter" and "litter" (*FW* 93.24), that metonymically presents itself as a urine-stained scrap of discarded writing rediscovered on a dungheap, and that finally shows more than simply its behind to the political father, as well as the behind *of* the political father—"How culious an epiphany" (*FW* 508.11)[11]—marking and remarking the Wolf-Man's blasphemous inspiration "God—shit," the Bataillean plunge of sacred enunciation into soiled enounced, as "a viridible goddinpotty" (*FW* 59.11–12). Troping Beckett's early essay on Joyce's work *en procès*, we might say that *Finnegans Wake* is not about a *Durchfall*, it is that

Durchfall itself—"due to a collupsus of his back promises, as others looked at it" (*FW* 5.27–28).[12] Is the rectum a grave? Is the pen a metaphorical penis? Is the pen(is) a metonymic anus? Joyce writes, "in gutter dispear I am taking up my pen toilet you know . . ." (Beckett, *Our Exagmination* n.p.).

In *James Joyce: Authorized Reader* Jean-Michel Rabaté comments on the "language of earse," the "ambiguities of the written word of anal production" (141) that pervade *Finnegans Wake*. Rabaté writes that "with this anal or analogical writing, endlessly multiplying the definitions that constitute the propriety of a language, [Joyce] frees the words from their frozen meanings; he thereby short-circuits the illusion that there can be a mastery over meaning, a mastery that would correspond to a fixed position of the subject in his discourse and in society" (144).[13] Of particular interest in this regard is the book's carnally ironic juxtaposition of Shem, the abject and temporalist penman who circulates in the text as errant litter(er), with his brother, Shaun, the logocentric, authoritarian, and spatialist postman—"My unchanging Word is sacred. The word is my Wife, to expose and expound, to vend and to velnerate" (*FW* 167.28–30)—who seeks to ensure that all letters reach their proper destinations. Joyce lets this juxtaposition serve a number of purposes in *Finnegans Wake*, perhaps most notably as a rejoinder to hostile, mainly class-based criticisms of *Ulysses* by Wyndham Lewis and Rebecca West, as well as to criticisms of *Finnegans Wake* itself from Joyce's brother Stanislaus.[14] My interest, however, is in Shem, his "bodily getup" (*FW* 169.11), his shifting position within a subversion of stable gender identity, and the relation of that subversion to what is perhaps the most explicit treatment in modern literature of male writing as abject bodily production.

"Shem is short for Shemus as Jem is joky for Jacob" (*FW* 169.1): so begins Shem's chapter, the "Jem" aligning Shem not only with Jim Joyce, or "Shame's Voice"—one of the many code names for Joyce that circulate in *Finnegans Wake*—but with "Jim the Penman," a famous Dublin forger. One of the book's many riddles follows, this one designated as "the first riddle of the universe," namely, "when is a man not a man?" (*FW* 170.4–5). Several "yungfries" attempt to answer and so win the prize, "a bitter-sweet crab, a little present from the past" (*FW* 170.7.8). But "All were wrong, so Shem himself, the doctator, took the cake, the correct solution being—all give up?—; when he is a—yours till the rending of the rocks,—Sham" (*FW* 170.21–24). Shem is then immediately designated as "a sham and a low sham," which suggests that Shem himself is therefore "not a man." The word *sham* relates to forgery, suggesting that a man is not a man when his shammed signature cannot authenticate his gendered identity in a fixed and stable representation. If identity is an effect of the flux of representation, however (and Joyce's writing indicates he was at some level aware of this), and if all writing is potentially sham(e)ful forgery and plagiarism, as *Finnegans Wake*—an "epical forged cheque" (*FW* 181.16) of "many piously forged palimpsests" (*FW* 182.2) or "the last word in stolentelling" (*FW* 424.35)—suggests throughout, then a man is never a man in any fixed, stable, and noncontradictory way, never really "constantly the same as and equal to himself and magnificently well worthy of any and all such universalisation" (*FW* 32.20–21). A man is never simply himself, never anything other than a sham.

Interestingly, however, Shem's shamminess, and hence his unmanliness, does not thereby locate him on the side of woman as the universal man's symmetrical other. Shem's sham(e)iness does not "castrate" or feminize him, does not situate him on either side of the alternatives "to be" or "to have." Rather, Shem's unmanly shamminess relates to an abject lowness, which contrasts with a masculinity on Shaun's part based less on phallic self-possession (cf. Blazes Boylan in *Ulysses*) than on purity: Shaun, as Jaun, is referred to as "Pure Yawn" (*FW* 474.1), as "the most purely human being that ever was called man" (*FW* 431.11). It is Shaun as Pure Yawn who vilifies Shem's "letter selfpenned to one's other" (*FW* 489.33–34) on the grounds that "it is not a nice production. It is a pinch of scribble, not wortha bottle of cabbis. Overdrawn! Puffedly offal tosh! . . . second class matter. The fuellest filth ever fired" (*FW* 419.31–36). Shaun the postman insists on "post purification" (*FW* 446.28) and prides himself on being completely "innocent of disseminating the foul emanation" (*FW* 425.10.11).

As for Shem's unmanly lowness, I let it speak for itself: "Shem was a sham and a low sham and his lowness creeped out first via foodstuffs" (*FW* 170.25–26). "O! the lowness of him was beneath all up to that sunk to" (*FW* 171.12–13). "Talk about lowness! Any dog's quantity of it visibly oozed out thickly from this dirty little blacking beetle" (*FW* 171.29–31). But "What . . . was this disinterestingly low human type, this Calumnious Column of Cloaxity . . . really at?" (*FW* 179.9–15). Writing, apparently, for "You see, chaps, it will trickle out, freaksily of course, but the tom and shorty of it is: he was in his bardic memory low" (*FW* 172.27–28). Shem resides at "The house O'Shea or O'Shame," also "known as the Haunted Inkbottle" (*FW* 182.30–31), and the content of this bottle, metonymically aligned with the resident himself, is described as "a stinksome inkenstink, quite puzzonal to the wrottel" (*FW* 183.6–7). Scattered or "persianly literatured" across the walls and "warpcd flooring" of this writer's "lair" (*FW* 183.9) are, among many other items, "burst loveletters . . . stickyback snaps . . . alphybettyformed verbage . . . fluefoul smut [a reference to the pornography that Stephen Dedalus hides in the fireplace flue in chapter 3 of *A Portrait*] . . . seedy ejaculations . . . spilt ink, blasphematory spits . . . worms of snot, toothsome pickings . . . [and] undeleted glete" (*FW* 183.11–36), this last word glossed as "gleet" by Roland McHugh and defined as "slimy matter; morbid discharge from urethra" (*Annotations to FW* 169).

As if this list were not enough to establish an abject, metonymic contiguity between Shem's lowly pens(un)manship and his body's sham(e)ful productions, there follows a description of how Shem "made synthetic ink and sensitive paper for his own end out of his wit's waste. You ask, in Sam Hill, how?" (*FW* 185.6–8). The description itself (*FW* 185.14–25) is in Latin. Here is McHugh's translation:

> First the artist, the eminent writer, without any shame or apology, pulled up his raincoat & undid his trousers & then drew himself close to the life-giving & allpowerful earth, with his buttocks bare as they were born. Weeping & groaning he relieved himself into his own hands. Then, unburdened of the black beast, & and sounding a trumpet, he put his own dung which he called his "downcastings" into an urn once used as an honoured mark of mourning. . . . He then passed water into it happily & melliflouously, while chanting in a loud voice the psalm which begins "My tongue is the pen of a scribe writing swiftly." Finally, from the foul dung mixed, as I have said, with the "sweetness of Irion" & baked & then exposed to the cold, he made himself an indelible ink. (*Annotations to FW* 185)

With this indelibly abject ink, this "no uncertain quantity of obscene matter not protected by copriright in the United Stars of Ourani or beeded and bedood and bedang and bedung to him" (*FW* 185.29–32), this ink which he makes not only for himself but of himself and as himself, as "squidself" (*FW* 186.6–7), Shem, "the first till last alshemist wrote over every square inch of the only foolscap available, his own body" (*FW* 185.34–36).

The "squirtscreen" of Latin camouflage notwithstanding, Shem's inkenstink, quite personal to the writer, represents one of the most explicit and explicitly valorized articulations in modern male literature of the contiguity between abject bodily production and the inscription of subjectivity. Moreover, Shem's ink-making passage is conspicuous in modernist male writing in that it confronts the anxiety of production without the usual mainstream displacement of that anxiety onto a devalued, feminized other. Shem's sham(e)ful unmanliness does not correspond to a symmetrical feminization, to a castration that can be teleologically narrativized, and so his mode of abjection is not one in which the other becomes shit. Ma(r)king himself as indelible ink, Shem writes (on) his own male body, the only foolscap available, thus remarking the ethical unavailability of other bodies as scenes of writing or inscription and so leaving open the discursive and political space in which those bodies might speak or write their own anxieties and desires.

This is another perhaps overly generous reading on my part, and we should not infer from it that Joyce "was always constitutionally incapable of misappropriating the spoken words [or anxieties and desires] of others" (*FW* 108.5–6). The least I want to argue here, however, is that in writing Shem, Joyce writes the modernist male body and its abjection directly and by that gesture at least articulates a conspicuous lack of enmity to, and anxiety about, the materiality of production.

If, however, Joyce's Shem is not an enemy of production in Brecht's sense or my own, the same point could not be made about his earlier product, Stephen Dedalus, for despite the way traditional criticism has figured him as the paradigm of the modernist artist, Stephen actually produces very little. By the end of *A Portrait* there is only the onanistic villanelle, in which, as Suzette Henke writes, Stephen "simultaneously achieves masturbatory emission and an ejaculatory outburst of *sèmes* lyrically simulating orgasmic *jouissance*. . . . Substituting pen for phallus, he penetrates the opaque image of woman as inaccessible Other and, through a series of seminal outpourings, gains onanistic satisfaction from an archetypal figure elevated beyond the unsettling immediacy of sexual difference" (81–82). By June 16, 1904, however, this semiotic/seminal outpouring has produced scarcely more than "a capful of light odes" (*U* 14:1119). There is something more and other to this low output than the usual charge against Stephen of artistic immaturity, even if the charge receives an ostensibly feminist refurbishing: "Joyce makes clear to his audience that Stephen's fear of women and his contempt for sensuous life are among the many inhibitions that stifle this young man's creativity. Before he can become a true priest of the eternal imagination, Stephen must first divest himself of the spiritual-heroic refrigerating apparatus that characterizes the egocentric aesthete. Narcissism and misogyny are adolescent traits he has to outgrow on the path to artistic maturity" (Henke 84).[15] In what follows I examine the way in which Stephen's fear of writing, as an anxiety about the Shemian lowness of output, is involved with and perhaps overdetermines his fear of women and contempt for sensuous life. I trace the constitutive textual tensions that produce Stephen and put him *en procès*, metonymically disrupting the metaphorically phallic substitutions that would allow his insertion into a masculine subject position elevated beyond the unsettling immediacy of sexual difference. I read the way in which Joyce's writing unsettles Stephen in the abject space opened up by the question of productive anxiety and the way in which Joyce foregrounds Stephen's anxiety of production so as to unground his own.

Re: Openings—or Hegel Will Come, and Pull out His Eyes

> Once upon a time and a very good time it was there was a moocow coming down along the road and this moocow that was coming down along the road met a nicens little boy named baby tuckoo. . . .
> His father told him that story: his father looked at him through a glass: he had a hairy face.
> He was baby tuckoo. The moocow came down the road where Betty Byrne lived: she sold lemon platt.
>
> > *O, the wild rose blossoms*
> > *On the little green place.*
>
> He sang that song. That was his song.
>
> > *O, the green wothe botheth.*
>
> When you wet the bed first it is warm then it gets cold. His mother put on the oilsheet. That had the queer smell.
> His mother had a nicer smell than his father. She played on the piano the sailor's hornpipe for him to dance. He danced:
>
> *Tralala lala (PA 7)*

Hugh Kenner has written, "It is no exaggeration to say that every theme in the lifework of James Joyce is stated in the first two pages of the *Portrait*" ("The *Portrait* in Perspective" 33). Colin MacCabe, in *James Joyce and the Revolution of the Word*, has called the opening of the novel "a juxtaposition of quotations which oppose the narrating father who fixes one in place with his look and his story . . . and the mother who opens up language as sound and movement, appealing to the nose and ear against the identifying eye" (56). Given the rather incredible density of the opening—the introduction in such a tightly packed discursive space of so many thematic and tropaic elements—one might agree that Kenner is not exaggerating. As MacCabe's observation makes clear, however, the important point is how these elements—the engagement of the five senses, the conditions of narrative and the subject positions offered by narration, and the conflictual mechanisms of parental identification and differentiation—are mobilized not only in the opening but along the trajectory of Joyce's lifework. Concerning that work, we can say that in the body of Joyce's writing there is a definite movement away from both classical narrative (surely one of the more formidable of the "ideal containers" lying in wait for discursive flow) and the Name of the Father and toward the more musical possibilities of language that Joyce associates more with the body of the mother. It is not simply a matter of Stephen's preference for the way his mother smells (although there is in Joyce an unconventional hierarchy of senses that grants smell and sound a greater privilege than sight).[16] Rather, the subject position that Stephen's narrating father offers him is one that disrupts its own possibility, defers itself along a dilatory axis of narrative, specular, and paternal identification that is prohibited by those very terms: "His father told him that story: his father looked at him through a glass: he had a hairy face. He was baby tuckoo."

The problem here is pronominal. The latter instance of the pronoun *he* marks Stephen's point of entry into the symbolic order of his father's narration. The former instance of the same pronoun, however, blocks that entry by designating the father's possession of a hairy face, a specular marker of difference that here stands in for *the* marker of sexual difference, the phallus itself. Here the Name of the Father presents itself as both *pronom du père* and *non du père*, simultaneous identification and division, both as lure and as threat of castration. Although the pronoun *he* marks a promise of identification between father and son, it also marks a prohibition: "he" cannot be, or rather shall not be, both baby tuckoo and the possessor of a hairy face at the same time, for the "he" who possesses the hairy face—the phallus and the Name of the Father— also possesses the body of the mother. As Freud puts it, "The superego['s] . . . relation to the ego is not exhausted by the precept: 'You *ought* to be like this' (like your father). It also comprises the prohibition: 'You *may not be* like this' (like your father)—that is, you may not do all that he does; some things are his prerogative" (*SE* 19:34–35).

We know, then, how this oedipal narrative will turn out: baby tuckoo must wait until he is grown up to shave (and here the threat of the razor, of retribution against the specular "I," looms large: Stephen must apologize or else "the eagles will come and pull out his eyes"). Baby tuckoo cannot be "he," must forestall possession of pronominal and narrative identity, a forestallment that, as Peter Brooks has argued, is the determinate instance of both the reality principle and classical narrative.[17] It is little wonder, then, that faced with the intolerable contradictions of being baby tuckoo, of deciding who "he" really is, of being the oedipal subject of his father's narrative economy (the narrative subject of his father's oedipal economy), Stephen would rather listen to his mother's piano and dance the sailor's hornpipe. Although Stephen can separate, or "tell himself," from baby tuckoo, how, as Yeats asks, can we tell the dancer from the dance?

Nonetheless, in this movement from paternal narration to the mother's music, the problems of identification and separation, of Stephen's "telling himself" both from and through significatory practice, have been figured only in roughcast. The problem of separation, not only of Stephen from his mother's body, but also of Stephen from himself, is prefigured in the sentence "When you wet the bed first it is warm then it gets cold." Echoing Kenner, I claim that it is not a complete exaggeration to say that every theme in the lifework of James Joyce is figured in this one sentence from *A Portrait*. Surveying Stephen's trajectory within that work, for example, and comparing it with my earlier discussion of Hegel's abjections of *Vorstellung* and of the Jews, one might note that Stephen first appears in the Joycean ouevre wetting the bed and vanishes from *Ulysses* only after having danced a *pisse de deux* with Leopold Bloom in that wandering Jew's backyard. Remaining at this end of the trajectory, we might posit the flat surface of Stephen's childhood bed as a blank space, a scene of writing, and the urinary stain itself as a transitional part-object, an inscription, a signifying trace. The urinary flow, externalizing itself from the body, at first still partakes of the body's warmth, remains a part-object that still seems connected to the body proper, and so guarantees the body's presence in much the same way that, according to Derrida, speech has been thought to guarantee the presence of the speaking subject. When the urine turns cold, however, the separation of the body from its own externalization seems complete: the stain becomes a trace of the body's having been there that—much like the commodity for Marx's alienated worker—confronts the still-present producing body as hostile and alien object, an inscription of the subject's absence. "When you wet the bed," then, becomes a sort of parable—in much the same way that Freud's *fort-da* is a parable—as well as a paradigm for the anxiety of production that the process of writing calls into play, the transmission of warm speech into cold script, living words into dead letters of waste.

I pause here to recall Kristeva's terms in *Revolution in Poetic Language*, where Kristeva designates the semiotic and the symbolic as the two major components of the signifying process. For Kristeva, the symbolic retains its largely Lacanian designation as the socioculturally arranged system of linguistic and representational meanings, governed by the Law of the Father, whereas the semiotic designates largely presymbolic discursive energies that Kristeva relates to the body, its pulsions and drives, and the mother's territoralization of them. Kristeva writes, "The semiotic is articulated by flow and marks: facilitation, energy transfers, the cutting up of the corporeal and social continuum as well as that of signifying material, the establishment of a distinctiveness and its ordering in a pulsating. . . . We shall [use] the term semiotic to designate the operation that logically and chronologically precedes the establishment of the symbolic and its subject" (*RPL* 40–41). As Roudiez explains, Kristeva takes a text to be "the effect of the dialectical interplay between semiotic and symbolic dispositions. . . . The nature of the [textual] 'threads' thus interwoven will determine the presence or absence of poetic language. Those that are spun by drives and are woven within the semiotic disposition make up what Kristeva has defined as a genotext; they are actualized in poetic language. Those that issue from societal, cultural, syntactical, and other grammatical constraints constitute the phenotext: they insure communication" (5). For Kristeva, what is revolutionary about poetic language is the extent to which it mobilizes semiotic and genotextual energies for incursions into the symbolic and phenotextual field, incursions that disrupt and reject those societal, cultural, syntactical, and grammatical constraints. Significantly, however, since those constraints are based largely on the demand placed on the subject "to renounce pleasure through symbolization by setting up the sign through the absence of the object, which is expelled and forever lost" (149), the revolutionary rejection of these constraints involves a radical reactivation of the pleasure of expulsion/rejection, what Kristeva calls a "reactivation of anality" (152).

Here I might add urethrality as well, for it is fairly easy to locate in the reactivating opening of *A Portrait* a negatively dialectical interplay between semiotic/genotextual and symbolic/phenotextual elements. The bed-wetting parable partakes of the former, whereas the narrative of baby tuckoo relates more to the latter. Nonetheless, although there is an apparent binary formation at work here, there is no clear breakdown among the various textual elements. According to a purely phenotextual logic, there should be an elemental convergence of warmth, nonseparation, music, the semiotic, the mother's body, and speech, all set against the cold comfort offered by the father's symbolic narrative, which demands separation and scripts Stephen in the role of castrato. The phenotext, however, also dictates that the phallic father owns the logos—as Derrida writes in *Dissemination*, the Western tradition "assigns the origin and power of speech, precisely of *logos*, to the paternal position" (*D* 76)—and that the body of the mother be relegated to the materiality of writing. As Henke puts it, Stephen "perceives his father as a primordial storyteller who inaugurates the linguistic apprenticeship that inscribes the boy into the symbolic order of patriarchal authority," as "a bearer of the law and the word, instruments of the will that promise psychological mastery over a hostile material environment" (50). Although Stephen is symbolically hailed as the one supposed to warm to his father and to give his mother the cold shoulder, however, his response to this call remains ambivalent. In his diary at the end of *A Portrait*, Stephen writes of opening up "the spiritual-heroic refrigerating apparatus, invented and patented in all countries by Dante Alighieri" (*PA* 252). In *Ulysses* he thinks of himself as "Gelindo" (*U* 9:941), an Italian name that Gifford translates as "he who must be cold" (*Notes for Joyce* 198).[18] The thought in which this name appears, however, suggests that Gelindo must be cold both to the body of the mother as object to be possessed and to the Name of the Father as the signifier of possession: "S.D.: *sua donna. Già: di lui Gelindo risolve do non amare S.D.*" (*U* 9:940–41)—"S.D.: his woman. Oh sure—his. Gelindo resolves not to love S.D." (*Notes for Joyce* 198).

I say more about Stephen's ambivalent resolutions vis-à-vis these initials in the next section. Here we can note that the juxtaposition of warmth and coldness with questions of language, liquidity, the mechanisms of parental separation and identification, and hence the gendering of environmental hostilities continues throughout *A Portrait* and *Ulysses*, if not to the negated finale of *Finnegans Wake*, where the river ALP dies by flowing into the oceanic arms of her "cold mad father" (*FW* 628.1–2). In book 1 of *A Portrait* this warm/cold juxtaposition becomes a rapid alternation, if not a collapse, due to the fever Stephen contracts at Conglowes after having been pushed into the "square ditch" (Gifford reports that "square was the school name for the urinal in the boys' lavatory" [*Joyce Annotated* 137], so that the square ditch seems to be a cesspool or open sewer). The first signs of fever come while Stephen is savoring the "nice sentences in Doctor Cornwell's Spelling Book," which are "like poetry but ... were only sentences to learn spelling from" (*PA* 10).

> It would be nice to lie on the hearthrug before the fire, leaning his head upon his hands, and think on those sentences. He shivered as if he had cold slimy water next his skin. That was mean of Wells to shoulder him into the square ditch. . . . How cold and slimy the water had been! A fellow had once seen a big rat jump into the scum. Mother was sitting at the fire with Dante. . . . She had her feet on the fender and her jewelly slippers were so hot and they had such a lovely warm smell! Dante knew a lot of things. She had taught him where the Mozambique Channel was and what was the longest river in America. . . . Father Arnall knew more than Dante because he was a priest but both his father and uncle Charles said that Dante

was a clever woman and a wellread woman. And when Dante made that noise after dinner and then put up her hand to her mouth: that was heartburn. (*PA* 10–11)

Here the warm thought of sentences—perhaps, with reference to Hegel, we might say the picture-thought, the *Vorstellung* or mental representation of sentences—plunges Stephen's memory into a cold cesspool and produces a shiver as a physical symptom of distress: the condition of fever allows the metonymic contiguity of the nice, warm sentences in his head with the "cold slimy water next his skin," a contiguity that can be traced back to Stephen's earlier contact with the warm-then-cold urinary stain of his bed-wetting. A somewhat similar effect occurs in the passage immediately following, where the sound of the word *suck*, here meaning "sycophant," provokes in Stephen what Sheldon Brivic calls a "bathroom vision of anxious mystery" (*Joyce between Jung and Freud* 24).

Suck was a queer word. . . . The sound was ugly. Once he had washed his hands in the lavatory of the Wicklow Hotel and his father pulled the stopper up by the chain after and the dirty water went down through the hole in the basin. And when it had all gone down slowly the hole in the basin had made a sound like that: suck. Only louder. To remember that and the white look of the lavatory made him feel cold and then hot. There were two cocks that you turned and water came out: cold and hot. He felt cold and then a little hot: and he could see the names printed on the cocks. That was a queer thing. (Joyce, *PA* 11–12)

Brivic interprets these passages as articulating Stephen's flight away from the threatening cold cut of castration and toward the fullness of the maternal lap, "the warmth of home and mom" (*Joyce between Freud and Jung* 23). Brivic's comments are suggestive, but they underplay the extent to which the ambivalence about parental identification that Brivic himself notes—Stephen's "desires are ambivalent, for he also feels attraction to the cold masculine side" (23)—are also related to an ambivalence about and within language.[19] He writes that in the first passage, the bully Wells "embodies the paternal threat visited on Stephen for thoughts of the 'hearth,'" that "Wells founds a series of father figures who emasculate Stephen by knocking him down, striking, degrading or dispossessing him," and that "the fall into the cesspool is not merely an image of virile disgrace; its features of coldness and a rat suggest death." Brivic goes on to say that "fear of castration often appears as fear of death, and the ditch as grave shows Stephen utterly negated by Wells's masculinity. At this point Stephen is impelled

toward comfort and the text returns suddenly to mother and hearth"
(23).

But this sudden textual return is tricky. Obviously, the first passage
associates mother with warmth and hearth. The problematic status of
sentences, however—the problem that inaugurates this series of memories—seems to qualify these associations, for Joyce's own sentences
juxtapose and thus to some extent identify the mother not simply with
warmth but with the cold slimy water: "How cold and slimy the water had been! A fellow had once seen a big rat jump into *the scum.
Mother* was sitting at the fire" (*PA* 10; emphasis added). The text, that
is, suddenly and simultaneously returns Stephen to the warm mother
as an escape *from* the square ditch and cloacally returns Stephen to the
cold mother *as* the square ditch. Again, we can read this return back
into the bed-wetting scene, for there the mother as provider of bodily
warmth is associated with the warm, just-externalized urine, whereas
her domestic status as sheet-changer simultaneously aligns her with
the impressive caesura—to misappropriate Freud's language—of the
cold. A similar collapse of warm and cold is inscribed on Dante's body
in the apparent association of the noise of after-dinner heartburn that
causes her to put her hand to her mouth with the sound that the lavatory drain makes after the cold, dirty water has disappeared down its
hole.

Obviously, the possibilities for misogyny in these associations of
maternal and female bodies with sewage ditches and drainage holes
are legion, and one might be led to agree with Gilbert and Gubar's
assessment (which puns on Joyce's poem "The Holy Office") that for
Joyce, "woman, both linguistically and biologically, is wholly orifice"
(*No Man's Land* 232). The point here, however, is the subject position
that Stephen comes to occupy in relation to these associations, his
abject and ambivalent identification of himself not with the secured
corps propre of the paternal metaphor but as an anxious producer with
and product of "the hole we all have" (Joyce, *SH* 163). In Dante's case,
the mutual resonance between her heartburn and the noise of the
drainage hole could be read as Joyce's disparaging commentary on
women's knowledge, an instance of his self-proclaimed hatred for
"women who know anything" (Ellmann, *James Joyce* 634), and thus as
his legitimation of the idea that the Fathers as fathers "knew more."
Alternatively, it might also be read as his carnally ironic commentary
on the necessarily embodied production of knowledge itself, on the
intrication of orificial noises with the "litteringture" of anyone's fall into
textuality, and thus on the question of what it means for any body to
be "wellread." As for Stephen's mother, if the text seems to return

Stephen to her as warm lap, thus oedipally figuring him as her reattached phallus, it also returns him to her as cold ditch, less womb-tomb than rectal grave, thus pre- or anti-oedipally figuring Stephen as the big rat that plops into the scum. This figuration of Stephen as rectal rodent has less to do with his being pushed by bullies than with his own attraction to a powerlessness devalued by phallocentrism, his own desire to fall: "He would fall. He had not yet fallen but he would fall silently, in an instant. Not to fall was too hard, too hard: and he felt the silent lapse of his soul, as it would be at some instant to come, falling, falling but not yet fallen, still unfallen but about to fall" (*PA* 162).

Stephen is less a Freudian Rat-Man than a sort of Bataillean Bat-Man, however, for he wants not simply to jump and fall but also to fly; his later image of Emma Clery as "a batlike soul waking to the consciousness of itself in darkness and secrecy and loneliness" (*PA* 221) refers not exclusively to the "temptress" of his villanelle but also to himself. The figuration of a falling Stephen as a rat jumping into scum is darkly transfigured into the image of the feminized soul, the "virgin womb of the imagination" (*PA* 217), as flying bat and is further embedded in Stephen's own identification of himself as an Icarus/Lucifer figure, a winged creature capable of both flight and fall. In the final chapter of *A Portrait*, Stephen, emerging from the masturbatory outpouring of the villanelle, with its "liquid letters of speech" that "flowed forth over his brain" (*PA* 223), stands on the steps of the library, "leaning wearily on his ashplant" (224) and watching the "dark flash" of circling birds. He listens to their cries, which he likens to "the squeak of mice behind the wainscot," and lets their cold "inhuman clamour" and "dark frail quivering bodies" soothe his ears and eyes, which are troubled by "his mother's sobs and reproaches" and by "the image of his mother's face" (an image that might be conflated with his own by virtue of the corporeal displacements of writing, for he has just penned a poem, and his first effort, ten years earlier, had left him so unsettled that to recuperate his sense of identity he "went into his mother's bedroom and gazed at his face for a long time in the mirror of her dressingtable" [71]). Stephen attempts to dissociate the sounds of the birds from "the cry of vermin" (i.e., mice) so as to conjure up "shapeless thoughts from Swedenborg on the correspondence of birds to things of the intellect" (224). Nonetheless, he retains "a fear of the unknown . . . a fear of symbols and portents, of the hawklike man whose name he bore soaring out of his captivity on osierwoven wings, of Thoth, the god of writers, writing with a reed upon a tablet and bearing on his narrow ibis head the cusped moon" (225).

Perhaps Stephen's anxiety here stems from his inability or failure—as well as his own attraction to this inability or failure—fully or finally to disintricate birds, vermin, and the written correspondence between such material things of the intellect and the nagging question of "Where did thots [thoughts, tots, Thoth] come from?" (*FW* 597:25). The figure of the bat conflates bird and vermin, and Stephen's designation of himself as a certain sort of bird, a lapwing, in the "Scylla and Charybdis" chapter of *Ulysses*—"Fabulous artificer. The hawklike man. You flew. Whereto? Newhaven-Dieppe, steerage passenger, Paris and back. Lapwing. Icarus. *Pater, ait.* Seabedabbled, fallen, weltering. Lapwing you are. Lapwing be" (*U* 9:952–54)—traces back to the bat, if not finally to the square ditch as well. Gifford notes that "the lapwing is so called in English after the jerky motions of its wings. In the Bible it is listed, together with the bat, as a bird 'to be held in abomination among the fowls' 'and not to be eaten' (Leviticus 11:19 and Deuteronomy 14:18)" (*Ulysses Annotated* 245). He also notes that "Ovid, in his account of the flight of Daedalus and the fall of Icarus, concludes by describing Daedalus's mourning and his burial of his son: 'As he was consigning the body of his ill-fated son to the tomb, a chattering lapwing looked out from a muddy ditch and clapped her wings uttering a joyful note' (Ovid, *Metamorphoses* 8:236–38)" (245). Stephen's reference to himself as lapwing in *Ulysses*, then, returns us by process of allusion to the opening problematics of *A Portrait*, reopening the abject association of the maternal lap as productively muddy ditch and the "thothful" bat as its abominably airborne product.

The problem that remains throughout Joyce's writing is the question of correspondence, of how and whether the "litter" of this airmail ever arrives at its destination. In the batlike figure of the lapwing, the womb-as-lap(se) itself takes wing, a dark flight and a bright, unvirgin fall. In *A Portrait* Stephen, misremembering a line from Nashe, is confused as to whether it is "darkness" or "brightness" that "falls from the air" (*PA* 234). This confusion is bound up with Stephen's feverish childhood alternation between warm and cold, for it is the warm brightness of the sun that melts Icarus's wings and causes him to plunge into the cold, dark sea, whereas Lucifer's proud disobedience plunges the fallen angel into the fires of hell.

This confusion is never completely resolved. The fever is textual, and for Joyce there is no final remedy. Joyce's text, like Stephen's fever, continues to collapse hot and cold, darkness and brightness, flying and falling, rectal gravity and solar anality. This confusion, this winged collapse or flying *Durchfall*, constitutes the primary semiotic or genotextual incursion of Joyce's writing into the symbolic and phenotextual domain of the Law of the Father. It suggests that, in relation to that phallogocentric Law, Joyce will always remain something of a "rotten sun." Joyce's incursion stages itself as more than just a problem of writing in relation to parental identification; it is even less simply a matter of the gendering of bodies along the teleologically narrativized masquerade of "to be" or "to have." Rather, Joyce's semiotic incursion presents itself as a matter of the properties and improprieties of male bodily production, a question, as I will continue to show, of the anxious tension between that semiotic, often fluidic production and the symbolic means of its containment. One of the mainstream means of containment, and hence sources of tension, is naming, and as I show in the next section, the uncanny "bathroom vision of anxious mystery" that Stephen experiences in the lavatory of the Wicklow Hotel when he sees the names on the taps from which the hot and cold water flows will be replicated in other scenes, in and out of bathrooms, where Stephen will confront the (di)visible inscription of his identity in a name.

Dispossession: The Initials of the Father

> All life lifts and longs toward its own name
> And toward fulfillment in the singleness of definition.
> —Robert Penn Warren, *Brother to Dragons*

> What's in a name? That is what we ask ourselves in childhood when we write the name that we are told is ours.
> —Stephen Dedalus in James Joyce, *Ulysses*

> The one who will not work . . . gives birth to the wind—but the one who will work gives birth to his own father.
> —Søren Kierkegaard, *Fear and Trembling*

> Count me out, [Stephen] managed to remark, meaning work.
> —James Joyce, *Ulysses*

Writing "against *Ulysses*" in *The Culture of Redemption*, Leo Bersani argues that "Joyce incarnates the enormous authority of sublimation in our culture—of sublimation viewed not as a non-specific eroticizing of cultural interests but as the appeasement and even transcendence of anxiety. *Ulysses* is modernism's monument to that authority, although—in what I take to be the most authentic risk Joyce takes in producing this monument—it also alludes to the anxiety from which we escape in our exegetical relocation of the work itself within the authorial consciousness at its origin" (176). Bersani goes on to say that "the anxiety that *Ulysses* massively struggles to transcend . . . is that of disconnectedness" (177). For Bersani, this massive struggle to transcend disconnectedness involves Joyce's effort to suture "cultural fragmentation"—the "immense panorama of futility and anarchy which is contemporary history" (Eliot 270)—by "giv[ing] us back our culture as *his* culture" (Bersani, *Culture* 177). Indeed, "Joyce's novel asks only that we reconstruct the structurally coherent fragments of Joyce's own cultural consciousness. It is not Western culture that matters, but the coherence of a particular broken version of it. Joyce is faithful to our humanist tradition at a deeper level, in his reenactment of its assumptions and promise that the possession of culture will transcend anxiety and perhaps even redeem history" (178). Bersani connects what he reads as Joyce's desire to transcend anxiety—by possessing, redeeming, and bequeathing cultural history to his readers as his—with paternity. If anxiety is about disconnectedness, "for authors, the anguish of paternity is experienced as an uncertainty about the property of their work, about who owns it and if it is indeed their own" (177). To the extent that *Ulysses* does transcend anxiety, then, "we should now be able to recognize [it] as modernism's most impressive example of the West's long and varied tribute to the authority of the Father" (177–78).

Fredric Jameson—who has his own interests, if not in transcending anxiety, then certainly in redeeming history—has a somewhat different critique of *Ulysses* and paternity. In his essay "*Ulysses* in History" Jameson identifies the theme of paternity as one of those "traditional interpretations" of *Ulysses* that "have become so sedimented into our text—*Ulysses* being one of those books which is 'always-already-read,' always seen and interpreted by other people before you begin—that it is hard to see it afresh and impossible to read it as though those interpretations had never existed" (126). Designating "the mythical, the psychoanalytical, and the ethical readings" as "those we can really make an effort to do without" (126), Jameson reduces psychoanalytic readings to an interest in the oedipalized "father-son relationship" and dismisses such readings on the grounds that "the father-son relationships in *Ulysses* are all miserable failures . . . ; and if more is wanted on this particular theme, one might read into the record here the diatribes against the very notion of an Oedipus complex developed by Deleuze and Guattari's *Anti-Oedipus*, which I do not necessarily endorse but which should surely be enough to put an end to this particular interpretive temptation" (131).

The theme of paternity in *Ulysses* was one of the first to be privileged by conservative Joyce criticism. Indeed, since many readers were exposed to Stuart Gilbert's study of Joyce's novel before they had legal access to the text itself, that theme, highly privileged by Gilbert, can be seen as part of the text's quite literal "always-already-read." In the traditional interpretation Stephen's need for a symbolic father interpenetrates with Bloom's need for a son, and the two characters' meeting constitutes an atonement that is an "at-one-ment," a reconciliation that securely positions each character's identity—and thus by implication, the reader's own. Nonetheless, as Stephen points out twice in the "Scylla and Charybdis" chapter, every reconciliation requires a prior sundering (*U* 9:334–35, 397–98). For Stephen, biological father and son are so "sundered by a bodily shame" (*U* 9:850) that any hope of a spiritual relationship between them—of "a mystical estate, an apostolic succession" (*U* 9:838) that would confer and secure identity—is compromised.[20] Paternity, as Stephen famously puts it, becomes "a legal fiction," founded "upon incertitude, upon unlikelihood," while "*Amor matris,* subjective and objective genitive, may be the only true thing in life" (*U* 9:840–45).

Stephen, then, might be the first to agree with Jameson that all the father-son relationships in *Ulysses* are "miserable failures," while I of course agree with him on the need—particularly in the age of Robert Bly—for rigorously anti-oedipal, antipaternal readings, and not only of Joyce.[21] I wonder, however, whether we can really do without a desedimented critical interrogation of the *failure* of paternity in Joyce, particularly when Joyce himself so relentlessly insists on it and when so many recent (and especially feminist) critics of Joyce have read him afresh precisely by scrutinizing this failure. Moreover, given Bersani's definition of phallocentrism as "the denial of the *value* of powerlessness in both men and women" ("Rectum" 217), I remain suspicious of a critical dictate that forecloses on the interpretive temptation of and attraction to failure, to powerlessness itself. If, as Bersani suggests, we should value passive or demeaning sex because "the value of sexuality itself is to demean the seriousness of efforts to redeem it" ("Rectum" 222), perhaps we should similarly value the theme of paternity in Joyce precisely because he presents it as failure, because he demeans it, defiles it through the bodily shame of writing.

We can read this de-meaning back into the matter of Joyce's own efforts at cultural paternity, his monumental sublimations and massive efforts to transcend anxiety and redeem history. Certainly Joyce was invested in paternity and self-paternity. Certainly he wanted his readers to become his sons and daughters, to enter the family business and become lifelong salespeople of his encyclopedic fictions, to spend the rest of their lives with him trying to understand his work. "The call," says Bersani, "is very hard not to heed" (*Culture* 178). But perhaps we can avoid this fate, the seduction of becoming "a Joycean," to the extent that we side with the unsublimated, acyclopedic Joyce, the authentically risky Joyce who ceaselessly alludes to anxiety, rather than the self-paternal Joyce who wants to help us transcend it. This siding would involve producing a debilitated, irredemptive, culturally nonviable interpretation of Joyce, a partial reading that can only limp along and pull up short. Since *Ulysses,* as Lacan puts it, "is a testimony of the way in which Joyce remains caught up, rooted in his father, while still disowning and denying him" ("Le Sinthome" 15; cited in Rabaté, *Joyce* 55), Bersani is probably right: a non-Joycean reading of Joyce would necessarily be "against *Ulysses,*" even though, or perhaps precisely because, such a move feels like "a fall from grace" (*Culture* 178).[22] As Joyce puts it, "It's something fails us. First we feel. Then we fall" (*FW* 627:11).

A Portrait not only alludes to anxiety but demolishes in advance any Ulyssean effort to transcend or redeem it by appeal to paternal positionality. The novel disrupts the notion of paternity as origin and thus by extension any "exegetical relocation of the work itself"—or of any subsequent work—within a paternalized, authorial, originary consciousness. In chapter 2 of *A Portrait* Stephen Dedalus accompanies his father, Simon, to Cork, the latter's place of origin, in what Maud Ellmann calls "an attempt—if the pun can be excused—to cork identity" ("Polytropic Man" 81). The originary and identificatory value of "Cork" as a proper name, however, has already been called into question by its status as an object, already been located as a site of expenditure, abjection, and powerlessness, well before Stephen's arrival at that destination. Earlier in the chapter, for example, Stephen conjectures that one of the things Uncle Charles might pray for is "that God might send him back a part of the big fortune he had squandered in Cork" (62). Stephen later wanders among the docks and quays of Dublin, "wondering at the multitude of corks that lay bobbing on the surface of the water in a thick yellow scum" (67). This scum becomes feminized shortly thereafter, during Stephen's conversation with Emma on the tram: "They seemed to listen, he on the upper step and she on the lower. She came up to his step many times and went down to hers again between their phrases and once or twice stood close beside him for some moments on the upper step, forgetting to go down, and then went down. His heart danced upon her movements like a cork upon a tide" (69). If, however, the proximity of this description to that of the yellow scum of the Dublin waterways figures Emma's ebb and flow on the tram steps as abject, it is significant that Stephen regards himself not as the subjective master of this feminine movement but rather as its helplessly bobbing object. These references to corks as scummy objects refer backward and forward to Cork as a site of squander; they factor a certain originary feminine movement into the construction of masculine subjectivity and work to crumble the power of Cork as a properly paternal name.

On the train to Cork (the "night mail") Stephen listens "without sympathy to his father's evocation of Cork and of scenes of his youth, a tale broken by sighs or draughts from his pocketflask whenever the image of some dead friend appeared or whenever the evoker remembered suddenly the purpose of his actual visit." This purpose is that Stephen's father's property "was going to be sold by auction and in the manner of his own dispossession he felt the world give the lie rudely to his phantasy" (*PA* 87). The masculine pronouns are ambiguous in the final clause, and I think intentionally so, for to use a word that will become very important in *Ulysses*, there is a supposed "consubstantiality" between father and son, so that in terms of the patrilineal transmission of the mantle of authority, the fantasy of one should be that of the other, and the dispossession of either dispossesses both. Simon's paternal authority is slipping away from him: he is becoming dispossessed of property and power, his tale or narrative broken by the knowledge of failure, loss, and death. Simon is thus the very emblem of the castrated father, and his search for his proper name, in the form of the initials "S.D." carved into a desk, represents his vain wish to regain the power inscribed therein, his desire to repossess the phallus. This phallus, in Lacan's sense of primary signifier or *nom du père*, embodied here in the initials "S.D.," should serve to position securely Stephen's identity as well as Simon's. However, a certain signifier of bodily shame inserts itself between Stephen and the initials that are supposed to guarantee this fixed mode of subjectivity:

> They passed into the anatomy theatre where Mr Dedalus, the porter aiding him, searched the desk for his initials. Stephen remained in the background, depressed more than ever by the darkness and silence of the theatre and by the air it wore of faded and formal study. On the desk before him he read the word *Foetus* cut several times in the dark stained wood. The sudden legend startled his blood: he seemed to feel the absent students of the college about him and to shrink from their company. A vision of their life, which his father's words had been powerless to evoke, sprang up before him out of the word cut in the desk. A broadshouldered student with a moustache was cutting in the letters with a jackknife, seriously. Other students stood or sat near him laughing at his handiwork. . . . Stephen's name

was called. He hurried down the steps of the theatre so as to be as far away from the vision as he could be and, peering closely at his father's initials, hid his flushed face. But the word and the vision capered before his eyes as he walked back across the quadrangle and towards the college gate. It shocked him to find in the outer world a trace of what he had deemed till then a brutish and individual malady of his own mind. (89–90)

Maud Ellmann refers to the word *foetus* as a "scarletter" that "precedes [the father's] initials in the narrative, and in a sense preempts the name that they imply" ("Polytropic Man" 81). She writes that Stephen's vision of the broad-shouldered student "incorporates the scar into the fiction of a single author, and resurrects a father for the letter" (96). Here we might say that fetus precedes both father and author in the narrative in two ways. Literally, Stephen sees the broad-shouldered student's handiwork before he sees that of his own father, and as I will show, the startling perception of the first undercuts any identification he might have had with the second. More important, however, and perhaps more literally as well, fetus always proceeds father *and* author in any narrative, in the sense that one must have been the former before one can ever become the latter, and it is this knowledge—that any paternal, authorial subject is "already constituted . . . as an object from before his birth" (Wilden 161)—that so disturbs Stephen.

It is not simply the word itself, however, but also its placement and mode of production that initiate and elaborate this distressing knowledge in Stephen's consciousness, indicating just what sort of object the subject already and constitutively may have been. Ellmann asks, "Why should such a word, or wound, evoke such dread, if not because the phallus has surrendered to the omphalos?" ("Polytropic Man" 96). Dread of another orifice, another surrender, may be at work here as well, for the wounding word takes its form as a carved "obscenity" on a desk top, thus assuming a position usually reserved for more phallic or fecal sexual expressions. This collapse of loci and functions brings us back to Freud's notion of a phantasmatic association of fetus (or baby), feces, and penis—"a unity," Freud writes, "the concept . . . of 'a little one' that can be separated from one's body" (*SE* 17:84). This unity also returns us to Freud's elaboration of the cloaca theory, the idea that "children are at one in thinking that babies must be born through the bowel; [that] they must make their appearance like lumps of faeces" (*SE* 16:319). These phantasmatic associations could be at work in Stephen's apprehension of, and about, the word *foetus* even if the broad-shouldered student had used the fecal pen rather than the phallic jackknife to inscribe it. How much more wounding for Stephen, then, that the letters are carved. Jacqueline Rose has noted the identification of the maternal body as "an undifferentiated space" ("Introduction II" 54). The desk top—like baby tuckoo's wetted bed, another "scene of writing"—is also an undifferentiated space that the broad-shouldered student differentiates with his jackknife, so that the carving reveals itself as a separation, a severance of the part-object-word *foetus* from its maternal body. It is only by undergoing this operation, this severance, that the word can assume its shape, its hollowed-out and wounded substantiality. Further, the word has been cut into the desk not once but several times, which means not that there are several instances of the word on the desk but that the same word has been repeatedly carved deeper, and, as Ellmann points out, not necessarily by the same hand. The originary "author" of the letter, although Stephen resurrects him singularly, thus has rather a multiple identity, a heterogeneity that gives the lie rudely to the unitary "singleness of definition" (Penn Warren 77) that Stephen hopes for when he images the strong, self-possessed wielder of the jackknife as a substitute for his own dispossessed father.

Stephen's recognition of the word *foetus* can thus be read as a loss for which the initials *S.D.* provide little compensation. Significantly, Stephen experiences this loss as the sort of *Vorstellung* that made Hegel uneasy—the externalization of a mental image, picture-thinking in transgression of the body's boundaries: "It shocked him to find in the outer world a trace of what he had deemed till then a brutish and individual malady of his own mind" (*PA* 90). In other words, Stephen discovers here an irreducible anteriority, the history of sexuality and the sexuality of his history: somebody else wet the bed first. The word that Stephen would speak has already been spoken by another, by many others. Words, in effect, have already spoken Stephen. He has lost them and been lost in and by them, and any word that he might thereafter speak or write, any attempt he might make to accede to himself by designating himself in a statement, is one in which he has always already suffered the same fate. Any cry that might issue from his lips, any mark that might flow from his pen, is already "but the echo of an obscene scrawl which he had read on the oozing wall of a urinal" (*PA* 100). As Ellmann puts it, "the wake of language—writing—is stained by urine, the wake of the flesh" ("Polytropic Man" 92).

What is enacted quite suggestively here is thus the Lacanian premise that the subject is an effect of the signifier, that subjectivity is passed through and produced by the defiles of signification and the materiality of language. Faced with the inadequate model of subjective mastery offered by Simon Dedalus, Stephen tentatively envisions a more ideal figure whose self-possession would enable Stephen to get a grip on himself. That vision, however, springs up out of a word cut on a desk, is itself an effect of a particularly overdetermined material signifier that precedes it and defiles it—even though the scene that Stephen defensively envisions is that of the word's ostensible initiation. Stephen's anxiety thus stems from the recognition of his irreducible inscription within a defiling semiotic flow of which he is not the punctual origin. Harold Bloom has called this a recognition of "lack of priority." We can see how disturbing this recognition is for Stephen, not simply as a young man, but also as the artist, for as Bloom points out, "what strong maker desires the realization that he has failed to create himself?" (5).

Of course, it is highly questionable whether Stephen ever becomes a Bloomian "strong maker," whether he is ever able, as the last words of the novel put it, to self-paternally "stand" himself "in good stead" (*PA* 253): in the "Oxen of the Sun" chapter of *Ulysses*, Lynch tells Stephen that the bardic "coronal of vineleaves . . . will adorn you more fitly when something more, and greatly more, than a capful of light odes can call your genius father" (*U* 14:1116–19), whereas the end of "Circe" finds Stephen sprawled on the Nighttown street. Nonetheless, Stephen *wants* to be a strong maker just as badly as he does *not* want the realization of his failure to create himself, his inability to take his stand. His gesture will therefore be not to surrender himself to the heterological materiality in which he is so dreadfully inscribed but rather to search for greater certainty within the symbolic itself. Thus, although he has no sympathy for Simon Dedalus, who has failed to pass on to his son the mantle of authority and fixed identity in the form of an unbroken narrative, Stephen still wants a symbolic father, yet not one who will have generated him as a son, for that would only repeat on the symbolic level the same problems inherent in mere physical procreation and would do nothing to assuage Stephen's anxieties of influence and exfluence. Rather, Stephen wants a figure who will act as guarantor for his own fantasy of self-generation and self-paternity—a fantasy whose main function is to disavow the anteriority of both maternal sexual agency and the materiality of language in the constitution of his subjectivity. In *Ulysses* the name of this particular wild goose is Shakespeare.[23]

As for Stephen's actual father, the feckless Simon "appears" only once more in *A Portrait*, an appearance in which he does not actually appear but rather is figured only as a disembodied voice resounding from above. The scene is at the beginning of chapter 5, just after

Stephen's epiphanous encounter with the "bird-girl" on the beach and his final decision not to take the Jesuit orders, not to become a father.[24] Stephen's mother, still performing what Cixous has called her "classical anal" function ("Reaching the Wheat" 6), is washing him at the basin.

> An earsplitting whistle was heard from upstairs and his mother thrust a damp overall into his hands, saying:
> —Dry yourself and hurry out for the love of goodness. A second shrill whistle, prolonged angrily, brought one of the girls to the foot of the staircase.
> —Yes, father.
> —Is that lazy bitch of a brother gone out yet?
> —Yes, father.
> —Sure?
> —Yes, father.
> —Hm!
> The girl came back making signs to him to be quick and go out quietly by the back. Stephen laughed and said:
> —He has a curious idea of genders if he thinks a bitch is masculine.
> —Ah, it's a scandalous shame for you, Stephen, said his mother, and you'll rue the day you ever set foot in that place. I know how it has changed you. (175)

Stephen's decision to forsake the church and enter the university has put him at odds with the mother and the father: ready to give himself over, to open the "virgin womb" of his imagination to the world, he has feminized himself in the eyes of both. The father calls him a bitch, while the mother's tropes of insertion and consequent change posit the university as a cross between a steel trap and a *vagina dentata*.

With these familial noises ringing in his ears, Stephen sets forth from his father's house:

> The lane behind the terrace was waterlogged and as he went down it slowly, choosing his steps amid heaps of wet rubbish, he heard a mad nun screeching in the nun's madhouse beyond the wall.
> —Jesus! O Jesus! Jesus!
> He shook the sound out of his ears by an angry toss of his head and hurried on, stumbling through the mouldering offal, his heart already bitten by an ache of loathing and bitterness. His father's whistle, his mother's mutterings, the screech of an unseen maniac were to him so many voices offending and threatening to humble the pride of his youth. (*PA* 175–76)

At this juncture in Stephen's trial, a significant reversal is at work: the phenotextual constraints that confront Stephen's semiotic flow—the parents' religiously motivated and rigidly gendered proscriptions and a primary signifier of the discourse of Catholicism—are all reduced to the same level of meaningless, nearly psychotic babble. The father's whistle and the mother's mutterings are equated with the screech of an unseen maniac who has herself been driven mad (presumably) by desire and for whom the Name of the Son—the detached and restored phallus of a dismembered God—is no more than a reified linguistic fetish. All these have become for Stephen just so many voices that he rejects, quite significantly, while negotiating his way along a water-clogged lane, stumbling through moldering offal and heaps of wet rubbish. It is precisely the rank materiality of the refuse in his path, however, that helps Stephen to unclog his own semiotic passage, to reject the oppressive phenotextual voices in a gesture that collapses vocal, corporeal, and spiritual expulsion: "He drove their echoes out of his heart with an execration: but, as he walked down the avenue and felt the grey morning light falling about him through the dripping trees and smelt the strange wild smell of the wet leaves and bark, his soul was loosed of her miseries." (*PA* 176) The issue that remains un-resolved throughout Stephen's trial is the extent to which he can keep his soul loosened of its heavy baggage and continue to ease himself out of his own semiotic self-retention. As I will show in the next section, the same semiotic elements that assist Stephen here return later to disturb the symbolic construction of his aesthetic theory.

Another disturbance occurs in his confrontation with Mr. Deasy in the "Nestor" episode of *Ulysses,* where Stephen makes what is perhaps his most famous pronouncement:

> —History, said Stephen, is a nightmare from which I am trying to awake.
> From the playfield the boys raised a shout. A whirring whistle: goal. What if that nightmare gave you a back kick?
> —The ways of the creator are not our ways, Mr Deasy said. All human history moves towards one great goal, the manifestation of God.
> Stephen jerked his thumb towards the window, saying:
> —That is God.
> Hooray! Ay! Whrrwhee!
> —What? Mr Deasy asked.
> —A shout in the street, Stephen answered. (*U* 2:378–86)

Here again we find the radical reduction of a major phenotextual sym-bol and constraint—*the* transcendental signified—into a mere vocal effect, a material signifier, a shout in the street. Given the apparent incoherence of the shout, this reduction has a certain resonance with the one previously described, in which Stephen equates the screech of the mad nun (another shout in the street) with his mother's mutterings and his father's earsplitting whistle. The father's whistle carries with it a command, the implication of a narrative/oedipal goal that corresponds to the idealist, Hegelian, teleologically narrativized goal that Mr. Deasy posits for human history: the manifestation of God the Father. Stephen hears from the soccer field, however, another "whirring whistle" that has as its referent not only the word *goal* but also, significantly enough, the image of a ball being caught in a net. It is this net, this phenotextual constraint, that Stephen wants to fly past, this history—a nightmare narrative of oedipal tyranny and politico-sexual oppression—from which he wants to awake. But Stephen's gesture is hardly an appeal to an idealist ahistoricism. Rather, his insistence on the materiality of signifying practice allows for an intervention into Mr. Deasy's idealist history and, at the same time, a more radical notion of historicity, one in which heterogeneity and discontinuity are preserved and concrete historical and signifying differences not effaced.

Stephen has made this sort of intervention before. In chapter 5 of *A Portrait*, in his conversation with the (British) dean of studies, Stephen interrupts the dean's metaphysical ruminations about Epictetus's lamp by pointing out that the part of a *real* lamp for which the dean is using the word *funnel* is, in Ireland, called the "tundish."

> The little word seemed to have turned a rapier point of his sensitiveness against this courteous and vigilant foe. He felt with a smart of dejection that the man to which he was speaking was a countryman of Ben Jonson. He thought:
> —The language in which we are speaking is his before it is mine. How different are the words *home, Christ, ale, master*, on his lips and on mine! I cannot speak or write these words without unrest of spirit. His language, so familiar and yet so foreign, will always be for me an acquired speech. I have not made or accepted its words. My voice holds them at bay. My soul frets in the shadow of his language. (189)

Stephen's anxiety here, however, has little to do with the political struggle between the imperial English language and the indigenous, colonized Gaelic (particularly since Stephen shows nothing but contempt for learning the latter). Stephen's problem, again, is that language itself was someone else's, everyone else's, before it was his. He cannot speak or write any words without unrest of spirit precisely because all speech is always acquired. Stephen's soul frets in the shadow of language itself, and he cannot accept its words precisely because he has not made them, because he cannot be the punctual origin and author of his own semiotic flow. Hence Stephen's insistence on the materiality of language confronts him once again with his own lack of priority, leads him not away from history but directly to the history of sexuality, the sexuality of history. Is it also this other history that Stephen has in mind when he speaks of wanting to wake from a nightmare? He has had, in any case, another nightmare, a terrifying vision of his own making and of the making of his own anterior alterity:

> [He saw] a field of stiff weeds and thistles and tufted nettlebushes. Thick among the tufts of rank stiff growth lay battered canisters and clots and coils of solid excrement. A faint marshlight struggled upwards from all the ordure through the bristling greygreen weeds. An evil smell, faint and foul as the light, curled upwards sluggishly out of the canisters and from the stale crusted dung. Creatures were in the field; one, three; six: goatish creatures were moving in the field, hither and thither. Goatish creatures with human faces, hornybrowed, lightly bearded and grey as india rubber. The malice of evil glittered in their hard eyes, as they moved hither and thither, trailing their long tails behind them. . . . Soft language issued from their spittleless lips as they swished in slow circles round and round the field, winding hither and thither through the weeds, dragging their long tails amid the rattlingcanisters. They moved in slow circles, circling closer and closer to enclose, to enclose, soft language issuing from their lips, their long swishing tails besmeared with stale shite, thrusting upwards their terrific faces. (138–39)

Here the innocent genotextual bed-wetting parable has been transmogrified, has been so phenotextually overcoded as to become Stephen's nightmare vision of his own material history and its goal: "his hell. . . . stinking, bestial, malignant, a hell of lecherous goatish fiends. For him! For him!" (139). Stephen's tormented soul frets in the shadows of warm, soft language and cold, stale shit, a monstrous collapse of oral and anal expulsion in which he sees himself eternally damned. Eventually Stephen will pray, hoping to recuperate his logos in good clean words that will fly straight up to heaven. His initial involuntary response, however, corresponding to the demonic energy that so terrifies him, is to enact his own collapse of oral and anal expulsion in a convulsively impure expenditure, a revolt of corporeal-poetic language: "he vomited profusely in agony" (139). Of course, this could hardly be called a pleasurable reactivation in the sense Kristeva intends, but then, no one ever said that écriture would be easy.

Excrementitious Intelligence: Stephen's Lousy Aesthetics

> But all these men of whom I speak
> Make me the sewer of their clique
> That they may dream their dreamy dreams
> I carry off their filthy streams
>
> —Joyce, "The Holy Office," in *Critical Writings*

Attempting to elaborate his theory of aesthetics in chapter 5, Stephen responds to Lynch's question about the nature of beauty: "To speak of these things and to try to understand their nature and, having understood it, to try slowly and humbly and constantly to express, to press out again, from the gross earth or what it brings forth, from sound and shape and colour which are the prison gates of our soul, an image of the beauty we have come to understand—that is art" (*PA* 206). But Stephen's own effort to press out this "dreamy dream" of artistic production is momentarily troubled by the sight of a "filthy stream": "They had reached the canal bridge and, turning from their course, went on by the trees. A crude grey light, mirrored in the sluggish water, and a smell of wet branches over their heads seemed to war against the course of Stephen's thought" (*PA* 207). Whereas earlier "the grey morning light falling about him through the dripping trees and . . . the strange wild smell of the wet leaves and bark" (*PA* 176) had helped Stephen to loosen his soul of its miseries, here sound, shape, and color—all aspects of representation itself—are figured as the soul's prison gates. Here an array of semiotic, genotextual elements—grey light mirrored in sluggish water, the smell of wet branches, all the disturbing appeal of the square ditch and the piss-warm bed, of the abject, maternal, and material over and against the proper, paternal, and narrative—wars against the symbolic, phenotextual course of Stephen's thought, suggesting Stephen's unconscious awareness of a tension between his theory and its production, art and its commission, between any ideal image of beauty and the always embodied effort to press out that image.

In the midst of another of Stephen's pressing efforts, he lists the following as one of the aesthetic questions he sets for himself: "*Can excrement or a child or a louse be a work of art? If not, why not?*" (*PA* 214). Freud's cloaca theory accounts quite handily for the first two items on the list. Freud notes that "this theory is not abandoned until all anal interests are deprived of their value" (*SE* 16:319). Given the problematic and faltering "reactivation of anality" in which Stephen is caught up, we can see how his inclusion of excrement and a child as conceivable works of art indicates a struggle against deprivation but, at the same time, an anxiety that such externalizations be recuperated under aesthetic, quasi-phenotextual constraints—constraints of his own making, but constraints nonetheless. As for the louse, we know that Stephen has lice on his body. Such disregard for hygiene is an aspect of Stephen's medievalism; it partakes of the logic of fleshly mortification that allowed medieval ascetics to cherish their bodily vermin as "pearls of God" (Russell 377). But there is something else at work here as well:

> A louse crawled over the nape of his neck and, putting his thumb and forefinger deftly beneath his loose collar, he caught it. He rolled its body, tender yet brittle as a grain of rice, between thumb and finger for an instant before he let it fall from him and wondered would it live or die. . . . The life of his body, illclad, illfed, louse-eaten, made him close his eyelids in a sudden spasm of despair: and in the darkness he saw the brittle bright bodies of lice falling from the air and turning often as they fell. . . . His mind bred vermin. His thoughts were lice born of the sweat of sloth. (PA 233–34)

Here we can see why Stephen is so anxious to recuperate even his own lice as objects of aesthetic contemplation and by what logic he groups them along with children and excrement as conceivably being works of art: Stephen's mind breeds the vermin; his thoughts are born as lice. Furthermore, mental production can enact itself only through language, through the externalization of speech, through words that, once written, tend, like lice, to assume a life of their own.

Thus, despite the fluid economy of writing, the masturbatory enthusiasm that he permits himself in penning his villanelle, despite the "liquid letters of speech" that "flowed forth over his brain" (PA 223), the "soft liquid joy" (PA 225) to which he can sometimes give himself over with pleasure, Stephen retains himself as the turd of his own fantasy within his anxiety of production. Stephen's subjectivity is such that he cannot begin to designate himself in the statement because he cannot admit the nature of the objectivity, the fundamental lack of priority, that never ceases to be inscribed within that designation. To "tell himself," to write "the mystery of his own body" (PA 168), Stephen must permit that body to become its own scene of writing; he must soil himself with his own semiotic flow, hollow himself out in a self-shattering gesture of dilapidation, dissemination, and impure expenditure. It is not the bird-girl's flesh, on which "an emerald trail of seaweed had fashioned itself as a sign" (PA 171), it is not Eve's skin—"Belly without blemish, bulging big, a buckler of taut vellum" (*U* 3:42)—but his own, the only foolscap available, that he must allow to become the blank page waiting for his traces. It is not woman's body but his own across which he must suffer the little letters to crawl.

Stephen, in short, must become Shem the Penman. If we were to follow Stephen more closely into *Ulysses*, however, we would see that his main projects in that novel—the disavowal of the mother's ghost and the concurrent quest for consubstantiality with a symbolic father whose logos will guarantee Stephen's self-paternity and negate his lack of priority—are fundamentally incompatible with that becoming, with the shameful writing of his body. Nonetheless, to say that Stephen fails, to render a final verdict at Stephen's trial, is to misapprehend radically the nature of Joyce's praxis, for Joyce is not offering up characters for anyone's moral judgment or aesthetic evaluation. Rather, he is articulating and disarticulating historical modes of subjectivity, of which Stephen's is only one. As Attridge and Ferrer state in their introduction to *Post-Structuralist Joyce*, Joyce's purpose "is not to explore the psychological depths of the author or characters, but to record the perpetual flight of the subject and its ultimate disappearance" (10). In the same volume Cixous comments on "how Joyce's work has contributed to the discrediting of the subject, how today we can talk about Joyce's modernity by situating him on that 'breach of the self' opened up by other writings whose subversive force is now undermining the world of western discourse; how his writing . . . [puts] a question mark over the subject and the style of the subject" ("Joyce" 15). Stephen and the mode of subjectivity he represents can carry Joyce only so far in his revolution in poetic language—to the end of *Ulysses* but not into *Finnegans Wake*. It is not that Stephen's trial reaches a verdict; it is not even that Stephen simply disappears, although of course Stephen does disappear. Rather, the venue of the trial of subjectivity changes from the insular, autonomous, phallicized ego to the self-shattering and irredeemably heterological materiality of history itself—There Goes Stephen, Here Comes Everybody. Joyce, in an authentically risky gesture of impure expenditure, sacrifices Stephen's high modernism on the altar/alter of Shem's postmodern body.

In so doing—that is, in producing *Finnegans Wake*, a production that, as Rabaté puts it, achieves "the symbolic liquidation of the father" (*James Joyce* 59)—Joyce, contra Derrida, reveals himself as the least Hegelian of modern novelists. He demonstrates that something great can indeed be discovered, and ceaselessly rediscovered, on a dunghill.

6

Closings: Desire and Interpretation in the Porno-House of Language, or "You Certainly Do Know What You Want, Sir"

> Desire, in fact, is interpretation itself.
> —Jacques Lacan, *The Four Fundamental Concepts*

> Desire . . . is eclipsed here, so swiftly, unnoticed, by the desire to kill.
> —Hélène Cixous, "Joyce: The (R)use of Writing"

> Satisfaction? Never. Every object resists becoming what the fascist wants to make of it. Only when destruction is absolute is he reasonably secure that nothing remains to ruffle him. To gain knowledge of the world without shifting from his own position, he organizes it to appear absolutely uniform—which is to say, dead. Now he can breathe a momentary sigh of relief: there's nothing in sight that might desire to penetrate him. Heil! . . . And now he turns on the radio: Twilight of the Gods. Liebestod. Eyes closed.
> —Klaus Theweleit, *Male Fantasies*

> You're not a writer—you're a killer.
> —Sergeant Hartman to Private Joker, in Stanley Kubrick, *Full Metal Jacket*

Lacan suggests that in a certain "defensive phase" desire and not wanting to desire "are the same thing" (*FFC* 235). For Lacan, the desire to masterfully end all desire entails not only the subject's own desire but also that of the other. Indeed, for Lacan, these two must also be the same thing, since, according to his famous formulation, "Man's desire is the desire of the Other" (*FFC* 235). Hence, the subject for whom desire and not wanting to desire are the same thing can end or master his own desire only by ending or mastering the desire of the other.

Here I have attempted to demonstrate that, in its most defensive phase, this desire to end all desire masterfully is at least partially the function of a symptomatically masculine anxiety, an unease about the production(s) of the male body, an unrest that is exacerbated by the materiality of writing, of inscription, of graphic notation on tangible material. I have argued that this anxiety is intricated with a certain anguish about traces of maternal determination in the constitution of male subjects, I have shown how this determination is figured as a stain on the tain of masculine self-reflection, and I have suggested that this anxiety of production is historically exacerbated, if not initiated, by modernity's disenframing of the feminine. I have also suggested that the production of material and the materiality of production call any bid toward representational mastery into question, always already depositing a devalued unmeaning into the processes of meaning's production, and that an emphasis on the materiality of signification, what Kristeva calls a "joying in the truth of self-division" (*PH* 89), opens a space for the possible disruption of representational mastery and hence the discursive boundaries of masculinity and patriarchy.

On the more ominous side, however, a masculine writing subject's bid toward the absolute mastery of his material, as a means of assuaging his own anxiety of production, can be in structural solidarity not only with a death-drive (the desire to end one's own desire) but also, as a discernible ideological and historical consequence, with the actual production of death itself, the desire to ends one's own desire by ending the desire of the other. If the absolute master is in fact death, as Lacan assert it is, what would it mean to be, or aspire toward being, an absolute master? Certainly not to die, for as Blanchot suggests, death itself is "the impossibility of dying." Rather, being an absolute master would mean being what death is—the agency of the death of others. This agency can be literal, entailing actual murder, or even mass murder (*Freikorps* member Rudolph Hoss, one of Theweleit's subjects, was not only a writer but eventually the commandant at Auschwitz), or "purely" literary, involving the absolutely masterful manipulation of the characters—either in the sense of letters themselves or of configurations of letters designed to represent human beings—that one has deposited on a blank sheet of paper. Writing itself, then, can become a certain sort of agency in which desire is eclipsed by the desire to kill, the process that Theweleit calls "devivification," the search for the killable other. The writer as master has the means at his own disposal. The anxiety of production can assuage itself in the mass production of death.

In *Thinker on Stage: Nietzsche's Materialism* Peter Sloterdijk writes of Nietzsche's discovery that "it is absolutely *impossible* for self-reflection and identity—in the sense of an experience of unity that could lead to contentment—to occur simultaneously" (206). Nietzsche's endlessly disruptive discovery of the noncoincidence of identity and self-reflection adumbrates Lacan's assertion of a split between the subject of an enunciation and the subject of a statement. For Lacan this split ensures that a subject can never simultaneously possess an identity and a representation of that identity, can never be and mean itself at the same time. The subject who wants to accede to him- or herself in a meaningful statement finds in that representation not the content(ment) of his or her own full identity but rather only alienation and *aphanisis*, or fading. Here alienation and *aphanisis* are other words for linguistic abjection, for the loss of being in meaning, for the subject's utter(ed) dismemberment in the production of the signifier. Alienation, writes Lacan, "condemns the subject to appearing only in that division which, it seems to me, I have just articulated sufficiently by saying that, if it appears on one side as meaning, produced by the signifier, it appears on the other as *aphanisis*" (*FFC* 210).

The distinction Lacan points out between being and meaning seems to be aligned, respectively, with another Lacanian distinction, that between the sign and the signifier. Drawing on Saussure's formulation, in which the signifier (acoustic image) and the signified (mental conception) join to make a sign, Lacan states that whereas a sign "represents something for someone," a signifier "is that which represents the subject for another signifier" (*FFC* 207). The sign, in Lacan's sense, resides in the domain of being, identity, and the *corps propre*. It is a function of Husserl's *Ausdruck*, or "expression," what Derrida calls a "voluntarist metaphysics" that assumes that something other, some other thing, is intentionally represented for someone, for some subject that prophylactically imagines itself as autonomous from both the other and its representation. Since the subject of the sign feels authorized to locate no part of itself in the other, it loses nothing by virtue of the other's representation in the sign. The sign, then, guarantees identity and being. Meaning, on the other hand, resides in the dominion of the signifier, of *Anzeichen*, or "indication." The subject, passing through the indicative defiles of signification, finds not something but rather itself represented as a thing, and not for itself but rather for another signifier. That is, the subject of meaning is drawn ineluctably into a metonymic chain of signification that never comes to rest in a full or transcendental signified. For Lacan, this movement is the movement of desire, and "Desire, in fact, is interpretation itself" (*FFC* 176).

That this movement is a matter of some anxiety is signaled by the deathly coincidence Lacan notes between wanting to desire and wanting not to desire: the reduction of desire, the reduction of an anxious and unpleasurable tension, corresponds with a reduction of indication, which as Derrida points out, is simply "another name for the relation with death" (*SP* 40). The difference between sign and signifier, between expression and indication, could correspond to a difference between a desire that desires not to desire and a desire that desires desire itself. As Bataille puts it, describing the latter, or indicative, mode, "Desire desires *not* to be satsified" (*G* xxi). If desire is in fact interpretation, however, the expressive coincidence that Lacan notes indicates that a certain subject's desire to interpret may be caught up with the desire *not* to interpret, to interpret or produce interpretation only on the condition of eventually being able to have done with interpretation, bringing interpretation to closure by an act of interpretative mastery. A major function of this interpretative mastery would be the effort to convert the signifier, which always materializes the subject's abject *aphanisis*, its relation to death, into the immaterial sign—to convert meaning into being (not to "let being be," as Heidegger so tenderly puts it, but to stabilize the indeterminacy of meaning by force, to *make* meaning be). Given the difference established earlier between death and the relation to death, however, one could say that this effort involves forcing that which means death to be dead, that it involves the devivifying desire to convert what is active, speaking, and subjective into a passive, mute, and masterable object. The subject of this desire does not want to desire, but neither does it want (itself) to die. It does not want to be dead. Rather, and much more ominously, this subject desires to be death, to actively produce death. To be death is to produce death, and just as death is that which has no relation to death, so too death—and only death—is that for which being and production are identical. Death produces itself without loss, without remainder, without any contamination or any loss of value. It is that absolute master for whom no anxiety about production obtains.

But the subject's anxious bid for absolute mastery, the desire to end all (interpretative) desire, is called into question by both the materiality of production and the other's desire—that is, whatever evidence the other gives of not being a passive, mute, and masterable object. We can read a certain anxiety about that evidence in what seems to me a particularly vicious but nonetheless quite suggestive formulation from Henry Miller. In *Tropic of Cancer* the Miller persona pauses during one of his virile reveries about a woman named Tania to make the following announcement: "I am fucking you, Tania, so that you'll stay fucked" (13). Whatever else might be said about this braggadocio, it clearly articulates a desire on the part of the Miller persona to have so sexually overmastered Tania that her desire is brought to an end, so that "time and the repetition of desire in time" are foreclosed.[1] And if the subject's desire is the desire of the other, as Lacan asserts, then the Miller persona's desire to end Tania's desire is a function of his desire to end his own (perhaps, shall we say, by coming into his own, by making Tania his very own). Miller's writing, then, which ostensibly expresses sexual desire, indicates more conspicuously the desire to master, to fuck only on the condition of fucking as master, so that fucking and mastery become indistinguishable. Whatever is being celebrated in Miller's passage, it certainly is not Tania's active and subjective desire. Indeed, Miller's intent here seems nothing less than murderous, betraying a need to reduce the other to a state of devivification that would be expressed by desire's absence.

Nonetheless, if desire is in fact interpretation, the possibly murderous intent that Miller expresses here seems to bear on reading as well as fucking, for would not a certain act of reading house the belief, or hope, that the text at hand *can* be interpreted once and for all? Is this not a condition under which a certain reader subjects him- or herself to the unpleasurable tension of interpretation—the condition, guaranteed from the outset, that interpretation eventually be satisfactorily brought to closure? Just as the Miller persona wants to fuck Tania so that she will stay fucked, this reader desires to read a text so that it will stay read.[2]

Just as sexual mastery can be disrupted by the object's resistance, however, by the active, speaking desire of the other, so interpretative mastery is ceaselessly subverted by the textuality of the text. Tania, one suspects, will not stay fucked, and the text—any text, even *Tropic of Cancer*—will not stay read. Desire desires desire and not its satisfaction. We continue to interpret, to produce interpretation and to shatter our proud subjectivities into interpretation, as long as our desires remain open to the possibility of their own nonsatisfaction.

If the endlessness of interpretive desire makes some of us anxious, perhaps we can begin to learn how to let that anxiety remain productive. Perhaps we can begin to speak and write *our* bodies, to put those bodies on the line, to let the desire(s) of the other(s) speak.

Notes

Introduction

1. Drawing on the Althusserian theory of ideology as interpellation, Silverman also writes that "the dominant fiction consists of the images and stories through which a society figures consensus; images and stories which cinema, fiction, popular culture, and other forms of mass representation presumably both draw upon and help to shape" (*Male Subjectivity* 30). She goes on to say that "our present dominant fiction is above all else the representational system through which the subject is accommodated to the Name-of-the-Father. Its most central signifier of unity is the (paternal) family, and its primary signifier of privilege the phallus. 'Male' and 'female' constitute our dominant fiction's most fundamental binary opposition. Its many other ideological elements . . . all exist in a metaphoric relation to those terms. They derive their conceptual and affective value from that relation" (34–35).

2. A note on terminology: although I intend the word *appropriation* in the positive or productive sense established by such practitioners of postmodernism as Kathy Acker, Cindy Sherman, Sherrie Levine, and Richard Prince, for all of whom appropriation entails rifling the dominant culture and subversively restaging its productions, the negative instance of the word—in the sense of absorbing and defusing alternative discourses so as to reinscribe and protect the status quo—also needs to be addressed. Since my writing is informed by feminist and to some extent queer theory, it is of course liable to charges of appropriation in the latter, negative sense, because I am also writing as a heterosexual man. I discuss this problem more fully in notes 4 and 5 to this chapter. Here I will say only that I hope my writing is more an instance of proliferation than of appropriation. For a helpful discussion of the distinction between the two, see Gloria Anzaldúa's introduction to *Making Faces*. A few words are in order also for the phrase *heterological materiality*. For Julian Pefanis, in *Heterology and the Postmodern*, the word *heterology* is roughly synonymous with poststructuralism and refers to the "*thought of nonidentity*" that aims "to preserve the difference of otherness, resisting the totalizing and totally compromised tendency of civilization" (5). Readers of this work, however, will be adequately forewarned about what I mean by "heterological materiality" if they are alerted to the fact that for Bataille the word *heterology* refers not only to

"the science of the completely other" but also to "scatology" (*VE* 102).

3. Leo Bersani, in *The Freudian Body,* describes Beckett's art as "culturally nonviable" (12).

4. To exacerbate the anxiety, let me suggest that in positing such a co-axiality, I am in effect asking for my work to be considered as an exercise not only in male feminism but also in what might be called (and I understand the umbrage some will take here) straight queer theory. This designation is possible only if queerness is construed as a function less of sexual orientation, experience, or identity than of sustained critical or dispositional opposition to compulsory heterosexuality, homophobia, the systemic oedipalization of desire, the right's current rhetoric of "family values," and so on—although such opposition/disposition of itself is not likely get one drummed out of the military or denied housing, employment, spousal benefits, or even life. Nonetheless, such a shift in construing queerness has been indicated in a number of discursive contexts. In the article "Radical Change," L. A. Kauffman writes of "a new kind of politics, a post-identity politics of sorts. Queerness, in this view, [is] more a posture of opposition than a simple statement about sexuality. It [is] about principles, not particularities. 'To me,' explained [Queer Nation/San Francisco activist Karl] Knapper, 'queerness is about acknowledging and celebrating difference, embracing what sets you apart. A straight person can't be gay, but a straight person can be queer'" (20). In his essay "Are We (Not) What We Are Becoming?" Ed Cohen advocates "abjuring our hard-won gay and lesbian 'identities' in favor of more relational, more mobile categories: 'gay dis-positions' or 'lesbian attitudes,' for example" (174). Cohen goes on to say that "to the extent that we can transform our ec-centricities into our strengths, utilizing our 'off-center' positions to challenge the concrete institutional arrangements whereby the 'center' is both defined and produced, then we create the possibility for interrupting these defining practices even as they reiterate our specific marginalities" (175). Following from these comments, the issue becomes the extent to which one can participate in a gay disposition or lesbian attitude, can help to challenge concrete institutional arrangements and interrupt defining practices, without having gay or lesbian identity as a specific marginality, without having access to the operative possessive pronouns (but also, please, without whining about "exclusion"). Of course, the danger here is that straight queer theory might simply be the appropriation of gay theory for straight ends (in much the same way that male feminism can amount to nothing more than mastering feminist discourses only to reinscribe patriarchy). Straight writing about queer theory can produce blind spots as well; it can exclude pressing questions of gay politics just as much as compulsory heterosexuality does. In this book, for example, I deal extensively with the notion of abjection and with abject bodily substances— urine, semen, shit. I do not allude at all, however, except right here, to the fact that these substances take on a different valence in the age of AIDS (not that AIDS is a "gay disease," but it is undeniably a concern of gay

politics); as Helen Molesworth points out in a recent discussion, "The fact that blood, sperm, and anality are the most charged terms of abjection now has to be understood in relation to HIV" (Foster et al. 16). Here I also frequently refer to the work of Leo Bersani, particularly to his brilliant essay "Is the Rectum a Grave?" I do so because Bersani's emphasis on anality in this essay and elsewhere helps to underscore my arguments about the anus as a point of significant leakage for the dominant fiction of heterosexual masculinity (particularly as that masculinity attempts to represent itself in writing). Nowhere in my numerous citations of Bersani, however, many of which are from that article, do I mention that this essay appeared in the AIDS issue of *October* and is concerned primarily with anal intercourse between men. The fact that my concern is with anality as a site of production, or unproductive expenditure, rather than as a site of penetration should not occlude the fact that for gay men anality involves a mode of sexual practice outlawed and despised by dominant culture, and hence a site of conscious political struggle. Writing as a straight man, however, I can only allude to and support that struggle; I cannot speak for it any more than I, as a male feminist, have a dispensation to speak for women's experience of oppression (see Linda Alcoff, "The Problem of Speaking for Others"). One final point: although I have from the beginning of this writing wanted and considered it to be a feminist intervention, the process of understanding its possible coaxiality with queer theory has been slower and more gradual. This tardiness speaks of the blind spots and resistances endemic to the subject position from which I write and that I continue to try to renegotiate (not, of course, that I have worked out "my" feminism entirely). In the end, I do not want to claim either "male feminist" or "straight queer" as an identity; rather, I want to let those terms designate me—and the subject position that this "I" supposedly represent(s)—as a site of irresolvable contradiction, anxiety, and desire, of proliferation (or so I hope) rather than appropriation.

5. See also Butler's comments in *Bodies That Matter*: "Although the political discourses that mobilize identity categories tend to cultivate identifications in the service of a political goal, it may be that the persistence of *dis*identification is equally crucial to the rearticulation of democratic contestation. Indeed, it may be precisely through practices which underscore disidentification with those regulatory norms by which sexual difference is materialized that both feminist and queer politics are mobilized" (4). Again, the point is not for the straight male to claim feminist or queer theory in the name of identity but rather that a straight male's disidentification with regulatory sexual norms potentially assists the mobilization of feminist and queer politics.

Chapter 1: Openings

1. For the problems in Kristeva's politics, particularly her theorizations of maternity, see Domna Stanton, "Difference on Trial"; Drucilla Cornell, *Beyond Accommodation*; Elizabeth Grosz, *Sexual Subversions* and "The Body

of Signification"; see also Jacqueline Rose, "Julia Kristeva—Take Two" (*Sexuality in the Field of Vision* 141–64); Judith Butler, "The Body Politics of Julia Kristeva" (*Gender Trouble* 79–92); Gayatri Spivak, "French Feminism" and the interview with Ellen Rooney, in which Spivak proclaims herself to be "repelled by Kristeva's politics" (145); Paul Smith, "Julia Kristeva et al." For a response to Spivak, see John Lechte, *Julia Kristeva* (204–5, 216, 219). As for Smith's article, although it has many virtues, one might respond to his charge that psychoanalysis is "chronically unable to politicize itself" (101) with two observations. (1) One of the most valuable contributions of psychoanalytically based inquiry to critical thought is the understanding that the process by which any subject or discursive practice attempts to "politicize itself" is hardly as transparent, voluntaristic, or free from unconscious motivation as we might like it to be. If psychoanalysis is unable to politicize itself, it still may give us certain analytical tools for examining the psychosexual underpinnings of a resistance to self-politicization. (2) There is more to politics than interlarding one's text with anguished italicized references to contemporary political atrocities and injustices. In terms of combating such instances of the latter as Georgia's antisodomy laws, to use one of Smith's concluding examples, prehistory (by which I mean the pre-oedipal) may have as much to tell us—something just as politically indispensable—as history. Smith shows more sensitivity to the need to interrogate the pre-oedipal in "Vas."

2. Although my treatment of abjection derives mainly from Kristeva and Bataille, it should be noted that a considerable amount of discourse about abjection, some of it claiming more distance from Kristeva than I do, has been produced since the principal work of writing this book. As Rosalind Kraus puts it, with some dismay, "Abjection has become a theoretical project." Notable in this proliferation of abject discourses and practices would be the October panel discussion "The Politics of the Signifier II," where Krauss's remarks appear (Foster et al., 5); the Whitney Museum's 1993 Abject Art exhibition, which resulted in the publication of *The Abject, America* (Liu); and *Abject Art* (Houser et al.). Perhaps most significant in the development of abjection as a theoretical project is Judith Butler's *Bodies That Matter*, where Butler elaborates on the matters of abjection touched on in her earlier work. Butler's is the most politicized notion of abjection, since for her it designates "those 'unlivable' and 'uninhabitable' zones of social life which are nevertheless densely populated by those who do not enjoy the status of the subject, but whose living under the sign of the 'unlivable' is required to circumscribe the domain of the subject" (3). Butler rightly advocates "the politicization of abjection in an effort to rewrite the history of the term, and to force it into a demanding resignification," and maintains that "the contentious practices of 'queerness' might be understood . . . as a specific reworking of abjection into political agency" (21). Although my deployment of abjection in this book derives, again, primarily from Kristeva (and Bataille), I feel that I use it in a way closer to Butler's sense of the political stakes and urgency of examining the mechanisms of abjection and

forcing it into a demanding resignification, and I hope that this book's compatibility or coaxiality with Butler's project will be evident. At the same time, although I hope that the book avoids Kristeva's universalizations and political evasions, I also think that it pays more specific attention to the matters that bodies produce than does *Bodies That Matter*. This attention, however, would earn my book few points with some of the participants in the *October* conversation. To them, such attention might seem a dismissably "childish move," a "necessarily infantile celebration of body fluids and excrement" (4). I would respond that my intent is less to celebrate abjection childishly than to examine the way its repression functions in the constitutive exclusions that found and reproduce normative masculinity. Given this intent, and my desire to intervene into that reproduction with every theoretical means at my disposal, I am strategically indifferent to Krauss's question of whether "the contemporary annexation of Bataille under the banner of abjection is an illegitimate move" (3). Furthermore, I am as bothered by the somatophobia (whether half-seriously admitted or not) and referent-phobia—the too easy conflation of reference with reification—that emerge in the *October* discussion as its participants might be with my illegitimate annexations of Bataille.

3. In *Technologies of Gender* Teresa de Lauretis identifies the "simple equation: women = Woman = Mother" as "one of the most deeply rooted effects of the ideology of gender" (20). One of the problems of this study will be to examine this effect without reproducing it.

4. See both volumes of Klaus Theweleit's *Male Fantasies*. There have been several studies charting the correspondences between Theweleit's findings and Kubrick's film, most notably Susan White's "Male Bonding." Susan Jeffords, in *The Remasculinization of America*, reads Theweleit favorably but unfortunately considers Kubrick's film not as a powerful critique but rather as an instance of the very remasculinization she so skillfully and persuasively analyzes. In *Feminism without Women* Tania Modleski notes that Kubrick's film "corroborates" Theweleit but also asserts that the film is "in complicity with the attitudes it attacks" (62). Modleski, however, fails to demonstrate adequately the complicity she asserts.

5. Gitlin's specific reference is to such films as *Terminator* and *Lethal Weapon*.

6. This phrase was employed by the Krokers in a talk/performance entitled "Male Hysteria" given at the Center for Twentieth Century Studies at the University of Wisconsin–Milwaukee in November, 1989. See Arthur Kroker and Marilouise Kroker, *The Hysterical Male*.

7. As Berger continues: "Men look at women. Women watch themselves being looked at. This determines not only most relations between men and women but also the relation of women to themselves [but not men to themselves?]. The surveyor of woman in herself is male: the surveyed female. Thus she [but never he] turns herself [but never himself] into an object—and most particularly as an object of vision: a sight." My interjections are meant to indicate how Berger reproduces the paradigm he identifies.

8. Cf. an interesting moment in Barthes's *Incidents*: "Driss A. doesn't know that sperm is called sperm—he calls it shit. 'Watch out, the shit's going to come now': nothing more traumatizing" (24).

9. I take up Irigaray's essay "The Mechanics of Fluids" in greater detail in chapter 3.

10. See Shannon Bell, "Feminist Ejaculations," in Kroker and Kroker, *The Hysterical Male* (155–69).

11. These are the last words of Jacques Lacan's seminar on "The Purloined Letter" (*The Seminars of Jacques Lacan, Book II*, 205). See Derrida's critique of Lacan's reading in "The Purveyor of Truth" (*The Post Card* 411–96), and Barbara Johnson's reading of Lacan and Derrida in "The Frame of Reference (496–97). All three are collected in Muller and Richardson, *The Purloined Poe*.

12. What Bataille has in mind here is not semen, although I think it fits the description, but rather decaying, maggot-ridden corpses.

13. The full quotation, from a footnote in *Three Essays on the Theory of Sexuality*, reads as follows: "The first prohibition which a child comes across—the prohibition against getting pleasure from anal activity and its products—has a decisive effect on his whole development. This must be the first occasion on which the infant has a glimpse of an environment hostile to his instinctual impulses, on which he learns to separate his own entity from this alien one and on which he carries out the first 'repression' of his possibilities for pleasure. From that time on, what is 'anal' remains the symbol of everything that is to be repudiated and excluded from life" (Freud, *SE* 7:187).

14. It is not abjection but phallocentrism that is the active mode of agency by which others become shit. As Butler writes in *Bodies That Matter*, "Abjection (in latin, *ab-jicere*) literally means to cast off, away, or out and, hence, presupposes a domain of agency from which it is differentiated. . . . The notion of abjection designates a degraded or cast out status within the terms of sociality" (243). We should, I think, be careful to distinguish between abjection as a self-implicating mode and abjecting as the phallocentric mode of agency that operates the process Butler describes. For more on Butler's take on abjection, see note 2 of this chapter.

15. Nonetheless, some other feminists have argued that porn, by virtue of its very explicitness, may not be the worst offender and in some instances may even have a great use-value for a dangerously feminist pleasure, particularly as more women sex workers assume, and thus subvert, the means of production and distribution. The feminist debate about pornography has abated somewhat, mainly because the antiporn forces have been largely discredited after the Mapplethorpe and NEA struggles exposed the dangers of a feminist alliance with the radical right. Still, the dispute is far from settled, and the following is an only partial list of relevant work. Among the classics of the antiporn side are Susan Griffin, *Pornography and Silence*; Andrea Dworkin, *Pornography*; Catharine A. MacKinnon, *Feminism Unmod-*

ified; Suzanne Kappeler, *The Pornography of Representation*; and Laura Lederer, ed., *Take Back the Night*. On the feminist anti-antiporn side, see Angela Carter, *The Sadeian Woman*; Carol S. Vance, ed., *Pleasure and Danger*; Kate Ellis et al., eds., *Caught Looking*; Linda Williams, *Hard Core*; Carla Freccero, "Notes of a Post–Sex Wars Theorizer"; and Judith Butler, "The Force of Fantasy." For essays by straight and gay men on both sides of the debate, see Michael S. Kimmel, ed., *Men Confront Pornography*, particularly as regards gay male porn, and the debate between John Stoltenberg and Scott Tucker. See also Scott Tucker, "Gender, Fucking, and Utopia," and Leo Bersani, "Is the Rectum a Grave?" Tania Modleski's *Feminism without Women* ends with a chapter named "Anti-anti-anti Porn" that is largely a critique of Bersani. As for my own position, some statement of which is no doubt called for, what I value most are those discourses that recognize a politically salutory sense of contradiction, and not just hypocrisy, in the ability to be erotically thrilled and ethically troubled by the same imagery.

16. The classic treatment of Lawrence and anality is of course Mark Spilka's "Lawrence Up-Tight."

17. The political stakes of Lawrence's anxiety assuagement become evident when we locate Lawrence in that considerable host of male modernist figures—Eliot, Pound, Yeats, Lewis, and Marinetti, not to mention Heidegger—who were drawn to or participated in fascism. As Guy Hocquenghem puts it, "in fascist ideology, the healthy confront the degenerate, in a battle on which the fate of our civilisation hangs" (*Homosexual Desire* 56). For general discussions of the problem of male modernist affiliations with fascism, see, for example, Andrew Ross, *The Failure of Modernism*; Cairns Craig, *Yeats, Eliot, Pound and the Politics of Poetry*; Andrew Parker, "Ezra Pound and the 'Economy' of Anti-Semitism"; and Fredric Jameson, *Fables of Aggression*. Works dealing with the problem of Heidegger's politics will be referenced in the chapter of this work devoted to Heidegger.

18. Lacan refers to death as the "absolute master" (*FFC* 27).

19. Walter Benjamin, "Conversations with Brecht" (97). "They" in this instance are adherents to a Lukácsian dogma of critical realism.

20. The appropriate reference here is to Lacan's famous diagram in *Écrits* of "the image of the twin doors ['Ladies' and 'Gentlemen'] symbolizing, through the solitary confinement offered Western Man for the satisfaction of his needs away from home, the imperative that he seems to share with the great majority of primitive communities by which his public life is subjected to the laws of urinary segregation" (*É* 151).

21. "The question of a general economy is located at the same level as that of political economy, but the science designated by the latter refers only to a *restricted* economy (to market values). The general economy deals with the essential problem of wealth. It underlines the fact that an excess is produced that, by definition, cannot be employed in a utilitarian manner. Excess energy can only be lost, without the least concern for a goal or objective, and therefore, without any meaning" (Bataille, *Oeuvres com-*

plètes 5:215–16; quoted in Richman, *Reading Georges Bataille* 69–70). See also Jean Baudrillard, *The Mirror of Production*: "The process of capitalism crosses the entire network of natural, social, sexual and cultural forces, all languages and codes. In order to function, capitalism needs to dominate nature, to domesticate sexuality, to rationalize language as a means of communication" (138).

22. The term "tropaic matrix" comes from Dominick LaCapra, "Psychoanalysis and History": "The body might well serve as tropaic matrix in the investigation of sociocultural processes, including the opposition between public and private spheres as well as the formation of disciplines on both discursive and institutional levels. What is good to 'ingest' in a given group or discipline, what should be 'expelled' as indigestible, and what metabolism is considered 'normal' in the rhythm of social life are only some of the most pressing questions in this respect" (247).

23. "And besides, the last word is not said—probably shall never be said. Are not our lives too short for that full utterance which through all our stammerings is of course our only and abiding intention?" (Conrad, *Lord Jim* 208).

24. For Kristeva's articulation of her differences from Lacan, see "Within the Microcosm." See also Shuli Barzilai, "Borders of Language."

25. In *Revolution in Poetic Language* Kristeva designates the semiotic and the symbolic as the two major components of the signifying process. I will be discussing these terms in greater detail in later chapters. For the moment, Elizabeth Grosz's comments can suffice: "The semiotic is understood by Kristeva as a pre-oedipal, maternal space and energy subordinated to the law-like functioning of the symbolic, but, at times, breaching the boundaries of the symbolic in privileged moments of social·transgression, when, like the repressed, it seeks to intervene into the symbolic and subvert its operations" (*Sexual Subversions* xxi).

26. Although I join Bersani here in examining Freud's domestications of his own discoveries, I also join Bersani in insisting on reading Freud as a critical discoverer of the domestications in which he participates. The problem, as Judith Butler puts it in *Bodies That Matter*, lies in Freud's "failure to read himself in precisely the ways he teaches us to read" (65). For an examination of how Freud's failure enables his finally affirmative reading of patriarchy, see John Brenkmann, *Straight Male Modern*.

27. In her essay "Moving Backward or Forwards" Jane Gallop reports her distance from the Lacanian insistence on "the split." Gallop writes: "I certainly do not want a kind of lovely utopic continuum where we are all happy in nature: I remain suspicious of that. But recurring across a range of feminist studies and theory is an understanding that what Europeans call 'western culture' is based on this kind of violent split from biology, on a certain heavily-policed border with nature, which has everything to do with the domination and exploitation of women. I thus find myself questioning the Lacanian insistence on the split. . . . The split, the division model is always fundamentally defensive, always an adversarial position. . . . I

think that the adversarial model is coming from a certain masculinist ideology in which Freud and Lacan are thinking" (38). It seems to me that the linguistic split between enunciation and enounced—between the speaking and the spoken "I"—is irreducible. The ideological question becomes how that irreducible linguistic split is figured, how it is gendered, and how it parses out into other sociopolitically maintained binaries and hierarchies. It is certainly a masculinist ideology that figures the split as castration, but as I will show, there are other masculinist figurations at work here as well.

28. I should stress here that I do not intend these proper names to stand in *tout court* for their associated discourses. Nor do I pretend that my examination will have been a "critique" of these huge discursive fields. I want only to suggest how productive anxiety symptomatically emerges in these fields. Quite obviously, these are discourses in which my argument participates.

29. Jardine quotes Philippe Lacoue-Labarthe, "L'Imprésentable."

30. I take up the problem of the incompatibility between phallicity and ejaculation in the next chapter, in regard to Irigaray and Hegel. Here, however, one might note as symptomatic the general paucity of reference to seminal discharge in the "Phallus Issue" of *Differences* (4, no. 1), even in Charles Bernheimer's interesting "Penile Reference in Phallic Theory" (116–32).

31. As Diana Fuss puts it in *Essentially Speaking*, "Bodily experiences may seem self-evident and immediately perceptible but they are always socially mediated" (25).

32. Cf. Freud, *Moses and Monotheism*: "Under the influence of external conditions—which we need not follow up here and which in part are also not sufficiently known—it happened that the matriarchal structure of society was replaced by a patriarchal one. This naturally brought with it a revolution in the existing state of the law. . . . This turning from the mother to the father, however, signifies above all a victory of spirituality over the senses—that is to say, a step forward in culture, since maternity is proved by the senses whereas paternity is a surmise based on a deduction and a premiss. This declaration in favour of the thought-process, thereby raising it above sense perception, was proved to be a step charged with serious consequences" (*SE* 23:113–14).

33. "Commanding the accession by gold, the father, and the phallus to normative sovereignty is the same genetic process, the same progressive structuring principle with discrete phases. The phallus is the general equivalent of objects, and the father is the general equivalent of subjects, in the same way that gold is the general equivalent of products. The constituent members of these sets differ, but in all three an identical syntax allows one of these members (following a historical process) to accede to power and govern the evaluations of the set from which it is excluded. We seem to have before us a growth pattern and a statute that regulate sociohistorical structuration as a whole. We may go so far as to say that they *are* history itself" (Goux, *Symbolic Economies* 24).

34. An alternative historicization could come out of Foucault's project in *The History of Sexuality*, where Foucault establishes that it was not until the nineteenth century that the homosexual was discursively and institutionally invented as a "personage," that homosexuality was deployed as the "truth" of identity. Following Foucault, one could submit that it was not until the nineteenth century that the heterosexual was invented as the dominant mode of sexual identity against that of the homosexual as type. In other words, the invention of homosexuality in the nineteenth century brings a new historical pressure to bear on the processes of identification by which normative heterosexuality is secured. As important as Foucault's project is, however, I give very little attention to him in this work for two reasons. The first is his own much commented-on neglect of sexual difference. The second is that Foucault's discourses about the body tend to examine it as the site of institutional inscription rather than of production (in the sense of the word that I use here). Foucault, to my knowledge, does not really speak about what comes out of bodies. For a discussion of Foucault's sublimation of the body, see Bersani ("Rectum" 219).

35. See in this regard Kaja Silverman's notion in *Male Subjectivity at the Margins* of "historical trauma," particularly her assertion that the main symptom of such trauma is the culture's inability to sustain its dominant fiction of the commensurability of phallus and penis.

36. See, for example, Jürgen Habermas, "Modernity—An Incomplete Project"; Marshall Bermann's chapter on Baudelaire in *All That Is Solid Melts into Air*; and Paul de Man, "Literary History and Literary Modernity."

37. See my essay "*Tristram Shandy*'s Consent to Incompleteness."

38. Diana Fuss, in a recent essay titled "Fashion and the Homospectatorial Look," calls photography "the very technology of abjection." Having first asserted that the "intimate codependency of fashion, fetishism, photography, and femininity suggests that in the dominant regime of fashion photography, femininity is itself an accessory: it operates as a repository for culture's representational waste" (720), Fuss then goes on to write that "abjection . . . is the psychical equivalent of photography's mechanical transformation of subjects into objects. Barthes writes 'the Photograph . . . represents that very subtle moment when . . . I am neither subject nor object but a subject who feels he is becoming an object: I then experience a micro-version of death (of parenthesis): I am truly becoming a specter' [*Camera Lucida* 14]. Photography, the very technology of abjection, functions as a mass producer of corpses [Kristeva calls the corpse "the utmost in abjection" (*PH* 4)], embalming each subject by captivating and fixing its image" (729).

39. The full quotation runs as follows: "Apart from some earlier attempts, it has been reserved in the main for our epoch to vindicate at least in theory the human ownership of the treasures formerly squandered on heaven; but what age will have the strength to validate this right in practice and make itself its possessor?" (Hegel, *ETW* 159).

40. Cf. Hocquenghem: "'Anal cleanliness' [is] the formation in the child

of the small responsible person; and there is a relation between 'private cleanliness' and 'private ownership [*propreté privée* and *propriété privée*] which is not merely an association of words but something inevitable. . . . Control of the anus is the precondition of taking responsibility for property. The ability to 'hold back' or to evacuate faeces is the necessary moment of the constitution of the self. 'To forget oneself' is the most ridiculous and distressing kind of social accident there is, the ultimate outrage to the human person. . . . 'To forget oneself' is to risk joining up, through the flux of excrement, with the non-differentiation of desire" (*Homosexual Desire* 84–85).

Chapter 2: Piss Hegel

1. For readings that do address Scotty as an instance of a particular subject or scopic position, see Laura Mulvey, "Visual Pleasure and Narrative Cinema"; Tania Modleski, *The Women Who Knew Too Much*; and Robin Wood, *Hitchcock's Films Revisited*, particularly "Male Desire, Male Anxiety: The Essential Hitchcock."

2. See Gayle Rubin, "The Traffic in Women." See also Irigaray, "Women on the Market" (*TS* 170–92).

3. Sandra Bartky delivered a paper on the feminization of shame at the Center for Twentieth Century Studies at the University of Wisconsin–Milwaukee in October 1989; see her *Femininity and Domination* (83–98).

4. See Jane Gallop's characterization of Lacan as "prick" in *The Daughter's Seduction* (37).

5. It should be stressed that, despite certain appearances, this will not have been a reading of Hegel or a critique of dialectics as such. As the reader may have surmised by now, I am strategically more interested in fluids than in philosophy.

6. It should be pointed out that in *The Sublime Object of Ideology* Žižek also takes up Hegel's critique of picture-thinking as urination but that he operates from rather different premises and so arrives at conclusions different from my own. One area of difference is in Žižek's dismissal of the Derridean reading of the *Phenomenology*; he rejects as "meaningless" the "usual reproach according to which Hegelian dialectics 'sublates' all the inert objective leftover, including it in the circle of dialectical mediation." On the contrary, he asserts, "the very movement of dialectics implies . . . that there is always a certain remnant, a certain leftover escaping the circles of subjectivation, of subjective appropriation-mediation, and *the subject is precisely correlative to this leftover*" (209). Although I agree with Žižek that this correlation between subjectivity and the leftover obtains, I do not know how to read Hegel with enough Lacanian finesse to see Hegel himself arguing for that correlation. Žižek's approach seems to overcathect the psychoanalyst back into the philosopher, a sort of "everything you always wanted to know about Lacan but were afraid to ask Hegel." Moreover, Žižek seems to erect his orthodox Lacanianism as a bulwark to protect not only Hegel but the phallus as well against the threat of deconstruction and

feminism. Judith Butler critiques Žižek more thoughtfully than I can, however; see her chapter "Arguing with the Real" in *Bodies That Matter* (187–222).

7. Hegel cited in Miller's translation of the *Phenomenology*, 210n.

8. As Alice Jardine puts it in *Gynesis*, quoting Derrida's *Glas*: "The Aufhebung, recognized as mediating between culture and nature, difference and identity, is also seen as that which fundamentally defines male and female through hierarchization: 'The *Aufhebung* is very precisely the relationship of copulation to sexual difference'" (138–39). Jardine's citation of Derrida is from *Glas* (Paris: Éditions Galilée, 1974), 127.

9. In fact, the *Aufhebung* may be not only "the relationship of copulation to sexual difference," as Derrida has it, but more precisely the relationship of imperative reproductivity to copulation itself. As Hegel writes in the chapter entitled "The ethical world. Human and Divine Law: Man and Woman," "The relationship of husband and wife is in the first place the one in which one consciousness immediately recognizes itself in another, and in which there is knowledge of this mutual recognition. Because this self-recognition is a natural and not an ethical one, *it is only a representation, an image of Spirit, not actually Spirit itself.* A representation or image, however, has its actual existence in something other than itself. This relationship therefore has its actual existence not in itself but in the child—an 'other,' whose coming into existence *is* the relationship" (*PS* 273; emphasis added).

10. See Goux's comments on Hegel's phallogocentrism in "The Phallus."

11. Note that "alternative" or "improper" receptacles, such as the mouth or anus, which could veil or reabsorb semen and thus keep it invisible, still inscribe a fundamentally or eventually excremental alignment. The way in which the incommensurability of penis and phallus brings the excremental into relief is the concern of the next chapter.

12. See also Irigaray: "Mother-matter-nature must go on forever nourishing speculation. But this re-source is also rejected as the waste product of reflection, cast outside as what resists it: as madness" (*TS* 77).

13. The adjectives are from a formulation by Serge Leclaire, "Sexuality" (46). The full quotation is of considerable interest: "Let us call the phallus 'God.' It's an old tradition. You don't have to see 'God,' properly speaking, you have no image of him. 'God' (the phallus) is invisible; therefore, the relation to the phallus is marked by a nonformalizable relation, a relation of exclusion. At the same time, everything is in relation to the phallus; everything is in relation to 'God.' Let's suppose that there is a child, Jesus, the son of God, who serves as mediator. Now, let's replace the 'child Jesus' with the penis, which happens to be the most convenient representative of the phallus. Because man has in his body a relation with his *penis as the representative of the phallus*, schematically, his natural inclination leads him to forget the fact that the phallus ('God') is invisible, unseizable, unnameable." See Kaja Silverman's analysis of Leclaire's deification of the phallus in *Male Subjectivity at the Margins* (43).

14. Two other formulations from Goux have direct bearing on the discussion of Hegel vis-à-vis the question of iconoclasm: "As long as we are in the theological space, the nonfigurative imperative appears as a superior path to transcendental realities; it provides an opening, an infinity, a sacred void, affording protection against the reductive interference of phantasy. Iconoclasm is first of all a rejection of the magico-religious beliefs that made the statue a replica of God, a material double animated by divine presence. But reconverted in rationalist space, nonfiguration . . . can become intellectual abstraction, the reduction of reality to a flat rationality" (*Symbolic Economies* 132). "Over and against the treasury of the imagination stands abstract thought, which, though it appears to paint gray on gray, is nonetheless richer. For Hegel and for all those who are opposed to empiricist philosophy, exchanging the image for the concept means a profit for the concept" (104).

15. See, for example, Jürgen Habermas, "Modernity—An Incomplete Project," as well as "Between Eroticism and General Economics: Georges Bataille" (*Philosophical Discourse of Modernity* 211–37). The latter essay was first published as "The French Path to Postmodernity: Bataille between Eroticism and General Economics," *New German Critique* 33 (Fall 1984): 79–102.

16. If one of the treasures that man had formerly attributed to heaven was the power of world destruction, then the story of modernity as a project of reappropriation could be said to have ended at Hiroshima. Actually, one might locate a certain end of modernity, and inauguration of postmodernity, somewhere in the historical space between Auschwitz and Hiroshima as, respectively, an industrial as opposed to a technological mode of genocide. This particularly deadly shift from industry to technology allows us to consider that shift in a more general way, relating modernity and postmodernity to their respective paradigmatic inventions. The paradigmatic invention of modernity is doubtless the engine, from steam to jet, that among other functions facilitates the increasingly rapid movement of bodies through space and time, with corresponding reconfigurations of consciousness. The paradigmatic invention of postmodernity, on the other hand, would have to be the screen, from cinema and television to the VDT and virtual reality displays, which facilitates the increasingly rapid movement of representations of space and time through stationary bodies, also with corresponding reconfigurations of consciousness. One index of the increased rapidity of postmodernism's motionless movement is pointed out by Anders Stephanson: "During the sixties, I was once told that the average camera movement—a change of view, a zoom, a pan— did not go below something like one per 7.5 seconds in an ordinary thirty-second commercial, the reason being that this was considered the optimum of what human perception could handle. Now, it is down to something like 3.5 or less. I have actually timed commercials in which there is about one change every two seconds, fifteen changes in a matter of thirty seconds" ("Conversation with Fredric Jameson" 5). The cognitive

consequences of postmodernism's collapse and inversion of the modernist sensibility of space and time include what Fredric Jameson identifies as the two major aspects of postmodernism: a loss of a sense of history (which was facilitated by a sense of spatial and temporal movement) and a waning of affect (postmodern subjects are never deeply "moved"); see Jameson, *Postmodernism*.

17. See Bataille, "The Psychological Structure of Fascism" (*VE* 137–60). For Bataille's troubled opposition to fascism, particularly in the novel *Blue of Noon*, see Allan Stoekl, *Politics, Writing, Mutilation*.

18. Cited in Melville, *Philosophy beside Itself* (81). In Hurley's translation, the statement appears as "energy can finally only be wasted" (*AS* I:11). I encountered Melville's translation first, however, and subsequent formulations of my own depend on its exact wording.

19. Cited in Michèle Richman, *Reading Georges Bataille* (138).

20. Nor is there anything explicitly scatological in "The Divinity of Laughter" (1943) (*Guilty* 89–119). Cf., however, the following from the erotic novel *My Mother*: "Dotingly, I repeated to myself 'Rhea's behind,' that being the part . . . which she had offered to my young virility. This part of Rhea which I longed to see with my eyes, and which, upon her invitation, I meant to abuse, it was taking shape in my mind: before me I beheld the shrine of mad laughter, simultaneously emblematic of, or redolent with the funereal aspects of, the flush toilet. I laughed, but it was a mirthless laugh: it was mad laughter all right, but it was toneless, it was morose, sly, it was hapless laughter. The idea of the part of herself Rhea had proposed to me, its location and the comic stink which everlastingly tokens our shame gave me the feeling of being happy, of a happiness more precious than any other, of that shameful happiness nobody else would have coveted" (67–68).

21. "To make reason shit" is Mark C. Taylor's translation of Denis Hollier's "Il faut faire chier la raison," in *La Prise de la Concorde* (187), cited in Taylor, *Altarity* (124). Betsy Wing's translation in *Against Architecture* appears as "reason has to be given shit" (98). Taylor's translation, which seems more approximate, carries the double sense of forcing reason *to* shit and turning reason *into* shit, while Wing's can mean both to present reason with shit as a gift and "to give reason some shit," that is, to give it a hard time.

Chapter 3: Dysgraphia I

1. I cite Beckett here in much the same way Bersani does in *The Freudian Body*—that is, as "a kind of terminal prologue to that collapse of theory which I wish to consider as a constitutive fact of both Freudian theory and esthetic practice" (7). Bersani's own formulation of Beckett can serve quite well as a terminal prologue to this chapter, in which I too attempt to produce what Bersani calls "A Beckettian consciousness of psychoanalytic thought" (9). Bersani writes that "Beckett's art of impoverishment is in part an attempt to save consciousness from the contingencies and the temptations of novelistic invention inherent in mobility. The best position

for pure thought is the reptilian one, with its severe restrictions of point of view; reptation is the mode of mobility most congenial to pure intellectuality. On the other hand, thought in Beckett is irresistibly drawn to that part of the body which seems most accurately to reflect its own dilemma. I refer of course to the anus which, like the mind, expels from the body substances which the body both produces and treats like waste. Thought, far from providing a guarantee of being in this radically non-Cartesian world, is the excrement of being" (8–9).

2. In "The Antithetical Meaning of Primal Words" Freud notes that *sacer* means both "'sacred' and 'accursed'" (*SE* 11:159).

3. Cf. "Coincidences" in the afterword to *Story of the Eye*, where Bataille explicates the pseudonym under which he wrote the novel: "The name Lord Auch [pronounced osh] refers to a habit of a friend of mine; when vexed, instead of saying 'aux chiottes' [to the shithouse], he would shorten it to 'aux ch.' *Lord* is English for God (in the Scriptures): Lord Auch is God relieving himself" (98).

4. The general point that God is idealized capital is elaborated throughout Goux's *Symbolic Economies*. The specific quotation, by Moses Hess, is cited on p. 154.

5. Although in my treatment of Freud I am stressing his normativizing and domesticating tendencies, I should also stress my understanding of the way Freud reveals all gender and sexual identity formation as only fragile and tenuous achievements. The problem, however, remains that despite such revelation, and despite the ample tools Freud gives us for critiquing patriarchy, there are numerous ways in which Freud still manages to give patriarchy an affirmative reading.

6. For readings that focus on the ontological and epistemological undecidability of the primal scene, see Peter Brooks, "Fictions of the Wolf Man" (*Reading for the Plot* 264–86), and Ned Lukacher, *Primal Scenes*.

7. Although Freud, in the essay entitled "Femininity" in the *New Introductory Lectures*, specifically warns against conflating activity and passivity with masculinity and femininity, respectively, it is a conflation that he himself never completely abandons; this is the problem, once again, of the conflict between description and prescription in Freudian theory. Juliet Mitchell writes that although Freud "clarified" the "uselessness" of terms such as these, "he returned to the erroneous terms with the fascination of a man who could not see his way through them as terms, though I believe he had come to an understanding of their meaning which surpassed them" (*Psychoanalysis and Feminism* 46).

8. Actually, feminists have turned Freud on his head here by arguing that the absence of castration anxiety, and hence of a strong superego, allows women a more fluid sense of both ethics and ego boundaries than men are afforded. In any case, it is not particularly flattering to masculinist cultural significance that it is shown to be motivated by a fear of castration; here as elsewhere Freud joins Nietzsche in revealing the shameful origins of significant cultural ideals.

9. See also "Some Psychical Consequences of the Anatomical Distinction between the Sexes" (Freud, *SE* 19:257–58): "I cannot evade the notion . . . that for women the level of what is ethically normal is different from what it is in men. Their super-ego is never so inexorable, so impersonal, so independent of its emotional origins as *we require* it to be in men." What I find most striking in this passage is the phrase I have emphasized, which marks the requirements for masculinity as being cultural rather than natural—for what would "we" refer to here other than culture? Although unfortunately Freud himself never adequately follows up on them, he provides hints throughout his work that psychical consequences are in fact *social* consequences.

10. Cf. a selection from the "Anal Erotism and the Castration Complex" section of "The Wolf Man": "The handing over of faeces for the sake of (out of love for) some one else becomes a prototype of castration; it is the first occasion upon which an individual gives up a piece of his own body in order to gain the favour of some other person whom he loves. So that a person's love of his own penis, which is in other respects narcissistic, is not without an element of anal erotism. 'Faeces,' 'child,' and 'penis' thus form a unity, an unconscious concept . . . the concept, namely, of a little thing that can become separate from one's body" (*SE* 17:84).

11. Cf. another moment, this time in *Civilization and Its Discontents*, where writing is inscribed in a heterosexually significant economy: "Writing was in its origin the voice of an absent person; and the dwelling-house was a substitute for the mother's womb, the first lodging, for which in all likelihood man still longs, and in which he was safe and felt at ease" (*SE* 21:91).

12. See the sections on metaphor and metonymy in Kaja Silverman, *The Subject of Semiotics*. See also the following formulation from Maud Ellmann, "Eliot's Abjection": "According to Freud [in *Totem and Taboo*], there are two ways in which taboo can spread, through resemblance or through contiguity. To touch a sacred object is to fall under its interdict, which is an instance of contiguous infection. But the offender must also be tabooed because of 'the risk of imitation,' for others may follow his example. These two forms of transference operate like rhetorical tropes, because the first, like metonymy, depends on contiguity, the second on similitude, like metaphor" (192). For a valuable discussion of the way the metaphor/metonymy and phallus/penis distinctions help to operate each other, see Bernheimer, "Penile Reference."

13. In "The Notion of Expenditure" Bataille notes the sacrificial logic underpinning the oppositional similarity between turds and diamonds "as sumptuous gifts charged with sexual love." He writes that "when in a dream a diamond signifies excrement, it is not only a question of association by contrast"—note how the hard, clear, dry, odorless, and eternal diamond is everything the soft, opaque, moist, smelly, and ephemeral turd is not—"in the unconscious, jewels, like excrement, are cursed matter that flows from a wound; they are a part of oneself destined for open sacrifice" (*VE* 119).

14. These are perhaps the guiding slogans of postmodernism. Or rather, the difference in response *to* them marks the difference between modernism and postmodernism. Both modernism and postmodernism agree with the slogans as diagnoses of alienation. Whereas modernism sees alienation as a breach to be healed by narrative, however—no, you are not yourself, but there was a time when you were yourself and there will be a time when you shall be yourself again—postmodernism sees no remedy, or rather sees all remedies in the light of coercive totalization: you are *not* yourself, you never *were* yourself, and you are never going to *be* yourself. So just get over it.

15. See also the letter of December 22, 1897, where Freud, commenting on the relationship between feces and money, writes to Fliess, "I can scarcely detail for you all the things that resolve themselves into—excrement for me (a new Midas!)" (*CL* 288). Strachey's translation in the *Standard Edition* ("I can scarcely enumerate for you all the things that I [a modern Midas] turn into—excrement" [*SE* 1:273]) is interesting in that it shows Freud more actively arrogating to himself the power to turn things into shit, whereas in the Masson translation it is the things that so resolve themselves. Perhaps the (maternal) source of the anxiety that Freud attempts to assuage here by turning himself into King Midas, and thus preventing himself from resolving, or dissolving, into excrement, will be indicated if the remainder of his paragraph is reproduced: "It fits in completely with the theory of internal stinking. Above all, money itself. I believe this proceeds via the word 'dirty' for 'miserly.' In the same way, everything related to birth, miscarriage, [menstrual] period goes back to the toilet via the word *Abort* [toilet] *Abortus* [abortion]. This is really wild, but it is entirely analogous to the process by which words take on a transferred meaning as soon as new concepts requiring a designation appear" (288 in Masson; Strachey's translation has "lavatory" for "toilet").

16. "Language acquisition implies the suppression of anality; in other words, it represents the acquisition of a capacity for symbolization through the definitive detachment of the rejected object, through its repression through the sign. Every return of rejection and of the erotic pleasure it produces in the sphincters disturbs this symbolic capacity and the acquisition of language that fulfills it. By inserting itself into the signifying system of language, rejection either delays its acquisition, or in the case of the schizoid child, prevents it altogether. In the adult, this return to nonsublimated, nonsymbolized anality breaks up the linearity of the signifying chain" (Kristeva, *RPL* 152).

17. In *Essentially Speaking* Diana Fuss argues that social constructionism cannot totalize itself without lapsing into essentialism, in effect turning construction into nature. Thus constructionism essentially depends on the essentialism from which it differs to construct itself as constructionism. For more on the essentialism/constructionism debate, see the "Essential Difference" issue of *Differences* 1, no. 2 (Summer 1989).

18. For Lacan, this is of course exactly what the symbolic order sup-

posedly does: dereify the fixations of the imaginary. As Teresa Brennan comments in *The Interpretation of the Flesh*, "The mirror stage is, for Lacan, a spatial phenomenon (the body-image is formed at a distance, through the eye of an imagined other). Language on the other hand is temporal; in the psychoanalytic situation, it takes the subject beyond its present fixed meanings into a new time. And given the question of identity, it should also be added that the imaginary continues to be the place in which identity is fixed, while the symbolic path is the means for shifting a fixed identity into one that is less fixed, more productive and truthful" (71). Brennan goes on to say, however, that the "problem with Lacan's account is that language is tied not only to the father, but to the phallus. The difference or empty space which is the condition of differentiation between words and phonemes is marked by the phallus, as 'signifier of lack.' This means that the phallus marks the difference which can never in itself be expressed. If it was, the gap or difference, ostensibly, would be erased. From this perspective, the phallus is a neutral signifier. The problem is that, in order that the subject maintain a fixed identity, this neutral signifier has to be tied to the body. So that while the symbolic is the path beyond [the imaginary's] fixity, it depends, paradoxically, on the fixity of sexual identity" (72).

19. Georg Lukács, in his preface to the 1967 edition of *History and Class Consciousness*, brings just such a charge against his own earlier work, criticizing himself for having failed adequately to distinguish among the terms *reification, objectification*, and *alienation*. For Lukács, this "crude error" inadvertently aligned *History and Class Consciousness* with the bourgeois philosophical and cultural criticism of Martin Heidegger, for whom "it was natural to sublimate a critique of society into a purely philosophical problem, i.e., to convert an essentially social alienation into an eternal 'condition humaine.' . . . This follows from the frequently stressed false identification of opposed fundamental categories. For objectification is indeed a phenomenon that cannot be eliminated from human life in society. If we bear in mind that every externalization of an object in practice (and hence, too, in work) is an objectification, then it is clear that we are dealing with a universal mode of commerce between men. And in so far as this is the case, objectification is a neutral phenomenon. . . . Only when the objectified forms in society acquire functions that bring the essence of man into conflict with his existence, only when man's nature is subjugated, deformed and crippled can we speak of an objective societal condition of alienation and, as an inexorable consequence, of all the subjective marks of an internal alienation" (xxiv). Here Lukács both distances himself from Heidegger's anguished fear of objectification and gives the lie to the notion of a Heideggerean historicity by pointing out that some degree of objectification is inextricable from the processes of externalization and production that enable human practice, sensual human activity, and hence, from the orthodox Marxist perspective, history itself (see Lucien Goldmann, *Lukács and Heidegger*). When he insists on the neutrality of the phenomenon,

however, Lukács thereby naturalizes objectification as a universal mode of commerce between men and necessarily fails to recognize how the long-patriarchal (and now capitalistic) history of this commerce subjugates, deforms, and cripples those women whose real essence as social agents is brought into conflict with their mystifying existence as commodified objects of exchange. The authors of *Dialectic of Enlightenment* are closer to the mark, and critically distance themselves from both Heidegger's anguish and Lukács's neutrality, when they state that "all objectification is a forgetting" (230). For Adorno and Horkheimer, what is forgotten is certainly not the question of Being, à la Heidegger, and is not only history itself, its constitutive tensions and struggles, but also "the importance of the body" (231–36). For Adorno in particular, remembering history does not entail the Lukácsian invocation and neutralization of a universal mode of commerce between men. As Robert Hullot-Kentor has recently pointed out, Adorno was "hardly obtuse to the situation of women" ("Back to Adorno" 11 n. 15). There is evidence enough in Adorno's writing that for him—despite his denunciations of a mass culture that some, according to Andreas Huyssen, devalue by gendering as feminine—the objectification that forgets history also necessarily occludes the question of women's subjective agency and desires. See my "A Knowledge That Would Not Be Power"; see also Gregory S. Jay's chapter entitled "Reification and Logocentrism" in *America the Scrivener,* in which Jay advocates "a reading of Marx [that] will stymie even the most sophisticated efforts to localize reification as the determined effect of a particular historical or socioeconomic condition" and suggests that "the phenomena of reification belong to an overdetermined history of 'object relations' which would include the contributions of ontology as well as psychoanalysis" (147).

20. At least one African-American woman, however, writes quite powerfully about both modes of possession. I refer of course to Toni Morrison, particularly in *The Bluest Eye, Sula,* and *Beloved.* See Kathryn Bond Stockton, "Heaven's Bottom."

21. Freud's notion of *Nachträglichkeit,* or deferred action, is crucial here. What I am suggesting, quite speculatively, is that for males it is not until "the transformations of puberty"—that is, the first experience of ejaculation—that the memories of earlier analized separations are reinvoked, reinvested, reconceptualized; this reinvocation, however, in turn reinvests the experience of ejaculation with a traumatic or scatontologically shattering cathexis that then becomes its ground. The most crucial point, however, is what the male has learned in the time *between* these two mutually determining moments—that is, everything his culture has taught him about its valuation of women and the feminine. That lesson is, in the final instance, the most crucial determination, but also the one most amenable to change.

22. I take the word *upstream* from Peter Dews. Dews writes that Derrida's Heideggerian "response to [the] collapse of Husserl's philosophical project is *not,* like that of Adorno or Merleau-Ponty, to move 'downstream'

towards an account of subjectivity as emerging from and entwined with the natural and historical world, but rather to move 'upstream,' in a quest for the ground of transcendental consciousness itself" (*Logics of Disintegration* 19). In the following section and in chapter 4 I attempt to show what sorts of streams may be involved here and how the Heideggerian desire to get upstream of metaphysics may be intricated with the desire, which Freud lays bare, to get beyond the pleasure/unpleasure principle. These intricated desires, which strive to get upstream of or beyond both sexual difference and abjection, can lead toward death, but they can also pull up short and become, instead, quite murderous.

23. Again, I should stress that my strategic appropriations of Bersani are not meant to foreclose on the fact that his discussions of anality in "Is the Rectum a Grave?" refer specifically to anal sex between men.

24. See, for example, "The Gesture in Psychoanalysis," *Between Feminism and Psychoanalysis*, ed. Teresa Brennan (London: Routledge, 1989), 127–38.

25. This foreclosure of the question of anality and gender in regard to the *fort-da* also obtains for Lacan and Derrida. Lacan, in *The Four Fundamental Concepts of Psychoanalysis*, appears markedly decided about the *fort-da*'s undecidability, declaring quite emphatically that the child's representational objectification of the mother in the reel is of only "secondary importance" and that the reel "is not the mother reduced to a little ball by some magical game worthy of the Jivaros—it is a small part of the subject that detaches itself from him while still remaining his, still retained" (62). Lacan insists that to say that the *fort-da* "is simply a question for the subject of instituting himself in a function of mastery is idiotic. . . . The function of the exercise . . . refers to an alienation, and not to some supposed mastery, which is difficult to imagine being increased in an endless repetition, whereas the endless repetition that is in question reveals the radical vacillation of the subject" (239). Here Lacan throws the supposed mastery of the *fort-da*'s subject into question by stressing a radical and alienating vacillation. Nonetheless, he reinstitutes a certain mastery—perhaps his own—by denying the possibility of any multiple or vacillating determinations or identifications for the reel, the *objet a* that for Lacan can be only a fill-in for the phallus. Although elsewhere Lacan admits a metaphorical fungibility (but not a metonymical contiguity) between phallus and feces—"The anal level is the locus of metaphor—one object for another, give the faeces in place of the phallus" (*FFC* 104)—even that exchange rate does not seem to be in currency here. By foreclosing, then, on the possibility of a coincidental anal/maternal identification for the reel, Lacan prophylactically separates subjective vacillation from a primontological reversibility that is the scene of a general anxiety about the (m)other's power to decide—the scene of a suspicion that it may originally have been she who decided to squeeze the subject into a little ball (perhaps to roll it toward some overwhelming question). Thus, despite the fact that for Lacan, man's desire is the desire of the Other, that "it is from the place of the Other that the subject's mes-

sage is emitted," here it appears that it is still the subject, and not the object, whom Lacan supposes to know.

There is no mention of anality in Derrida's lengthy explication of the *fort-da* in *The Post Card* either, not the slightest trace. *Pas de pas dans le merde*—not a single step. On whatever proper route Derrida limps along with Freud in "Freud's Legacy," it certainly is not the road on which the Wolf-Man saw the excremental trinity that plunged his thoughts to a Bataillean comparison. There is no intersection. Just as in *Writing and Difference* Derrida cleans up Bataille's apish rump and dries out the laughter of the Bataillean notion of expenditure, so here Derrida seems oblivious to the absent presence of fecality in Freud. Derrida seems curiously fastidious about materializing partiality, divisibility, that which falls, even though he gives us in his critique of Lacan the following indispensable formulation of "phallogocentric transcendentalism": "Especially if within *metalanguage*, language is centered on the voice, that is, on the ideal site of the phallus. If by some misfortune the phallus were divisible or reduced to the status of a part object, the entire edifice would collapse, and this must be avoided at all cost. This can always happen if its occurrence, its taking-place, does not have the ideality of a phonematic letter. . . . This always does *happen*, but the voice is there to deceive us about this strange event, and to leave to us the ideal guardianship of that which falls to the rank of partial or divisible object: a disseminable bit" (*PC* 478–79). He elaborates the term *part-object* only as being "subject like any other to the chain of substitutes" (478 n. 57) without acknowledging Lacan's much more material list of likely candidates for part-object status in *Écrits*: "the mamilla, faeces, the phallus . . . the urinary flow . . . the phoneme, the gaze, the voice—the nothing" (315). This list not only is more generous, or general, than the one Lacan restricts himself to in his formulation of the *fort-da*'s reel but also, including as it does both the phallus and the voice as part-objects, seems to problematize the terms of Derrida's charge of phono/phallogocentrism against Lacan in the previous quotation. If Lacan, in the seminar on "The Purloined Letter," gives us the signifier's *material indivisibility,* Derrida seems to answer with a *divisible immateriality.* This immaterialism suggests Derrida's own repression of writing, which I examine more fully in chapter 4.

26. "One day the child's mother had been away for several hours and on her return was met with the words 'Baby o-o-o-o!' which was at first incomprehensible. It soon turned out, however, that during this long period of solitude the child had found a method of making *himself* disappear. He had discovered his reflection in a full-length mirror which did not quite reach to the ground, so that by crouching down he could make his mirror-image 'gone'" (*SE* 18:15 n. 1).

27. As Helen Molesworth points out in the *October* discussion on abjection, there are moments in Bataille when "you can't tell the difference between an eye and an asshole" (Foster et al. 6). Interesting in this regard is the fact that the muscle that surrounds the eyeball is also called a sphincter.

Chapter 4: Dysgraphia 2

1. The number of texts dealing with Heidegger's politics is growing exponentially, and the following list is not exhaustive. See, to begin with, Victor Farias, *Heidegger and Nazism*. For discussions of Heidegger's politics and Farias's study by such theorists as Habermas, Derrida, Levinas, Gadamer, Lacoue-Labarthe, and others, see "Symposium on Heidegger and Nazism." See also "Special Section on Martin Heidegger," which includes translations of Heidegger's Freiburg addresses, particularly Richard Wolin's excellent article "The French Heidegger Debate"; Wolin expands that article in *The Politics of Being*. See "Heidegger: Art and Politics," a special issue of *Diacritics*; Günther Neske and Emil Kettering, *Martin Heidegger and National Socialism*; Derrida, *Of Spirit*; Jean-François Lyotard, *Heidegger and "the Jews"*; Michael E. Zimmerman, *Heidegger's Confrontation with Modernity*; Tom Rockmore, *On Heidegger's Nazism and Philosophy*; and Tom Rockmore and Joseph Margolis, eds., *The Heidegger Case*.

2. For Lyotard, as for me, this abjection is what remains the unthought of Heidegger's questioning of the unthought of metaphysics. "It is no longer a question of what is lacking in Heidegger's (political) thought so as to turn into effective politics, but it becomes a question of what it lacks quite simply in order to think, of what it misses, as thought, even in 'turning.' For it turns short." Lyotard then goes on to say of this lack that "Derrida cannot address [it] in any way, nor can he identify it, at least as long as he holds on to deconstruction" (*Heidegger and "the Jews"* 76). In the next section I examine what I consider the stakes and consequences of Derrida's "hold."

3. Lukacher's formulations of Heidegger in this important article are quite appropriate to my points and I therefore quote him at length: "Heidegger's determination to shake thinking out of its sclerotic condition by turning to poetic experience nevertheless leaves intact thinking's predominance over the differance between spirit and matter. The madness of words notwithstanding, Heidegger still appears committed to an ideational order that, while perhaps leaving traces in the resonant phenomenality of language, remains distinct from its matter. That poetic experience might register some absolutely resistant materiality that cannot be purged as thinking winnows its way through the phenomenality of poetry seems to be precisely the notion that most intrigues Heidegger and against which he must struggle most mightily" (142). Lukacher continues, "Poetry releases language into its estrangement, its otherness, but that otherness is for Heidegger finally retrievable only by thinking and not by the senses or some other noncognitive capacity. The unthought is for Heidegger entirely separate from the resistant noncognitive materiality of language. . . . Our estrangement before the other materiality that is language's essence may or may not entail the preeminence of thinking. Heidegger invariably leads us to this liminal point before succumbing himself to the need for reattachment" (143).

4. Derrida characterized Heidegger's problem with metaphysics thus in

a presentation at a conference on Heidegger at Loyola University in Chicago, September 22, 1989.

5. In *Being and Time* Heidegger designates Being as *"the transcendens pure and simple"* (62). Heidegger reemphasizes this transcendental purity in "Letter on Humanism" (216). For *Ereignis,* see Heidegger, *Identity and Difference* (36).

6. The privileging of verbals over noun forms is perhaps the characteristic gesture by which Heidegger always hopes to arrive at the "even more primordial": more primordial than any mere appearance is the appearing, more primordial than temporality is temporalizing, more primordial than any unconcealed truth is the unconcealing, more primordial than any unconcealed gift is the "It gives," and so on. To carnalize that gesture ironically, to allude to coming without come or shitting without shit, is only to give a twist to Adorno's charge that the Heideggerian "invocation of being" is animated by the need for "a repudiation of any content as unclean" (*Negative Dialectics* 7). For what I consider an unconvincing rebuttal of Adorno's critique of Heidegger, see Fred Dallmayr, "Adorno and Heidegger."

7. In *Epistemology of the Closet* Eve Kosofsky Sedgwick writes, "Deconstruction, founded as a very science of *différ(e/a)nce,* has both so fetishized the idea of difference and so vaporized its possible embodiments that its most thoroughgoing practitioners are the last people to whom one would now look for help in thinking about particular difference*s*" (23).

8. I am referring to the following, which is apparently Heidegger's sole reference to the Holocaust: "Agriculture is now a mechanized food industry. As for its essence, it is the same thing as the manufacture of corpses in the gas chambers and the death camps, the same thing as the blockades and the reduction of countries to famine, the same thing as the manufacture of hydrogen bombs" (cited in Blanchot, "Thinking the Apocalypse," 478). Blanchot joins Philippe Lacoue-Labarthe, whom he paraphrases here, in calling Heidegger's formulation "a scandalously inadequate statement, because all it retains of the extermination of the Jews is a reference to a certain technology and mentions neither the name nor the fate of the Jews. It is indeed true that at Auschwitz and elsewhere Jews were treated as industrial waste and that they were considered to be the effluvia of Germany and Europe (in that, the responsibility of each one of us is at issue). What was unthinkable and unforgivable in the event of Auschwitz, this utter void in our history, is met with Heidegger's determined silence" (478–79). Ferry and Renaut comment that Heidegger's formulation puts Hitler on a par with the French minister of agriculture.

9. In *Of Spirit* Derrida examines Heidegger's attempt to "spiritualize" National Socialism, particularly its racism. In Heidegger, says Derrida, "the thought of race . . . is interpreted in metaphysical and not biological terms. . . . By thus inverting the direction of determination, is Heidegger alleviating or aggravating this 'thought of race'? Is a metaphysics of race more or less serious than a naturalism or a biologism of race?" (74). These

are important questions that, among others, Derrida unfortunately insists on "leaving suspended."

10. Avital Ronnell, "The Differends of Man" (65); see also, in the same issue of *Diacritics*, Derrida, "How to Concede." See also Derrida's "Heidegger's Silence" and Herman Rapaport, *Heidegger and Derrida*. One might agree with Derrida that only attentive, "active" readers of Heidegger have the right to speak about his silence. One gets the feeling, however, that for Derrida and company *only* such readers have any business speaking not only about Heidegger's supposedly as-yet-unreadable silence but about the Holocaust itself; everyone else is a "loudmouth" (Ronnell) or a "show-off" (Derrida).

11. For Heidegger's appropriations of Jünger, see Zimmerman, *Heidegger's Confrontation with Modernity* (46–93), and Wolin, *The Politics of Being* (77–83, 88–92).

12. See Heidegger's tribute to Schlageter in the special section on Heidegger in *New German Critique* 45 (1988).

13. Cited in Derrida, "*Geschlect* II" (165).

14. In *Heidegger's Confrontation with Modernity* Zimmerman, following the lead of Heidegger's indebtedness to Jünger, mentions in a footnote the correspondence between aspects of Heidegger's philosophy and the subjects of Theweleit's study. Zimmerman traces this correspondence in greater detail in "Ontological Aestheticism." See also Daniel T. O'Hara, "Mask Plays."

15. This judgment is, for me at least, not qualified by a reading of Jean Graybeal's *Language and "the Feminine" in Nietzsche and Heidegger*. Graybeal attempts to link Kristeva's notions of the semiotic and the symbolic with, respectively, the authentic and the inauthentic in the first part of *Being and Time* and argues for the subversive effects of Heidegger's feminization of the figure of *Cūra* or "Care" in *Being and Time*, part 2. In doing so, she dismisses as misinterpretations Kristeva's own critiques of Heidegger in *Revolution in Poetic Language*, where Kristeva considers Heidegger as offering only "a stasis in which the unitary subject takes cover as if in a religion" and calls Heidegger's recourse to *Cūra* a "regressive mythological travesty" (*RPL* 129). Graybeal thinks Heidegger expresses a Kristevan "joy in the truth of self-division." But one has to wonder about a Heideggerian "joy" that in *Being and Time* remains unshakably "armed" (*gerüstete*), a rather conspicuous adjective considering Heidegger's "blunder" into fascism, which Graybeal never mentions. Furthermore—and perhaps this is not an accident—she does not address the more corporeal aspects of abjection.

16. My language here tropes and quotes the first page of Derrida's *Glas*.

17. Thanks to Gregory S. Jay for his assistance in formulating this "vulgar" point.

18. I leave that to the scholars and media pundits of the American right, who are currently reducing and transmogrifying both deconstruction and postmodernism into fascistically inspired denials of the "objective truth" that the Holocaust occurred. See, for example, George F. Will's column

entitled "Fascism's Second Spring," in which he introduces de Man simply as "a founder of 'deconstructionism'" and "a Belgian fascist" (72). For Derrida on de Man, see "Like the Sound of the Sea," but see also David Carroll, "The Temptation of Fascism."

19. There has been considerable discussion of Derrida's gender politics in regard to his stance(s) toward feminism, his treatment of the question of woman in *Spurs*, his deployment of terms such as *hymen, invagination,* and so on. See Gayatri Spivak, "Displacement and the Discourse of Woman"; Spivak, "Feminism and Deconstruction, Again: Negotiating with Unacknowledged Masculinism"; Sally Robinson, "Deconstructive Discourse"; Robert Scholes, "Reading Like a Man"; and Scholes, "Éperon Strings."

20. For Rorty this reading of the early Derrida is typified best by Rodolphe Gasché.

21. Although much has been written on Derrida's relationship to psychoanalysis, it is worth noting here the relative or even complete absence of any discussion of that relationship in predominantly Heideggerian readings of Derrida. Rodolphe Gasché's *The Tain of the Mirror: Derrida and the Philosophy of Reflection* is perhaps the foremost example, but see also Herman Rapaport's *Heidegger and Derrida*. Ned Lukacher's *Primal Scenes* is a notable exception.

22. See Medard Boss, "Martin Heidegger's Zollikon Seminars" (9); cited in Ned Lukacher, *Primal Scenes* (44).

23. Perhaps symptomatic is Derrida's treatment of the fart in *Glas:* "How could ontology lay hold of a fart?" (58). In her essay "Acting Bits" Gayatri Spivak writes that "Derrida is here marking the difference between *Geist* and *Gäschen*, between spirit and a fart, between the transcendent breeze and the wind that makes us embarrassed, which is marked by the body's materiality. . . . He rewrites the ontico-ontological difference by reminding us of the body's being: the ontic, which in Heidegger is the intimacy of being, to which the being is so proximate or close that no ontology can lay hold of it, in the late Heidegger becomes a certain kind of fetish. His politics change, he invokes an originary or primordial language" (797). Spivak goes on to say that "an ontology can always put its hand on whatever remains in the john—the shit—but never on the whiffs let out by roses. So the text is a gas, the mark of the spirit in one's body. . . . The ontic as fart or belch, the signature of the subject at ease with itself decentered from the mind to the body, which writes its inscription" (797). This discussion seems to problematize my critique—but then, not only does the fart remain *invisible;* it does not even *remain*. It is significant that Derrida focuses on such an effervescent anal product, one that always erases itself. Eve Sedgwick's comments reproduced in note 7, in which deconstruction is charged with "vaporizing" differences, seem oddly pertinent here.

24. Nietzsche's own will to power, his active nihilism, is relentlessly opposed to all forms of philosophical idealism. As *On the Genealogy of Morals* makes clear, however, the "ascetic ideal" is also a form of the will to pow-

er as practiced by the man of *ressentiment.* Theweleit's study suggests what happens when the passive nihilist actively performs his idealizations/devivifications on the body of the other. As Daniel T. O'Hara points out, "the fascist imagination is one modern enactment of a radical asceticism whose origins are saturated in blood" ("Mask Plays" 136).

25. Cornell's formulation (her "sink into the same old shit" is from Beckett's *Happy Days*) marks in an interesting way the differing stakes of Derridean deconstruction for men and women. Perhaps women, whom men have so long relegated to "the same old shit," can and should find utopian value in deconstruction's transcendental promise that "we might yet fly away." But the transcendental flights of masculinity historically have been predicated on the relegation of women and others to the same old shit (cf. again Hegel's fecalization of the Jews), so there is a political danger in men's too easy assumption of deconstruction's transcendental promise of flight. From a feminist perspective, I think there is just cause for suspicion when deconstruction hands out its boarding passes to masculinity: men still need to dirty their own wings.

26. The critique of Derrida's "there is nothing outside the text" hinges on whether one accepts Cornell West's assertion that Derrida "can actually be understood to claim that there is nothing outside social practices: intertextuality is a differential web of relations shot through with traces, shot through with activity. For a pragmatist, that activity is always linked to human agency and the context in which that agency is enacted. If he is read that way, I am in agreement" ("Interview" 270). For a refutation of the idea that Derrida can be read in this way, see Thomas McCarthy, "The Politics of the Ineffable."

Chapter 5: Not a Nice Production

1. H. G. Wells, "James Joyce" (159); cited in Don Gifford, *Ulysses Annotated* (137), and in Deming, ed., *James Joyce* (86). In *James Joyce and Sexuality* Robert Brown situates Wells among those early critics of Joyce who "rarely had a clear distinction in their minds between Joyce's treatment of sexuality and what they considered to be his exaggerated interest in all the workings of the body" (1). This "clear distinction," on which Brown insists and his book is based, seems to me particularly unproductive in reading Joyce.

2. "How right Wells was!" See Richard Ellmann, *James Joyce* (414).

3. For commentary on Pound's "rejection of the materiality of the letter and anality as both subversive of an identity guaranteed by the penis," see Colin MacCabe, *James Joyce and the Revolution of the Word* (170). Pound, of course, was not the only fascist-friendly modernist to base his rejection of Joyce on a rejection of the materiality of the letter and anality: Wyndham Lewis in *Time and Western Man* compares *Ulysses* to "a record diarrhoea" (109). For an overview of phallic, squeamish, or class-based rejections of Joyce by Pound, Lewis, Wells, West, Woolf, and others, see Patrick Parrinder, "The Strange Necessity."

4. Speculating on the relation between Joyce's cloacal obsession and his life and writing, Brenda Maddox writes "Joyce came to find everything connected with excretion unusually pleasurable. Morevover, if the Freudian view be taken—that the unconscious associates defecation with spending money or with childbirth—Joyce had formidable influences within his own home. His father's wild extravagance was the very opposite of anal retentiveness; Joyce himself linked his father's 'spendthrift habits' with his own and with 'any creativity I may possess.' As for his fertile mother, fat brown things [a reference to Joyce's 1909 erotic letters to Nora] popped from her body with a regularity that must have awed her impressionable first child" (*Nora* 102).

5. Derrida bases his characterization of Joyce on the line "Jewgreek is greekjew. Extremes meet" from *Ulysses* (15:2097–98). In *The French Joyce* Geert Lernout points out that since this line occurs in the hallucinatory "Circe" chapter and is "spoken" by Lynch's cap, it can hardly be taken as representing Joyce's philosophical views (59). Derrida's need to appropriate Joyce to Hegelianism may stem again from his retention of Heidegger, which I explore more fully in chapter 4. In "Two Words for Joyce" Derrida speaks of being "haunted by Joyce" but of not being sure "of liking him all the time" (146). Derrida rather unfavorably compares Joyce's "greatness" with "the greatness of s/he who writes in order to give, in giving, and therefore in order to give to forget the gift and the given, what is given—and impossible—way" (146). Derrida then goes on to drop the ambiguous "s/he" and to say that "once the gift is received, the work having worked to the extent of changing you through and through, the scene is other and you have forgotten the gift and the giver. Then the work is loveable, and if the 'author' is forgotten, we have for *him* . . . a gratitude without ambivalence. This is what's called love" (147; emphasis added). I suggest that any time Derrida goes into a riff about "incalculable gifts," he is sending a love letter or thank-you card to Heidegger, who in this passage is unnamed but not, I think, forgotten. Derrida characterizes Joyce's second-order greatness as always inescapably "*being memory of him*" (147), whereas Heidegger's greatness is, one supposes, simply that of Being itself: Derrida's assertion that "the gift I'm describing can never be a present" (147), which seems to ascribe Joyce's greatness to the metaphysical realm of presence and to locate Heidegger's beyond it, also has the effect of effacing the abject materiality of the gift that Joyce's writing celebrates.

6. That Joyce leaned politically in a different direction from many of his male modernist contemporaries is not merely coincidental. In this regard see Dominic Manganiello, *Joyce's Politics*, and Ira B. Nadel, *Joyce and the Jews*.

7. Monnier's commentary, from *Les Gazettes d'Andrienne Monnier*, May 1940, is cited in Robert McDougal, *The Very Rich Hours of Adrienne Monnier* (118), and in Bonnie Kime Scott, *Joyce and Feminism* (103).

8. See Burton A. Waisbren and Florence L. Walzl, "Paresis and the

Priest." In "Silence in *Dubliners*" Jean-Michel Rabaté uses language resonant with my discussion when he writes, "*paralysis* etymologically conveys an idea of dissolution, of an unbinding (*para-lyein:* to release, to unbind) which is coupled with an anguishing immobility, while *paresis* means 'to let fall'" (53).

9. See Stanislaus Joyce, *Complete Dublin Diary* (11n). One wonders to what degree this statement subverts itself by so evidently parading its patent ignorance: surely Joyce understood that women shit more than once a week. One also has to question the extent of Joyce's investment in other of his directly sexist statements. For instance, Joyce apparently enjoyed Mary Colum's rebuttal to his proclamation "I hate women who know anything" (see Ellmann, *James Joyce* 634). None of this, however, should be taken as a suggestion that Joyce did not participate in sexism. For discussions of Joyce's misogyny from a feminist/Joycean perspective, see Kime Scott, *Joyce and Feminism* and *James Joyce*; Suzette Henke and Elaine Unkeless, eds. *Women in Joyce*; Henke, *James Joyce*; and Karen Lawrence, "Joyce and Feminism."

10. Not only what is said in "The Sisters" but what is deleted from it, the ellipses, work toward the prevention of paralysis: cf. the deleted original last words of the story as it first appeared in the *Irish Homestead:* "God rest his soul."

11. My reference is to Barthes's "The text is (should be) that uninhibited person who shows his behind to the *Political Father*" (*Pleasure of the Text* 53). "Culious" from *Finnegans Wake* mixes "curious" with the Latin *culus*, or "fundament," whereas *epiphany* of course means "showing forth." See Roland McHugh, *Annotations to Finnegans Wake* (508).

12. "His writing is not *about* something; *it is that something itself*," Samuel Beckett, "Dante . . . Bruno . Vico . . Joyce" (Beckett et al., *Exagmination* 14).

13. Other treatments of the "language of earse" in *Finnegans Wake* include Rabaté, "Lapsus ex machine"; Margot Norris, *Decentered Universe*; Colin MacCabe, "An Introduction"; Stephen Heath, "Joyce in Language"; and Heath, "Ambiviolences." See also Susan Brienza, "Krapping Out."

14. See Patrick Parrinder, "The Strange Necessity." Margot Norris also spoke to these matters in a paper called "Clean and Dirty Prose: Joyce's Stylistic Self-Critique of Modernism," delivered at the 1991 MLA Convention.

15. My problem with Henke's formulation is not that Joyce's writing fails to deconstruct Stephen's misogyny but that this deconstruction does not take the teleological form or "path" of growth and maturity that Henke posits. Further, there is a problem in making misogyny a function of adolescence, of age or personal temperament rather than of social and psychosymbolical structures of oppression—as if there were not a significant number of very mature men and male artists who remain resolutely misogynist.

16. Cf. Freud's discussion of the sense of smell in the famous footnote in *Civilization and Its Discontents* (*SE* 21:99n-100n). Cf. also Horkheimer and

Adorno: "The multifarious nuances of the sense of smell embody the archetypal longing for the lower forms of existence, for direct unification with circumambient nature, with the earth and mud. Of all the senses, that of smell—which is attracted without objectifying—bears clearest witness to the urge to lose oneself in and become the 'other.' As perception and the perceived—both are united—smell is more expressive than the other senses. When we see we remain what we are; but when we smell we are overtaken by otherness" (*Dialectic of Enlightenment* 184).

17. Peter Brooks, "Freud's Masterplot: A Model for Narrative" (*Reading for the Plot* 90–113). For a response to Brooks, see Susan Winette, "Coming Unstrung."

18. Gifford, in his revised edition of this work, *Ulysses Annotated,* glosses "Gelindo" simply as "a man's name" (245), but an Italianist colleague informs me that the root *Gel* in "Gelindo" is the same as that in *"gelato"* and so does imply a certain coldness.

19. In his latest book on Joyce, *The Veil of Signs,* Brivic does rather unavoidably pay more attention to the problematic of language. Unfortunately, he also marshals a great deal of Lacanian-inflected discourse only to support some quite conventional arguments that attempt to justify "the idea of Joyce as a transcendent presence in his work" (24). Brivic's relentless investment in "transcendent value" (23) and "the transcendent level of perception" (51) is perhaps a holdover from his earlier interest in Jung, whom he in his first book calls "the psychologist of transcendence," over the materialism of Freud. This investment leads to what I consider some misdirected readings of Joyce. Commenting, for example, on Stephen's composition of the villanelle, in which "the liquid letters of speech, symbols of the element of mystery, flowed over his brain" (*PA* 223), Brivic is correct to say that "the formless form of 'liquid letters' corresponds to what Freud called primary process thinking, the indiscriminate flow of associations in the id." He buys into Stephen's own romanticizations, however, when writes that "the depth of Stephen's immersion in fluidity here allows him to discern that all of the signs that swirl by are only symbols of a primal mystery beyond expression" (47). Primal and primary, yes: mysterious and transcendent, no.

20. Rabaté comments that "the 'bodily' shame is confirmed by the common 'transgression' of the mother's sex" (*James Joyce* 69)—that is, both the father's penis and the son-as-fetus pass through the same maternal defile.

21. For a good explication of the utterly regressive nature of Bly's project, see Philomena Mariani, "'God Is a Man.'"

22. Here I am less writing "against *Ulysses*" than more or less steering clear of it, and for reasons rather different from those of Bersani. First of all, I do not think *Ulysses* is all that sublimated (and Bersani's positing of *Women in Love* as a more authentically avant-garde novel leaves me quite cold). Further, I think that the liquidation of the father, and of authorial consciousness, that begins in *A Portrait* and continues throughout *Finne-*

gans Wake is also enacted in *Ulysses,* particularly in Joyce's demolition of Stephen's self-paternal theory of Shakespeare in "Scylla and Charybdis" and in Stephen's and Bloom's anti-ephiphanic, anti-oedipal meeting in "Ithaca." I am avoiding *Ulysses* here not only because otherwise this chapter would become a book in itself but also because I think that the question of writing *Joyce's* body, which begins with Stephen and culminates with Shem the Penman, is taken up in a more authentically risky and radically desublimated way with those two figures than it is in *Ulysses'* rather more suspect (appropriative) gesture of writing from the position of woman (Molly) or from that of the Jew as new womanly man (Bloom).

23. If *Ulysses* is modernism's monument to the authority of sublimation, Stephen's theory of Shakespeare in the "Scylla and Charybdis" chapter of that novel represents his own monumental effort to transcend anxiety. Indeed, if Stephen has a monument, it is his theory—which MacCabe, in "The Voice of Esau," calls "a performance which [Stephen hopes] will both wrest a meaning from Shakespeare and confer an identity on himself" (111). The tension, the authentic risk, however, lies less in the content of the theory than in its production, in the way the theory becomes a lost object, an *objet petit a,* for Stephen even in his effort to press out this monument. Stephen cannot accede to himself, confer an identity on himself, by designating himself in this statement; he can only end up writing his own abjection. See Patrick McGee's excellent analysis of this writing in *Paperspace* (37–68).

24. In a footnote to a recent "condensation" of his earlier work, Sheldon Brivic writes of the bird-girl scene, "Thomas Flanagan has suggested in conversation that the girl's position and the 'noise of gently moving water' that issues from her probably indicate that she is urinating. The stream of her urine could constitute a phallic symbol and so add to the fetishism of the scene." See his "The Disjunctive Structure of Joyce's *Portrait*" (261). Actually, Flanagan's suggestion is much more interesting than what Brivic makes of it. It suggests how not only Stephen's "profane joy" but the whole epiphanic conversion to aesthetic heroism that this scene is usually taken to register become an *effect* of the woman's urinary production, thus marking the imminently nonoriginary status of anything the male artist-as-hero might himself thereafter produce. Thus, just as in the anatomy theater Stephen's vision of the broad-shouldered student as originary "strong maker" is revealed as the afterbirth of textual inscription, metonymically linked to oozing scrawls on urinal walls, so here Stephen's ontology as strong-maker wannabe is similarly stained, given the lie of its cloacal origin. On a corresponding note, it is only *after* Stephen imagines Emma Clery's first menstrual period that he is finally able to let the liquid letters of speech flow over his brain and to pen his villanelle. Although this scene ostensibly articulates a compassion on Stephen's part born of "commonality"—after all, menstrual blood and semen, like snow at the end of "The Dead, are general all over Ireland—it also cedes a certain material priority to the body of the other.

Chapter 6: Closings

1. This comes from a formulation of Lacan that I still find useful: "This is to say that neurosis for Lacan is essentially a failure to accept castration, a failure to accept the primal lack which is at the center of life itself: a vain and impossible nostalgia for that first essential plenitude, a belief that one really can in one form or another repossess the phallus. Genuine desire, on the other hand, is a consent to incompleteness, to time and to the repetition of desire in time; whereas the disorders of desire result from an attempt to keep alive the delusion and the fiction of ultimate satisfaction" (Jameson, *Prison-House* 172).

2. In *Marginal Forces* Michael Bérubé refers to "a pornographic mode of reading, a mode of reading that seeks above all else to restore unity and order to an ostensibly fragmented and challenging text; it would be a reading that meets the challenge by mastering the text, taking it apart, fighting its radical 'incompleteness'" (256–57).

Works Cited

Acker, Kathy. *Great Expectations*. New York: Grove, 1982.

Adorno, Theodor W., and Max Horkheimer. *Dialectic of Enlightenment*. Trans. John Cumming. New York: Continuum, 1987.

———. *Minima Moralia: Reflections from Damaged Life*. Trans. E. F. N. Jephcott. London: Verso, 1974.

———. *Negative Dialectics*. Trans. E. B. Ashton. New York: Continuum, 1987.

Alcoff, Linda. "The Problem of Speaking for Others." *Cultural Critique* 20 (Winter 1991–92): 5–32.

Althusser, Louis. *Lenin and Philosophy and Other Essays*. Trans. Ben Brewster. New York: Monthly Review, 1971.

Anzaldúa, Gloria. "Haciendo caras: una entrada." In *Making Faces, Making Soul/Haciendo Caras: Creative and Critical Perspectives by Feminists of Color*, ed. Gloria Anzaldúa, xv–xxviii. San Francisco: Aunt Lute, 1990.

Attridge, Derek, and Daniel Ferrer. "Introduction: Highly Continental Evenements." In *Post-Structural Joyce: Essays from the French*, ed. Attridge and Ferrer, 1–14. Cambridge: Cambridge University Press.

Barthes, Roland. *Camera Lucida: Reflections on Photography*. Trans. Richard Howard. New York: Noonday, 1981.

———. *Incidents*. Trans. Richard Howard. Berkeley: University of California Press, 1992.

———. *On Racine*. Trans. Richard Howard. New York: Hill and Wang, 1964.

———. *The Pleasure of the Text*. Trans. Richard Miller. New York: Noonday, 1975.

Bartky, Sandra. *Femininity and Domination: Essays on the Phenomenology of Oppression*. New York: Routledge, 1990.

Barzilai, Shuli. "Borders of Language: Kristeva's Critique of Lacan." *Publications of the Modern Language Association* 106, no. 2 (March 1991): 294–305

Bataille, Georges. "L'Abjection et les formes misérables." *Essais de sociologie*. Vol. 2 of *Oeuvres complètes*. 12 vols. Paris: Gallimard, 1970.

———. *The Accursed Share, Vol I: Consumption*. Trans. Robert Hurley. New York: Zone, 1991.

———. *The Accursed Share, Vols. II & III: The History of Eroticism & Sovereignty*. Trans. Robert Hurley. New York: Zone, 1991.

———. *Erotism: Death and Sensuality*. Trans. Mary Dalwood. San Francisco: City Lights, 1986.

———. *Guilty.* Trans. Bruce Boone. Venice, Calif.: Lapis, 1988.

———. "Hegel, Death and Sacrifice." Trans. Jonathan Strauss. *Yale French Studies* 78:9–28.

———. *Inner Experience.* Trans. Leslie Anne Boldt. Albany: SUNY Press, 1988.

———. *My Mother.* Trans. Austryn Wainhouse. London: Marion Boyars, 1989.

———. *Story of the Eye.* Trans. Joachim Neugroschel. San Francisco: City Lights, 1987.

———. *Visions of Excess: Selected Writings, 1927–1939.* Ed. Allan Stoekl. Minneapolis: University of Minnesota Press, 1985.

Baudrillard, Jean. *Forget Foucault.* New York: Semiotext(e), 1987.

———. *The Mirror of Production.* Trans. Mark Poster. St. Louis: Telos, 1975.

Beckett, Samuel. *Disjecta: Miscellaneous Writings and a Dramatic Fragment.* Ed. Ruby Cohn. New York: Grove, 1984.

———. *Three Novels: Molloy, Malone Dies, The Unnameable.* New York: Grove, 1965.

Beckett, Samuel, et al. *Our Exagmination round His Factification for Incamination of Work in Progress.* London: Faber and Faber, 1972.

Benjamin, Jessica. *The Bonds of Love: Psychoanalysis, Feminism, and the Problem of Domination.* New York: Pantheon, 1988.

Benjamin, Walter. "Conversations with Brecht." In *Aesthetics and Politics,* ed. New Left Books, 86–99. London: Verso, 1977.

———. *Reflections: Essays, Aphorisms, Autobiographical Writings.* Trans. Edmund Jephcott. New York: Harcourt, 1979.

Berger, John. *Ways of Seeing.* New York: Viking, 1973.

Bermann, Marshall. *All That Is Solid Melts into Air: The Experience of Modernity.* New York: Penguin, 1982.

Bernheimer, Charles. "Penile Reference in Phallic Theory." *Differences: A Journal of Feminist Cultural Studies* 4, no. 1 (Spring 1992): 116–32.

Bersani, Leo. *The Culture of Redemption.* Cambridge, Mass.: Harvard University Press, 1990.

———. *The Freudian Body: Psychoanalysis and Art.* New York: Columbia University Press, 1986.

———. "Is the Rectum a Grave?" *October* 43 (Winter 1987): 197–222.

Bérubé, Michael. *Marginal Forces/Cultural Centers: Tolson, Pynchon, and the Politics of the Canon.* Ithaca, N.Y.: Cornell University Press, 1992.

Blanchot, Maurice. *The Gaze of Orpheus and Other Literary Essays.* Trans. Lydia Davis. Barrytown, N.Y.: Station Hill, 1981.

———. "Thinking the Apocalypse: A Letter from Maurice Blanchot to Catherine David." *Critical Inquiry* 15, no. 2 (Winter 1989): 475–80.

Bloom, Harold. *The Anxiety of Influence: A Theory of Poetry.* Oxford: Oxford University Press, 1973.

Boothby, Richard. *Death and Desire: Psychoanalytic Theory in Lacan's Return to Freud.* New York: Routledge, 1991.

Boss, Medard. "Martin Heidegger's Zollikon Seminars." Trans. Brian Kenney. *Review of Existential Psychology and Psychiatry* 16 (1987/89): 7–20.

Brenkmann, John. *Straight Male Modern: A Cultural Critique of Psychoanalysis.* New York: Routledge, 1993.

Brennan, Teresa. *The Interpretation of the Flesh: Freud and Femininity.* New York: Routledge, 1992.

Brienza, Susan. "Krapping Out: Images of Flow and Elimination as Creation in Joyce and Beckett." In *Re: Joyce'n Beckett,* ed. Phyllis Carey and Ed Jewinski, 117–46. New York: Fordham University Press, 1992.

Brivic, Sheldon. "The Disjunctive Structure of Joyce's *Portrait.*" In James Joyce, *A Portrait of the Artist as a Young Man: Complete, Authoritative Text with Biographical and Historical Contexts, Critical History, and Essays from Five Contemporary Critical Perspectives,* 251–67. Ed. R. B. Kershner. Boston: Bedford/St. Martin's, 1993.

———. *Joyce between Freud and Jung.* Port Washington, N.Y.: Kennikat, 1980.

———. *The Veil of Signs: Joyce, Lacan, and Perception.* Urbana: University of Illinois Press, 1991.

Brooks, Peter. *Reading for the Plot: Design and Intention in Narrative.* New York: Vintage, 1985.

Brown, Robert. *James Joyce and Sexuality.* Cambridge: Cambridge University Press, 1985.

Butler, Judith. *Bodies That Matter: On the Discursive Limits of "Sex."* New York: Routledge, 1993.

———. "The Force of Fantasy: Feminism, Mapplethorpe, and Discursive Excess." *Differences: A Journal of Feminist Cultural Studies* 2, no. 2 (1990): 105–25.

———. *Gender Trouble: Feminism and the Subversion of Identity.* New York: Routledge, 1990.

Carroll, David. "The Temptation of Fascism and the Question of Literature: Justice, Sorrow, and Political Error (An Open Letter to Jacques Derrida)." *Cultural Critique* 15 (Spring 1990): 39–82.

Carter, Angela. *The Sadeian Woman and the Ideology of Pornography.* New York: Pantheon, 1978.

Cixous, Hélène. "Joyce: The (R)use of Writing." In *Post-Structuralist Joyce: Essays from the French,* ed. Derek Attridge and Daniel Ferrer, 15–30. Cambridge: Cambridge University Press, 1984.

———. "The Laugh of the Medusa." In *New French Feminisms,* ed. Elaine Marks and Isabelle de Courtivron, 245–64. New York: Schocken, 1981.

———. "Reaching the Wheat, or A Portrait of the Artist as a Maturing Woman." *New Literary History* 19, no. 1 (1987): 1–22.

Cohen, Ed. "Are We (Not) What We Are Becoming?: 'Gay' 'Identity,' 'Gay Studies,' and the Disciplining of Knowledge." In *Engendering Men: The Question of Male Feminist Criticism,* ed. Joseph A. Boone and Michael Cadden, 161–75. New York: Routledge, 1990.

Conrad, Joseph. *Lord Jim.* New York: Penguin, 1989.

Cornell, Drucilla. *Beyond Accommodation: Ethical Feminism, Deconstruction, and the Law.* New York: Routledge, 1991.

Coward, Rosalind. *Female Desires: How They Are Sought, Bought and Packaged.* New York: Grove, 1985.

Craig, Cairns. *Yeats, Eliot, Pound and the Politics of Poetry: Richest to the Richest.* Pittsburgh: University of Pittsburgh Press, 1982.

Dallmayr, Fred. "Adorno and Heidegger." *Diacritics* 19, nos. 3–4 (Fall-Winter 89): 82–100.

De Lauretis, Teresa. *Technologies of Gender: Essays on Theory, Film, and Fiction.* Bloomington: Indiana University Press, 1987.

———. "Upping the Anti (sic) in Feminist Theory." In *Conflicts in Feminism,* ed. Marianne Hirsch and Evelyn Fox Keller, 255–70. New York: Routledge, 1990.

De Man, Paul. "Literary History and Literary Modernity." *Blindness and Insight: Essays in the Rhetoric of Contemporary Criticism,* 142–65. Minneapolis: University of Minnesota Press, 1983.

Deming, Robert H., ed. *James Joyce: The Critical Heritage, Volume One: 1902–1927.* New York: Barnes and Noble, 1970.

Derrida, Jacques. *Dissemination.* Trans. Barbara Johnson. Chicago: University of Chicago Press, 1981.

———. *The Ear of the Other: Otobiography, Transference, Translation.* Ed. Christie McDonald. Lincoln: University of Nebraska Press, 1985.

———. "*Geschlecht:* Sexual Difference, Ontological Difference." *Research in Phenomenology* 13 (1983): 65–84.

———. "*Geschlecht* II: Heidegger's Hand." *Deconstruction and Philosophy: The Texts of Jacques Derrida,* 161–96. Ed. John Sallis. Chicago: University of Chicago Press, 1987.

———. *Glas.* Trans. John P. Leavey and Richard Rand. Lincoln: University of Nebraska Press, 1986.

———. *Of Grammatology.* Trans. Gayatri Spivak. Baltimore: Johns Hopkins University Press, 1974.

———. "Heidegger's Silence." In *Martin Heidegger and National Socialism: Questions and Answers,* ed. Günther Neske and Emil Kettering, 145–48. New York: Paragon House, 1990.

———. "How to Concede, with Reasons?" *Diacritics* 19, nos. 3–4 (Fall-Winter 1989): 4–9.

———. "Like the Sound of the Sea Deep within a Shell: Paul de Man's War." *Critical Inquiry* 14, no.3 (Summer 1988): 590–652.

———. *Margins of Philosophy.* Trans. Alan Bass. Chicago: University of Chicago Press, 1982.

———. *Positions.* Trans. Alan Bass. Chicago: University of Chicago Press, 1981.

———. *The Post Card: From Socrates to Freud and Beyond.* Trans. Alan Bass. Chicago: University of Chicago Press, 1987.

———. *Speech and Phenomena and Other Essays on Husserl's Theory of Signs.* Trans. David B. Allison. Evanston, Ill.: Northwestern University Press, 1973.

———. *Of Spirit: Heidegger and the Question.* Trans. Geoff Bennington and

Rachel Bowlby. Chicago: University of Chicago Press, 1989.

————. "Two Words for Joyce." In *Post-Structuralist Joyce: Essays from the French*, ed. Derek Attridge and Daniel Ferrer, 145–60. Cambridge: Cambridge University Press, 1984.

————. "Women in the Beehive: A Seminar." In *Men in Feminism*, ed. Alice Jardine and Paul Smith, 189–203. New York: Methuen, 1987.

————. *Writing and Difference*. Trans. Alan Bass. Chicago: University of Chicago Press, 1978.

Dews, Peter. *Logics of Disintegration: Post-Structuralist Thought and the Claims of Critical Theory*. New York: Verso, 1987.

A Dictionary of Marxist Thought. Ed. Tom Bottomore. Cambridge, Mass.: Harvard University Press, 1983.

Dworkin, Andrea. *Pornography: Men Possessing Women*. New York: Dutton, 1979.

Eagleton, Terry. *The Ideology of the Aesthetic*. Oxford: Blackwell, 1990.

Easthope, Anthony. *What a Man's Gotta Do: The Masculine Myth in Popular Culture*. London: Paladin, 1986.

Eliot, T. S. "*Ulysses*, Order and Myth." In *James Joyce: The Critical Heritage, Volume One: 1902–1927*, ed. Robert H. Deming, 268–71. New York: Barnes and Noble, 1970.

Ellis, Kate, et al., eds. *Caught Looking: Feminism, Pornography, and Censorship*. Seattle: Real Comet, 1988.

Ellmann, Maud. "Eliot's Abjection." In *Abjection, Melancholia and Love: The Work of Julia Kristeva*, ed. John Fletcher and Andrew Benjamin, 178–200. New York: Routledge, 1990.

————. "Polytropic Man: Paternity, Identity and Naming in *The Odyssey* and *A Portrait of the Artist as a Young Man*." In *James Joyce: New Perspectives*, ed. Colin MacCabe, 73–104. Sussex: Harvester, 1982.

Ellmann, Richard. *James Joyce*. Oxford: Oxford University Press, 1982.

————. *Ulysses on the Liffey*. Oxford: Oxford University Press, 1972.

Farias, Victor. *Heidegger and Nazism*. Philadelphia: Temple University Press, 1990.

Ferry, Luc, and Alain Renaut. *Heidegger and Modernity*. Trans. Franklin Philip. Chicago: University of Chicago Press, 1990.

Fish, Stanley. "Withholding the Missing Portion: Power, Meaning and Persuasion in Freud's 'The Wolf-Man.'" *Times Literary Supplement*, Aug. 29, 1986, 935–38.

Foster, Hal, et al. "The Politics of the Signifier II: A Conversation on the *Informe* and the Abject." *October* 67 (Winter 1994): 3–21.

Foucault, Michel. *The History of Sexuality*. Vol. 1. New York: Vintage, 1978.

Freccero, Carla. "Notes of a Post–Sex Wars Theorizer." In *Conflicts in Feminism*, ed. Marianne Hirsch and Evelyn Fox Keller, 305–25. New York: Routledge, 1990.

Freud, Sigmund. *The Complete Letters of Sigmund Freud to Wilhelm Fliess: 1887–1904*. Trans. and ed. Jeffrey Moussaieff Masson. Cambridge: Harvard University Press, 1985.

———. *The Standard Edition of the Complete Psychological Works.* Trans. James Strachey. 24 Vols. London: Hogarth, 1953–74.

Fuss, Diana. *Essentially Speaking: Feminism, Nature and Difference.* New York: Routledge, 1989.

———. "Fashion and the Homospectatorial Look." *Critical Inquiry* 18, no. 4 (Summer 1992): 713–37.

Gallop, Jane. *The Daughter's Seduction: Feminism and Psychoanalysis.* Ithaca, N.Y.: Cornell University Press, 1982.

———. *Intersections: A Reading of Sade with Bataille, Blanchot, and Klossowski.* Lincoln: University of Nebraska Press, 1981.

———. "Moving Backward or Forwards." In *Between Feminism and Psychoanalysis,* ed. Teresa Brennan, 27–39. New York: Routledge, 1989.

———. *Thinking through the Body.* New York: Columbia University Press, 1988.

Gasché, Rodolphe. *The Tain of the Mirror: Derrida and the Philosophy of Reflection.* Cambridge: Cambridge University Press, 1986.

Gifford, Don. *Joyce Annotated: Notes for Dubliners and A Portrait of the Artist as a Young Man.* Berkeley: University of California Press, 1982.

Gifford, Don, with Robert J. Seidman. *Notes for Joyce: An Annotation of James Joyce's Ulysses.* New York: Dutton, 1974.

———. *Ulysses Annotated: Notes for James Joyce's Ulysses.* Berkeley: University of California Press, 1988.

Gilbert, Sandra M., and Susan Gubar. *The War of the Words.* Vol. 1 of *No Man's Land: The Place of the Woman Writer in the Twentieth Century.* 3 vols. New Haven, Conn.: Yale University Press, 1988.

Gitlin, Todd. "World Leaders: Mickey, et al." *New York Times,* May 3, 1992, 2:30.

Goldmann, Lucien. *Lukács and Heidegger: Towards a New Philosophy.* Trans. William Q. Boelhover. London: Routledge and Kegan Paul, 1977.

Goux, Jean-Joseph. "The Phallus: Masculine Identity and the 'Exchange of Women.'" *Differences* 4, no. 1 (Spring 1992): 40–75.

———. *Symbolic Economies: After Marx and Freud.* Trans. Jennifer Curtiss Gage. Ithaca, N.Y.: Cornell University Press, 1990.

Graybeal, Jean. *Language and "the Feminine" in Nietzsche and Heidegger.* Bloomington: Indiana University Press, 1990.

Griffin, Susan. *Pornography and Silence: Culture's Revenge against Nature.* New York: Harper and Row, 1981.

Grosz, Elizabeth. "The Body of Signification." In *Abjection, Melancholia and Love: The Work of Julia Kristeva,* ed. John Fletcher and Andrew Benjamin, 80–103. New York: Routledge, 1990.

———. *Jacques Lacan: A Feminist Introduction.* New York: Routledge, 1990.

———. *Sexual Subversions: Three French Feminists.* Sydney: Allen & Unwin, 1989.

Groult, Benoîte. "Night Porters." In *New French Feminisms,* ed. Elaine Marks and Isabelle de Courtivron, 68–75. New York: Schocken, 1981.

Habermas, Jürgen. "Modernity—An Incomplete Project." In *The Anti-Aes-*

thetic: Essays on Postmodern Culture, ed. Hal Foster, 3–15. Port Towsend, Wash.: Bay, 1983.

———. *The Philosophical Discourse of Modernity: Twelve Lectures.* Trans. Frederick Lawrence. Cambridge, Mass.: MIT Press, 1987.

———. "Work and Weltanschauung: The Heidegger Controversy from a German Perspective." *Critical Inquiry* 15, no. 2 (Winter 1989): 43–56.

Heath, Stephen. "Ambiviolences: Notes for Reading Joyce." In *Post-Structuralist Joyce: Essays from the French,* ed. Derek Attridge and Daniel Ferrer, 31–68. Cambridge: Cambridge University Press, 1984.

———. "Joyce in Language." In *James Joyce: New Perspectives,* ed. Colin MacCabe, 129–50. Sussex: Harvester, 1982.

———. "Male Feminism." In *Men in Feminism,* ed. Alice Jardine and Paul Smith, 1–32. New York: Methuen, 1987.

Hegel, G. W. F. *Early Theological Writings.* Trans. T. M. Knox. Chicago: University of Chicago Press, 1948.

———. *The Phenomenology of Spirit.* Trans. A. V. Miller. Oxford: Oxford University Press, 1977.

———. *Philosophy of Mind.* Trans. W. Wallace. New York: Oxford University Press, 1971.

Heidegger, Martin. *Basic Writings.* Ed. David Farrell Kell. New York: Harper, 1977.

———. *Being and Time.* Trans. John Macquarrie and Edward Robinson. New York: Harper and Row, 1962.

———. *Discourse on Thinking.* Trans. J. M. Anderson and E. H. Freund. New York: Harper and Row, 1966.

———. *Identity and Difference.* Trans. J. Stambaugh. New York: Harper and Row, 1969.

———. *An Introduction to Metaphysics.* Trans. Ralph Manheim. New Haven, Conn.: Yale University Press, 1959.

———. *Poetry, Language, Thought.* Trans. Albert Hafstadter. New York: Harper and Row, 1971.

———. *The Question concerning Technology and Other Essays.* Trans. William Lovitt. New York: Harper, 1977.

———. *On Time and Being.* Trans. J. Stambaugh. New York: Harper and Row, 1972.

"Heidegger: Art and Politics." Special issue. *Diacritics* 19, nos. 3–4 (Fall-Winter 1989).

Henke, Suzette A. *James Joyce and the Politics of Desire.* New York and London: Routledge, 1990.

Henke, Suzette, and Elaine Unkeless, eds. *Women in Joyce.* Urbana: University of Illinois Press, 1982.

Hollier, Denis. *Against Architecture: The Writings of Georges Bataille.* Trans. Betsy Wing. Cambridge, Mass.: MIT Press, 1989.

———. *La Prise de la Concorde: Essais sur Georges Bataille.* Paris: Gallimard, 1974.

Hocquenghem, Guy. *Homosexual Desire.* Trans. Daniella Dangoor. London: Allison and Busby, 1978.

Houser, Craig, et al. *Abject Art: Repulsion and Desire in American Art.* Independent Study Program Papers, no. 3. New York: Whitney Museum of American Art, 1993.

Hullot-Kentor, Robert. "Back to Adorno." *Telos* 81 (Fall 1989): 5–29.

Huyssen, Andreas. *After the Great Divide: Modernism, Mass Culture, Postmodernism.* Bloomington: Indiana University Press, 1986.

Irigaray, Luce. "The Gesture in Psychoanalysis." In *Between Feminism and Psychoanalysis,* ed. Teresa Brennan, 127–38. London: Routledge, 1989.

———. *Speculum of the Other Woman.* Trans. Gillian G. Gill. Ithaca, N.Y.: Cornell University Press, 1985.

———. *This Sex Which Is Not One.* Trans. Catherine Porter. Ithaca, N.Y.: Cornell University Press, 1985.

Irwin, John T. *Doubling and Incest/Repetition and Revenge: A Speculative Reading of Faulkner.* Baltimore: Johns Hopkins University Press, 1975.

Jameson, Fredric. *Fables of Aggression: Wyndham Lewis, The Modernist as Fascist.* Berkeley: University of California Press, 1979.

———. *Late Marxism: Adorno, or the Persistence of the Dialectic.* London: Verso, 1990.

———. *Marxism and Form: Twentieth Century Dialectical Theories of Literature.* Princeton: Princeton University Press, 1971.

———. "Pleasure: A Political Issue." In *Syntax of History,* 61–74. Vol. 2 of *The Ideologies of Theory: Essays 1971–1986.* Minneapolis: University of Minnesota Press, 1988.

———. *The Political Unconscious: Narrative as a Socially Symbolic Act.* Ithaca, N.Y.: Cornell University Press, 1981.

———. *Postmodernism, or, The Cultural Logic of Late Capitalism.* Durham, N.C.: Duke University Press, 1991.

———. *The Prison-House of Language.* Princeton: Princeton University Press, 1972.

———. "*Ulysses* in History." In *James Joyce and Modern Literature,* ed. W. J. McCormack and Alistair Stead, 126–41. London: Routledge and Kegan Paul, 1982.

Jardine, Alice. *Gynesis: Configurations of Woman and Modernity.* Ithaca, N.Y.: Cornell University Press, 1985.

———. "Men in Feminism: Odor di Uomo or Compagnons de Route?" In *Men in Feminism,* ed. Alice Jardine and Paul Smith, 54–61. New York: Menthuen, 1987.

Jay, Gregory S. *America the Scrivener: Deconstruction and the Subject of Literary History.* Ithaca, N.Y.: Cornell University Press, 1990.

Jeffords, Susan. *The Remasculinization of America: Gender and the Vietnam War.* Bloomington: Indiana University Press, 1989.

Johnson, Barbara. "The Frame of Reference: Poe, Lacan, Derrida." In *Literature and Psychoanalysis: The Question of Reading: Otherwise,* ed. Shoshana Felman, 457–505. Baltimore: Johns Hopkins University Press, 1982.

———. *A World of Difference.* Baltimore: Johns Hopkins University Press, 1987.

Joyce, James. *The Critical Writings of James Joyce*. Ed. Ellsworth Mason and Richard Ellmann. New York: Viking, 1959.

———. *Dubliners*. New York: Penguin, 1967.

———. *Finnegans Wake*. New York: Penguin, 1967.

———. *A Portrait of the Artist as a Young Man*. New York: Penguin, 1977.

———. *Selected Letters*. Ed. Richard Ellmann. New York: Viking, 1975.

———. *Stephen Hero*. New York: New Directions, 1963.

———. *Ulysses*. Ed. Hans Walter Gabler. New York: Vintage, 1986.

Joyce, Stanislaus. *The Complete Dublin Diary of Stanislaus Joyce*. Ed. George H. Healey. Ithaca, N.Y.: Cornell University Press, 1971.

Kappeler, Suzanne. *The Pornography of Representation*. Minneapolis: University of Minnesota Press, 1986.

Kauffman, L. A. "Radical Change: The Left Attacks Identity Politics." *The Village Voice* 37, no. 26 (June 30, 1992).

Kenner, Hugh. "The *Portrait* in Perspective." In *Joyce's Portrait: Criticisms and Critiques*, ed. Thomas E. Connolly, 25–59. New York: Appleton-Century-Crofts, 1962.

Kierkegaard, Søren. *Fear and Trembling/Repetition*. Ed. and trans. Howard V. Hong and Edna H. Hong. Princeton: Princeton University Press, 1983.

Kimmel, Michael S., ed. *Men Confront Pornography*. New York: Meridian, 1990.

Kristeva, Julia. "Joyce 'the Gracehopper' or the Return of Orpheus." In *James Joyce: The Augmented Ninth*, ed. Bernard Benstock, 167–80. Syracuse: Syracuse University Press, 1988.

———. *Powers of Horror: An Essay on Abjection*. Trans. Leon S. Roudiez. New York: Columbia University Press, 1982.

———. *Revolution in Poetic Language*. Trans. Margaret Waller. New York: Columbia University Press, 1984.

———. "Within the Microcosm of 'The Talking Cure.'" In *Interpreting Lacan*, ed. Joseph H. Smith and William Kerrigan, 33–48. New Haven, Conn.: Yale University Press, 1983.

Kroker, Arthur, and Marilouise Kroker, eds. *The Hysterical Male: New Feminist Theory*. New York: St. Martin's, 1990.

Lacan, Jacques. *Écrits: A Selection*. Trans. Alan Sheridan. New York: Norton, 1977.

———. *The Four Fundamental Concepts of Psychoanalysis*. Trans. Alan Sheridan. New York: Norton, 1978.

———. *The Seminars of Jacques Lacan, Book II: The Ego in Freud's Theory and in the Technique of Psychoanalysis 1954–55*. Ed. Jacques-Alain Miller. Trans. Sylvana Tomaselli. New York: Norton, 1988.

———. "Le Sinthome." *Séminaire* of January 13, 1976, published in *Ornicar* 7 (1976): 3–18.

———. "Of Structure as an Inmixing of Otherness Prerequisite to Any Subject Whatever." In *The Structuralist Controversy: The Languages of Criticism and the Sciences of Man*, ed. Richard Macksey and Eugenio Donato, 186–200. Baltimore: Johns Hopkins University Press, 1970.

LaCapra, Dominick. "Psychoanalysis and History." *Critical Inquiry* 13, no. 2 (1987): 222–51.

Lacoue-Labarthe, Philippe. "L'Imprésentable." *Poétique* 21 (1975): 74.

Lawrence, D. H. "Obscenity and Pornography." In *Selected Literary Criticism*, ed. Anthony Beal, 32–51. New York: Viking, 1956.

Lawrence, Karen. "Joyce and Feminism." In *The Cambridge Companion to James Joyce*, ed. Derek Attridge, 237–58. Cambridge: Cambridge University Press, 1990.

Lechte, John. *Julia Kristeva.* New York: Routledge, 1990.

Leclaire, Serge. "Sexuality: A Fact of Discourse, an Interview by Hélène Klibbe." In *Homosexualities and French Literature: Cultural Contexts/Critical Texts*, ed. George Stambolian and Elaine Marks, 42–55. Ithaca, N.Y.: Cornell University Press, 1979.

Lederer, Laura, ed. *Take Back the Night: Women on Pornography.* New York: William Morrow, 1980.

Lernout, Geert. *The French Joyce.* Ann Arbor: University of Michigan Press, 1990.

Lewis, Wyndham. *Time and Western Man.* London: Chatto and Windus, 1927.

Liu, Catherine, ed. *The Abject, America, Lusitania: A Journal of Reflection and Oceanography* 1, no. 4 (n.d.).

Lukacher, Ned. *Primal Scenes: Literature, Philosophy, Psychoanalysis.* Ithaca, N.Y.: Cornell University Press, 1986.

———. "Writing on Ashes: Heidegger *Fort* Derrida." *Diacritics* 19, nos. 3–4 (Fall-Winter 1989): 128–48.

Lukács, Georg. *History and Class Consciousness: Studies in Marxist Dialectics.* Trans. Rodney Livingstone. Cambridge, Mass.: MIT Press, 1968.

Lyotard, Jean-François. *Heidegger and "the Jews."* Trans. Andreas Michel and Mark S. Roberts. Minneapolis: University of Minnesota Press, 1990.

———. *The Postmodern Condition: A Report on Knowledge.* Trans. Geoff Bennington and Brian Massumi. Minneapolis: University of Minnesota Press, 1984.

MacCabe, Colin. "An Introduction to *Finnegans Wake*." In *James Joyce: New Perspectives*, ed. Colin MacCabe, 29–44. Sussex: Harvester, 1982.

———. *James Joyce and the Revolution of the Word.* New York: Harper and Row, 1979.

———. "The Voice of Esau: Stephen in the Library." In *James Joyce: New Perspectives*, ed. Colin MacCabe, 111–28. Sussex: Harvester, 1982.

MacKinnon, Catharine A. *Feminism Unmodified: Discourses on Life and Law.* Cambridge, Mass.: Harvard University Press, 1987.

Maddox, Brenda. *Nora: The Real Life of Molly Bloom.* Boston: Houghton Mifflin, 1988.

Manganiello, Dominic. *Joyce's Politics.* London: Routledge and Kegan Paul, 1980.

Mariani, Philomena. "'God Is a Man.'" In *Critical Fictions: The Politics of Imaginative Writing*, ed. Philomena Mariani, 3–12. Seattle: Bay, 1991.

Marx, Karl. *Grundrisse: Foundations of the Critique of Political Economy*. Trans. Martin Nicolaus. New York: Vintage, 1973.

McCarthy, Thomas. "The Politics of the Ineffable: Derrida's Deconstructionism." *The Philosophical Forum* 21, nos. 1–2 (Fall-Winter 1989–90): 146–68.

McDonald, Scott. "Confessions of a Feminist Porn Watcher." In *Men Confront Pornography*, ed. Michael S. Kimmel, 34–42. New York: Meridian, 1990.

McDougal, Robert. *The Very Rich Hours of Adrienne Monnier*. New York: Scribner's, 1976.

McGee, Patrick. *Paperspace: Style as Ideology in Joyce's Ulysses*. Lincoln: University of Nebraska Press, 1988.

McHugh, Roland. *Annotations to Finnegans Wake*. Baltimore: Johns Hopkins University Press, 1991.

Meghill, Allan. *Prophets of Extremity: Nietzsche, Heidegger, Foucault, Derrida*. Berkeley: University of California Press, 1985.

Melville, Stephen. *Philosophy beside Itself: On Deconstruction and Modernity*. Minneapolis: University of Minnesota Press, 1986.

Miller, Henry. *Tropic of Cancer*. London: Granada, 1965.

Mitchell, Juliet. *Psychoanalysis and Feminism: Freud, Reich, Laing, and Women*. New York: Vintage, 1975.

Mitchell, W. J. T. "An Interview with Barbara Kruger." *Critical Inquiry* 17, no. 2 (Winter 1991): 434–48.

Modleski, Tania. *Feminism without Women: Culture and Criticism in a "Postfeminist" Age*. New York: Routledge, 1991.

———. *The Women Who Knew Too Much: Hitchcock and Feminist Theory*. New York: Methuen, 1988.

Muller, John P., and William J. Richardson. *The Purloined Poe: Lacan, Derrida, and Psychoanalytic Reading*. Baltimore: Johns Hopkins University Press, 1988.

Mulvey, Laura. "Visual Pleasure and Narrative Cinema." *Screen* 16, no. 3 (Autumn 1975): 6–18. Reprinted in *Film Theory and Criticism: Introductory Readings*, ed. Gerald Mast and Marshall Cohen, 803–16. Oxford: Oxford University Press, 1985.

Nadel, Ira B. *Joyce and the Jews: Culture and Texts*. Iowa City: University of Iowa Press, 1989.

Nelson, Cary. "Men, Feminism: The Materiality of Discourse." In *Men in Feminism*, ed. Alice Jardine and Paul Smith, 153–72. New York: Methuen, 1987.

Neske, Günther, and Emil Kettering, eds. *Martin Heidegger and National Socialism: Questions and Answers*. New York: Paragon House, 1990.

Norris, Margot. *The Decentered Universe of Finnegans Wake*. Baltimore: Johns Hopkins University Press, 1974.

O'Hara, Daniel T. "Mask Plays: Theory, Cultural Studies, and the Fascist Imagination." *Boundary 2* 17, no. 2 (Summer 1990): 129–54.

Parker, Andrew. "Ezra Pound and the 'Economy' of Anti-Semitism." *Post-

modernism and Politics, ed. Jonathan Arac, 70–90. Minneapolis, University of Minnesota Press, 1986.

Parrinder, Patrick. "The Strange Necessity: James Joyce's Rejection in England (1914–1930)." In *James Joyce: New Perspectives,* ed. Colin MacCabe, 151–67. London: Harvester, 1982.

Pefanis, Julian. *Heterology and the Postmodern: Bataille, Baudrillard, and Lyotard.* Durham, N.C.: Duke University Press, 1991.

Pound, Ezra. *Pound/Joyce: The Letters of Ezra Pound to James Joyce, with Pound's Essays on Joyce.* Ed. Forrest Read. New York: New Directions, 1967.

Power, Arthur. *Conversations with Joyce.* Ed. Clive Hart. New York: Harper and Row, 1974.

Rabaté, Jean-Michel. *James Joyce: Authorized Reader.* Baltimore: Johns Hopkins University Press, 1991.

———. "Lapsus ex machine." In *Post-Structuralist Joyce: Essays from the French,* ed. Derek Attridge and Daniel Ferrer, 79–102. Cambridge: Cambridge University Press, 1984.

———. "Silence in Dubliners." In *James Joyce: New Perspectives,* ed. Colin MacCabe, 45–72. London: Harvester, 1982.

Rapaport, Herman. *Heidegger and Derrida: Reflections on Time and Language.* Lincoln: University of Nebraska Press, 1989.

Restuccia, Frances L. *Joyce and the Law of the Father.* New Haven, Conn.: Yale University Press, 1989.

Richman, Michèle. *Reading Georges Bataille: Beyond the Gift.* Baltimore: Johns Hopkins University Press, 1982.

Rimbaud, Arthur. Letter to Georges Izambard. *Complete Works and Selected Letters.* Trans. Wallace Fowlie. Chicago: University of Chicago Press, 1966.

Robinson, Sally. "Deconstructive Discourse and Sexual Politics: The 'Feminine' and/in Masculine Self-Representation." *Cultural Critique* 13 (Fall 1989): 203–28.

Rockmore, Tom. *On Heidegger's Nazism and Philosophy.* Berkeley: University of California Press, 1992.

Rockmore, Tom, and Joseph Margolis, eds., *The Heidegger Case: On Philosophy and Politics.* Philadelphia: Temple University Press, 1992.

Ronnell, Avital. "The Differends of Man." *Diacritics* 19, nos. 3–4 (Fall-Winter 1989): 63–75.

Rorty, Richard. *Contingency, Irony, Solidarity.* Cambridge: Cambridge University Press, 1989.

Rose, Jacqueline. Introduction II. In *Feminine Sexuality: Jacques Lacan and the école freudienne,* ed. Juliet Mitchell and Jacqueline Rose; trans. Jacqueline Rose, 27–57. New York: Norton, 1982.

———. *Sexuality in the Field of Vision.* London: Verso, 1986.

Ross, Andrew. *The Failure of Modernism: Symptoms of American Poetry.* New York: Columbia University Press, 1986.

Roudiez, Leon S. Introduction. In Julia Kristeva, *Revolution in Poetic Language,* 1–10. Trans. Margaret Waller. New York: Columbia University Press, 1984.

Rubin, Gayle. "The Traffic in Women: Notes on the 'Political Economy' of Sex." In *Toward an Anthropology of Women*, ed. Reyna Reiter, 157–210. New York: Monthly, 1975.

Russell, Bertrand. *A History of Western Philosophy*. London: Clarion, 1945.

Scholes, Robert. "Éperon Strings." *Differences* 1, no. 2 (Summer 1989): 93–104.

———. "Reading Like a Man." In *Men in Feminism*, ed. Alice Jardine and Paul Smith, 204–18. New York: Methuen, 1987.

Scott, Bonnie Kime. *James Joyce*. Brighton: Harvester, 1987.

———. *Joyce and Feminism*. Bloomington: Indiana University Press, 1984.

Sedgwick, Eve Kosofsky. *Epistemology of the Closet*. Berkeley: University of California Press, 1990.

Silverman, Kaja. *Male Subjectivity at the Margins*. New York: Routledge, 1992.

———. *The Subject of Semiotics*. Oxford: Oxford University Press, 1983.

Sloterdijk, Peter. *Thinker on Stage: Nietzsche's Materialism*. Trans. Jamie Owen Daniel. Minneapolis: University of Minnesota Press, 1989.

Smith, Paul. "Julia Kristeva et al.; Take Three or More." In *Feminism and Psychoanalysis*, ed. Richard Feldstein and Judith Roof, 84–104. Ithaca, N.Y.: Cornell University Press, 1989.

———. "Vas." *Camera Obscura* 17 (May 1988): 89–111.

"Special Section on Martin Hedegger," *New German Critique* 45 (Fall 1988): 91–161.

Spilka, Mark. "Lawrence Up-Tight, or the Anal Phase Once Over." *NOVEL* 4, no. 3 (Spring 1971): 252–70.

Spivak, Gayatri. "Acting Bits/Identity Talk." *Critical Inquiry* 18, no. 4 (Summer 1992): 770–803.

———. "Displacement and the Discourse of Woman." In *Displacement: Derrida and After*, ed. Mark Krupnick, 169–95. Bloomington: Indiana University Press, 1983.

———. "Feminism and Deconstruction, Again: Negotiating with Unacknowledged Masculinism." In *Between Feminism and Psychoanalysis*, ed. Teresa Brennan, 206–24. New York: Routledge, 1989.

———. "French Feminism in an International Frame." *In Other Worlds: Essays in Cultural Politics*, 134–53. New York: Methuen, 1987.

———. Interview (with Ellen Rooney). *Differences* 1, no. 2 (Summer 1989): 124–56.

Stanton, Domna. "Difference on Trial: A Critique of the Maternal Metaphor in Cixous, Irigaray, and Kristeva." In *The Poetics of Gender*, ed. Nancy K. Miller, 157–82. New York: Columbia University Press, 1986.

Stephanson, Anders. "A Conversation with Fredric Jameson." In *Universal Abandon?: The Politics of Postmodernism*, ed. Andrew Ross, 3–30. Minneapolis: University of Minnesota Press, 1988.

Stockton, Kathryn Bond. "Heaven's Bottom: Anal Economics and the Critical Debasement of Freud in Toni Morrison's *Sula*." *Cultural Critique* 24 (Spring 1993): 81–118.

Stoekl, Allan. *Politics, Writing, Mutilation: The Cases of Bataille, Blanchot, Roussel, Leiris, and Ponge*. Minneapolis: University of Minnesota Press, 1985.

———. "Truman's Apotheosis: Bataille, 'Planisme,' and Headlessness." *Yale French Studies* 78:181–205.

"Symposium on Heidegger and Nazism," *Critical Inquiry* 15, no. 2 (Winter 1989): 407–88.

Taylor, Mark C. *Altarity.* Chicago: University of Chicago Press, 1987.

Theweleit, Klaus. *Psychoanalyzing the White Terror.* Trans. Erica Carter and Chris Turner. Vol. 2 of *Male Fantasies.* 2 vols. Minneapolis: University of Minnesota Press, 1989.

———. *Women, Floods, Bodies, History.* Trans. Stephen Conway. Vol. 1 of *Male Fantasies.* 2 vols. Minneapolis: University of Minnesota Press, 1987.

Thomas, Calvin. "A Knowledge That Would Not Be Power: Adorno, Nostalgia, and the Historicity of the Musical Subject." *New German Critique* 48 (Fall 1989): 155–75.

———. "*Tristram Shandy's* Consent to Incompleteness: Discourse, Disavowal, Disruption." *Literature and Psychology* 36, no. 3 (1990): 44–62.

Tucker, Scott. "Gender, Fucking, and Utopia." *Social Text* 27:3–34

Vance, Carol S., ed. *Pleasure and Danger: Exploring Female Sexuality.* London: Routledge, 1984.

Waisbren, Burton A., and Florence L. Walzl. "Paresis and the Priest: James Joyce's Symbolic Use of Syphilis in 'The Sisters.'" *Annals of Internal Medicine* 80 (June 1974): 758–62.

Warner, Michael. "*Walden's* Erotic Economy." In *Comparative American Identities: Race, Sex, and Nationality in the Modern Text,* ed. Hortense Spillers, 157–74. New York: Routledge, 1991.

Warren, Robert Penn. *Brother to Dragons.* New York: Random House, 1979.

Watney, Simon. *Policing Desire: Pornography, AIDS, and the Media.* Minneapolis: University of Minnesota Press, 1987.

Wells, H. G. "James Joyce." *New Republic* 10 (Mar. 10, 1917).

West, Cornell. Interview. In *Universal Abandon: The Politics of Postmodernism,* ed. Andrew Ross, 269–86. Minneapolis: University of Minnesota Press, 1988.

White, Susan. "Male Bonding, Hollywood Orientalism, and the Repression of the Feminine in Kubrick's *Full Metal Jacket.*" *Arizona Quarterly* 44, no. 3 (Autumn 1988): 121–44.

Wilden, Anthony. "Lacan and the Discourse of the Other." *Speech and Language in Psychoanalysis.* Baltimore: Johns Hopkins University Press, 1968.

Will, George F. "Fascism's Second Spring." *Newsweek,* May 2, 1994.

Williams, Linda. *Hard Core: Power, Pleasure and the "Frenzy of the Visible."* Berkeley: University of California Press, 1989.

Winette, Susan. "Coming Unstrung: Women, Men, Narrative, and Principles of Pleasure." *Publications of the Modern Language Association* 105, no. 3 (May 1990): 505–18.

Wolin, Richard. "The French Heidegger Debate." *New German Critique* 45 (1988): 135–61.

———. *The Politics of Being: The Political Thought of Martin Heidegger.* New York: Columbia University Press, 1990.

Wood, Robin. *Hitchcock's Films Revisited*. New York: Columbia University Press, 1989.

Wyschogrod, Edith. *Spirit in Ashes: Hegel, Heidegger, and Man-Made Mass Death*. New Haven, Conn.: Yale University Press, 1985.

Zimmerman, Michael E. *Heidegger's Confrontation with Modernity: Technology, Politics, Art*. Bloomington: Indiana University Press, 1990.

———. "Ontological Aestheticism: Heidgger, Jünger, and National Socialism." In *The Heidegger Case: On Philosophy and Politics*, ed. Tom Rockmore and Joseph Margolis, 52–92. Philadelphia: Temple University Press, 1992.

Žižek, Slavoj. *The Sublime Object of Ideology*. New York: Verso, 1989.

Index

Abjection, 14–15, 22–29 passim, 38, 44,
46, 49, 50, 51, 53, 58, 81, 86, 97–101
passim, 117, 127, 149, 152, 153, 158,
165, 198*n2*, 200*n14*, 204*n38*, 218*n15*
Acker, Kathy, 20, 195*n2*
Adorno, Theodor, 39–40, 61–62, 64–65,
213*n19*, 217*n6*, 222–23*n16*
Althusser, Louis, 30
Anal penis, 85–89, 91, 158–60
Anus/anality, 23, 31, 35, 41, 42, 45, 61–
73, 74–116 passim, 136, 149, 161–65,
169, 180, 186, 200*n13*, 204–5*n40*,
208*nn20,21*, 209*nn1,3*, 211*n16*, 215*n27*,
220*n3*. *See also* Feces/defecation
Attridge, Derek, 189

Barthes, Roland, 1, 4, 11, 18, 45, 156–
57, 200*n8*, 204*n38*
Bartky, Sandra, 50
Bataille, Georges, 1, 4–6, 8, 19, 23, 30,
45, 46, 61, 66–75, 81, 114–15, 125,
142, 153, 161, 173, 193, 195*n2*, 198–
99*n2*, 200*n12*, 201*n21*, 208*n20*n,
209*n3*, 210*n13*, 215*n27*
Baudrillard, Jean, 13, 34, 202*n21*
Beckett, Samuel, 1, 4, 74, 89, 101, 116,
117, 136, 152, 161, 208–9*n1*
"Being-death," 29, 108, 110, 113, 142,
191–93
Benjamin, Jessica, 93–94, 96
Benjamin, Walter, 29, 67
Berger, John, 3, 18, 19, 27, 199*n7*
Bermann, Marshall, 24, 65
Bernheimer, Charles, 5, 27
Bersani, Leo, 20–22, 24, 26–27, 32, 35,
62, 65–66, 72–73, 81, 87, 102, 117,
175–76, 196*n3*, 197*n4*, 202*n26*, 208–
9*n1*, 214*n23*, 223*n22*
Bérubé, Michael, 225*n2*

Blanchot, Maurice, 11, 12, 18, 108
Bloom, Harold, 14, 88, 182
Bly, Robert, 177
Brecht, Bertold, 29, 116, 161
Brivic, Sheldon, 171–72, 223*n19*,
224*n24*
Brooks, Peter, 167
Butler, Judith, 7, 23, 35, 82, 197*n5*, 198–
99*n2*, 200*n14*, 202*n26*

Castration anxiety, 18, 27–28, 33, 79–
116 passim, 167
Cixous, Hélène, 37, 153–61, 183, 189,
190
Clitoris envy, 150
Cohen, Ed, 196*n4*
Conrad, Joseph, 31, 202*n23*
Coward, Rosalind, 15

De Lauretis, Teresa, 6, 199*n3*
Derrida, Jacques, 8, 11, 18, 28, 29, 33,
34, 55, 68–72, 87, 102–4, 117, 131–
51, 153, 168, 169, 189, 192, 215*n25*,
217–18*n9*, 219*n23*, 220*n26*, 221*n5*
Dews, Peter, 133, 213–14*n22*
Durchfall, 71, 83, 88, 89, 144, 174
Dysgraphia: defined, 32

Eagleton, Terry, 55, 120, 121
Easthope, Anthony, 17
Ehrenreich, Barbara, 130
Ellmann, Maud, 178, 180, 181, 210*n12*
Ellmann, Richard, 61

Fascism, 18, 43, 66, 67, 117, 119, 127–
30, 153, 201*n17*, 218*n15*, 218–19*n18*
Faulkner, William, 18, 27
Feces/defecation, 2, 14, 18–19, 23, 27–
29, 30, 32–34, 46, 54, 60–61, 61–73,

74–116 passim, 164, 210nn10,13, 211n15, 214–15n25, 217n6, 219n23, 220n25, 221n4
Ferry, Luc, 119, 124, 128
Fish, Stanley, 77
Fort/da, 77–78, 102, 104–9, 125, 214–15n25
Foucault, Michel, 19, 204n34
Freud, Sigmund, 8, 17, 19, 20, 27, 31, 32–33, 34, 40, 41, 55, 74–115, 119, 125, 134, 136, 137, 140–45, 167, 168, 180, 187, 200n13, 202n6, 203n32, 209nn2,5,7,8, 210nn9–12, 211n15, 215nn25,26, 222n16
Fuss, Diana, 203n31, 204n38, 211n17

Gallop, Jane, 12, 19, 35–36, 47, 62, 99, 202–3n27, 205n4
Gilbert, Sandra, 43–44, 172
Gubar, Susan, 43–44, 172
Goux, Jean-Joseph, 40–42, 52, 64, 203n33, 207n14, 209n4
Grosz, Elizabeth, 37, 71–72, 86

Habermas, Jürgen, 44, 66, 68, 122, 123
Heath, Stephen, 36–37
Hegel, G. W. F., 8, 34, 46, 51, 54–73, 93, 125, 127, 139, 144, 153, 168, 185, 204n39, 205–6n6, 206n9, 207n14, 221n5
Heidegger, Martin, 8, 27, 34, 44, 108, 116–51, 193
Henke, Suzanne, 156, 165, 169–70
Hitchcock, Alfred, 8, 47–49, 131
Hocquenghem, Guy, 35, 204–5n40
Hollier, Denis, 5, 71, 125
Homophobia, 37, 63, 88
Homosexuality, 38, 204n34
Huyssen, Andreas, 16, 22, 43–44, 119

Irigaray, Luce, 8, 19, 47–48, 52–54, 79, 83, 85, 100, 101, 107–9, 111–12, 146, 147–48, 206n12
Irwin, John T., 18

Jameson, Fredric, 4, 16, 38–42, 55, 176–78, 208n16, 225n1
Jardine, Alice, 11, 37–38, 43–45, 206n8
Jay, Gregory S., 213n19, 218n17
Jeffords, Susan, 199n4

Johnson, Barbara, 131, 138
Joyce, James, 8, 17, 34, 71, 128, 145, 152–89

Kenner, Hugh, 166, 168
Kristeva, Julia, 14–15, 17, 18, 28, 31–33, 44, 51, 57, 85–86, 89, 92, 93, 97–99, 148, 152, 153, 158, 160, 168–69, 186, 191, 197–99nn1,2, 202nn24,25, 211n16, 218n15
Kroker, Arthur, 18
Kroker, Marilouise, 18
Kubrick, Stanley, 18, 28, 190

Lacan, Jacques, 8, 29, 31, 33, 49–51, 56, 60, 74, 88, 90, 104, 108, 109–14, 125, 126, 139, 151, 155, 190–94, 205n6, 211–12n18, 214–15n25
LaCapra, Dominick, 76, 202n22
Lawrence, D. H., 25–26, 43, 61
Lawrence, Karen, 160
Lewis, Wyndham, 220n3
Lukacher, Ned, 118, 137, 216n3
Lukács, Georg, 116–17, 212–13n19
Lynch, David, 101
Lyotard, Jean-François, 65, 72–73, 117, 123, 216n2

MacCabe, Colin, 166
Male feminism, 5, 8, 36–38
Marx, Karl, 40, 41, 49, 168
Maternal agency/authority, 14–15, 28, 75, 87–89, 91–98 passim, 122, 182
Meghill, Allan, 117–18
Melville, Stephen, 140
Miller, Henry, 193–94
Mirror stage, 44–46, 95, 109–15 passim, 126
Modernity/postmodernity, 24–25, 32, 42–46, 51, 52, 65–66, 72–73, 117, 119, 152, 189, 207–8n16, 211n14
Modleski, Tania, 13, 17, 199n4, 201n15
Morrison, Toni, 213n20

Nelson, Cary, 36
Nietzsche, Friedrich, 141, 191–92, 209n8, 219–20n24

Orgasm/ejaculation split, 22, 98, 113, 121, 145. See also Semen/ejaculation

Pefanis, Julian, 195*n2*
Penis, 19–20, 51, 52–61, 77–78, 81–82, 162. *See also* Phallus/penis distinction
Phallocentrism/phallogocentrism, 21–29, 35, 52, 177
Phallus, 19, 31, 41, 47, 49–51, 52–61, 82, 152, 158, 195*n1*, 212*n18*. *See also* Phallus/penis distinction
Phallus/penis distinction, 34–36, 51, 52–61 passim, 99, 121, 204*n35*, 206*n13*
Photography, 8, 34, 45, 204*n38*
Pornography, 19–26, 200–201*n15*
Pound, Ezra, 43, 152
Primontological reversal, 83–84, 86–89, 106–7, 122

Queer theory, 7, 37, 196–97*nn4,5*

Rabaté, Jean-Michel, 162, 189
Rapaport, Herman, 130–31
Renaut, Alan, 119, 124, 128
Representation (*Vorstellung,* "picture thinking"), 2, 8, 16, 19, 22, 24, 34, 38, 44–46, 55–61, 125–27
Restuccia, Frances, 160
Richman, Michèle, 70, 75
Rorty, Richard, 123, 132, 151
Rose, Jacqueline, 45, 86

Sedgwick, Eve Kofosky, 217*n7*, 219*n23*
Semen/ejaculation, 14, 19–24, 26, 28, 32, 34, 38, 46, 53–61, 86, 146–51, 159, 165, 200*n12*, 213*n21*. *See also* Orgasm/ejaculation split
Silverman, Kaja, 3, 13, 34, 61, 195*n1*
Sloterdijk, Peter, 191–92
Smith, Paul, 198*n1*
Spivak, Gayatri, 138–39, 219*n23*
Stoekl, Allan, 69, 70, 128

Taylor, Mark C., 57–58, 62–63, 124
Theweleit, Klaus, 18, 29, 129–30, 190, 191, 220*n24*

Urine/urination, 1, 8, 14, 30, 32, 34, 46, 55–61, 86, 168–69, 201*n20*, 224*n24*

Warner, Michael, 39
Williams, Linda, 19–20, 23, 112
Writing, 2–3, 13, 16, 28, 32–34, 46, 56, 88–89, 98–101, 138–51 passim, 161–65, 210*n11*

Zimmerman, Michael E., 117
Žižek, Slavoj, 51–52, 56, 205–6*n6*

Calvin Thomas is an assistant professor of English at the University of Northern Iowa, where he teaches modern literature, critical theory, and gender studies. He holds a Ph.D. in Modern Studies from the University of Wisconsin–Milwaukee, where he was an Uihlein Fellow at the Center for Twentieth Century Studies, and has been an Emerson Distinguished Faculty Fellow in Modern Letters at Syracuse University. He has published essays in *Literature and Psychology, NOVEL, New German Critique,* and other journals.